WALKING EASY

WALKING EASY

IN THE SWISS AND AUSTRIAN ALPS

Chet Lipton

Fourth Edition

iUniverse, Inc.
New York Lincoln Shanghai

WALKING EASY
IN THE SWISS AND AUSTRIAN ALPS

Copyright © 2007 by Chet Lipton

iUniverse books may be ordered through booksellers or by contacting:

iUniverse
2021 Pine Lake Road, Suite 100
Lincoln, NE 68512
www.iuniverse.com
1-800-Authors (1-800-288-4677)

ISBN-13: 978-0-595-41330-0 (pbk)
ISBN-13: 978-0-595-85683-1 (ebk)
ISBN-10: 0-595-41330-7 (pbk)
ISBN-10: 0-595-85683-7 (ebk)

Printed in the United States of America

Every effort has been made to by the author and editors to make this guide as accurate and useful as possible. However, many things can change after a guide is published—trails are rerouted, regulations and facilities come under new management. We would love to hear from you. Please e-mail your comments and suggestions to the following address: walkingez@aol.com.

To Barbara, Arnie. Dustin, Sue, and Steve,
the next generation of *Easy Walkers*.

And a special, heavenly hug to Carolee, my hiking and life partner.

Photographs, including front cover by Chet Lipton, except page 16,
courtesy of Fritz Lauener and used with his kind permission.

Maps and illustrations by Chet Lipton.

ACKNOWLEDGMENTS

A special thank you to Switzerland Tourism and The Austrian National Tourist Offices in New York and throughout the many beautiful villages in the Swiss and Austrian Alps. Another note of thanks goes to all the hotel owners and their staffs for providing the author with local village history, general background information, and helpful hints about their best walking trails.

We also wish to acknowledge the support of RAIL EUROPE and the SWISS TRAVEL SYSTEM.

Help us keep this guide up to date. Every effort has been made by the author and editors to make this guide as accurate and useful as possible. However, many details can change after a guide is published…trails are rerouted and facilities can change management.

We would like to hear from you concerning your experiences and suggestions. Please e-mail your comments to: walkingez@aol.com.

CONTENTS

BECOMING AN EASY WALKER

Timing is Everything, xv • Switzerland and Austria by Train and Bus, xv
• Discount Travel, xvi • Comfortable Inns and Hotels, xvii • Where to Eat
and Drink, xvii • Dressing for the Trail-From Boots to Backpack, xviii
• Rules of the Trail, xix

SWITZERLAND

AUSTRIA

BECOMING AN EASY WALKER

Lush green valleys, filled with the clanging bells of placidly grazing cattle. Dramatic snow-covered peaks. Pine forests surrounding crystal-clear glacial lakes. These are part of the landscape of the Swiss and Austrian countryside, but it is the townspeople who are the vibrant heart and soul of the villages tucked into these valleys and alps. A varied network of summer hiking trails and cableways complete this pastoral scene, attracting walkers from around the world. This is the setting of *Walking Easy Swiss and Austrian Alps*, written for active adults who enjoy walking, prefer the exhilarating outdoors, and have the need to fill a quest for discovery. This is a how-to-book containing carefully detailed day walks based out of charming villages and towns; sight-seeing suggestions for lazier days including special side-trip itineraries to Vienna, Salzburg, Innsbruck, and Lucerne; suggestions for comfortable accommodations; and helpful hints to benefit the recreational walker.

Every activity described in the following chapters has been experienced and edited by the author to meet the needs of the active adult walker (and those juniors who think they can keep up!). Travelers of all ages walk on the intricate and fascinating network of alpine hiking trails and use the clean and efficient Swiss and Austrian public transportation systems.

Each section in this guide is devoted to a particularly beautiful village or mountain area and includes a brief description of its location, access by car and public transportation, excursions to nearby points of interest, and detailed instructions for each walk. In Switzerland, our base villages are Appenzell, Arosa, Engelberg, Gstaad, Kandersteg, Lauterbrunnen/Wengen, Lenk, Saas-Fee, Samedan/St. Moritz, Verbier, and Zermatt. Base villages in Austria include Alpbach, Badgastein, Kaprun, Kitzbuhel, Mieming, Neustift, Seefeld, and Zell am Ziller. These mountain areas were selected because of their proximity to great walking and exciting excursions, local charm, availability of public transportation, and comfortable accommodations.

Every walk in the book is preceded by an overview, followed by directions on how to arrive at the start of the walk from the base village. Many walks begin with a mountain railway or thrilling cable car ride, while others are gentle walks though the forest or around a tranquil lake. Some are above the tree line or across a glacier, while others descend though alpine meadows resounding with the harmonious ringing of cowbells—all within the capability and range of most active adults and planned to give *Easy Walkers* maximum visual and physical pleasure.

The walks are graded into one of three classifications: gentle—low-level walks with few ascents and descents, through valleys and around lakes and rivers; comfortable—ascents and descents over mixed terrain; more challenging—steeper and longer ascents and descents on narrower, rockier trails. All walks can be accomplished in two to six hours by recreational walkers of any age and in good health.

Walk at a pace you are comfortable with, depending on the terrain and your own reaction to the altitude. Hiking in the alps should not be treated as a fitness test. Enjoy the spectacular scenery and rest as often as needed. Most *Walking Easy* hikes are under 7500 ft. (2285 m.) at altitudes most walkers find comfortable. Each walk description includes the degree of altitude change and the ratings reflect these conditions. Generally, it's a good idea to walk more slowly at higher altitudes until your body adjusts. There are easy-guide maps in some of the more detailed walks. They are not drawn to scale, but act as a general guide to major trail markings. You will also find a recommended hiking map listed at the beginning of each village's Walks section. These and other maps can be purchased at the local Tourist Information Office or newspaper/magazine stores. While a detailed local hiking map and a whistle for emergencies are necessities, you may also find it fun to carry a compass to check direction, a pedometer to keep track of walking distances and a cell phone for communications.

The *Walking Easy* time listed before each walk is time spent actually walking. It does not include time spent for lunch, resting, photography, scenery breaks, sight-seeing and transportation. This additional time is left to the discretion of each *Easy Walker,* so that an average day with a four-hour walk could begin by 9:00 a.m. and end back at your hotel in the late afternoon.

The Swiss and Austrian Alps have thousands of miles of *trails—wanderwege* (comfortable walking paths) and *bergwege* (narrower, rockier mountain trails)— most well signed, well maintained, and easily followed. But be warned: Not all hikes are easy. Many will challenge your capabilities with ascents and descents over mixed terrain. However, it is not uncommon for people of all ages to be steadily wending their way along a favorite trail, and it is said that the first pair of shoes that proud Swiss and Austrian parents purchase for their children is a pair of tiny hiking boots. Europeans love to walk—and love walkers. The Swiss and Austrians have created wonderful trail systems—it is the best way to see the countryside—and walkers are welcome almost everywhere in their hiking boots and backpacks.

You can do it—just tuck a copy of *Walking Easy Swiss and Austrian Alps* in your backpack and you're on your way.

TIMING IS EVERYTHING

The weather can vary tremendously within the small countries of Switzerland and Austria. The tree line is about 6500 ft. (1980 m.) and the snow line in summer can be at 9000 ft. (2745 m.) or lower.

Deciding the best time of year to walk in the Alps depends on what you enjoy most in the way of scenery and weather. The alpine flowers begin to bloom in late May and are at their peak from the beginning of June to mid-July. Snow can cover some of the higher trails in mid-June and some cable lifts are still closed, but the riotous colors of alpine wildflowers, framed against the white mountain peaks, are breathtaking.

HINT: Insulated or Polartec-type jackets are a necessity in mountain areas, even during summer.

July, and especially August are the most popular tourist months. September offers fewer tourists, lower temperatures, and clearer skies. Hiking season usually begins mid-June and lasts through the end of September—but it is very important to check lift schedules in each village—some stay open until October, while others close after the first week in September. Whichever month you choose, walking on the network of alpine trails will be an exhilarating experience.

SWITZERLAND AND AUSTRIA BY TRAIN AND BUS

HINT: Train cars are marked with a large "1" or "2" to denote travel class. Second-class rail travel is as clean and almost as comfortable as first class—we recommend taking advantage of second-class fare savings.

The efficient Swiss and Austrian public transportation systems are among the best in the world, linking trains, buses, and boats, and *Easy Walkers* will find that it may not be necessary to rent a car. It can be a welcome change to sit back and enjoy the superb views without worrying about hairpin turns or city traffic.

HINT: *Gepack,* or baggage forwarding, is an invaluable and reliable traveler's aid. Bring your luggage to the train station and, for a small fee, have it sent on to your next destination. However, it may be necessary to check your luggage through the night before to ensure timely arrival.

Buses are one class and can take *Easy Walkers* to trail heads, across remote valleys, and through high alpine passes. Boats traverse major lakes and rivers from May to October.

DISCOUNT TRAVEL

Swiss Pass: This is the most convenient of the Swiss discounts. It entitles users to unlimited first or second class travel on the entire public transportation systems—trains, buses and boats—and to purchase 25 percent discount tickets on selected lift systems and mountain railways. You can choose a period of consecutive days—4, 8, 15, or 21 days or one month—with savings for two adults traveling together and free travel for children under sixteen when traveling with adults (the family card).

Swiss Flexi-Pass: Within a one-month period you can travel on any three days of your choice without restrictions. You can also purchase up to six additional days of unlimited transportation. There are additional savings for two adults traveling together and no charge for children under sixteen traveling with adults.

If you're planning a *Walking Easy* trip to Switzerland, we recommend buying a Swiss Pass. These passes can by purchased only in the United States. Call Rail Europe at 800-438-7245, or visit www.raileurope.com

Swiss Card: You travel free of charge from the border or airport to your destination and back. In other words, one free round trip, plus 50 percent discount for all additional trips by train, bus, or boat, and 25 to 50 percent discount on most cableways. This card is valid for one month, and children under sixteen travel free with you.

Austrian Railpass: This pass is valid for any three days of unlimited travel, without charge, in a given fifteen-day period; you can also buy up to five extra days of travel. If sold in the United States though Rail Europe.

HINT: Travel with extra passport-size photos, as some local transportation discount passes may also require them.

COMFORTABLE INNS AND HOTELS

HINT: For best rates when making reservations, fax, write, e-mail, or call the hotel directly and ask if a *"Walking Easy* Special Hiking Package" is available. Remember, all taxes and gratuities are included in the room rate.

Accommodations in the Alps range from five-star deluxe hotels to comfortable rooms in rural farmhouses. The quality of a hotel, or *pension,* and its prices can be judged by the number of stars awarded to it: Five stars denote deluxe; four stars, first class; three stars, superior; two stars, standard; and one star, minimum. The recommended *Walking Easy* three-and four-star Swiss and Austrian hotels listed for each base village have been used by the authors on their walking trips. All these hotels offer half-board (breakfast and dinner) unless otherwise noted, and most have excellent kitchens. For convenience, quality, and savings, we suggest making hotel reservations with half-board, unless otherwise indicated. All listed three-star hotels offer comfortable rooms with private facilities, buffet breakfast, and are scrupulously clean and well located. Our recommended four-star hotels, while more expensive, generally feature more luxurious accommodations, a wider menu choice at breakfast and dinner, and a variety of other guest services such as swimming pools and health and beauty facilities. Many of these three-and four-star hotels have been owned and operated by the same family for generations.

To call or fax Switzerland and Austria from the United States, first dial the international access number (011), followed by the country code—41 for Switzerland, 43 for Austria—followed by the telephone or fax number. Most of the listed hotels now have e-mail.

HINT: Except where listed, all *Walking Easy* hotels accept credit cards, unless otherwise noted.

WHERE TO EAT AND DRINK

Hotels: Hotels in the Alps offer buffet breakfast included in the room rate and a three-to five-course meal for dinner, if you take *halbpension* (half-board). Hotel food is usually delicious, and *Easy Walkers* can take advantage of lower costs by booking with dinner.

HINT: Always carry bottled water in your backpack when hiking, even when planning to lunch in a restaurant.

Restaurants: If you decide to eat in a restaurant outside your hotel, check the special of the day *(tagesteller or plat du jour)*, representing the best value on the menu. A 15 percent service charge is always included in your bill but a few coins should be left on the table if you were pleased with the service.

Picnicking: When planning a day of walking, we recommend taking along a picnic lunch. Many local supermarkets will prepare sandwiches for you.

DRESSING FOR THE TRAIL—FROM BOOTS TO BACKPACK

Walking Easy clothing should be lightweight and layerable. All clothing is not suitable for all types of walking—climate, altitude, and time of day during the alpine hiking season are points to consider.

Hiking Boots: The most important item for a successful *Walking Easy* experience is a pair of broken-in, medium-weight hiking boots, preferably waterproof and above the ankle, providing more support on rocky or steep trails. Do not wear sneakers or sneakers that look like hiking boots, as they do not provide the foot support and traction needed.

HINT: Wear your hiking boots for overseas and intercity travel—they can be heavy and bulky to carry or pack. You can remove them on the plane or train for comfort. Custom dictates that hiking boots are *never* worn in the hotel dining room. At breakfast, sneakers, sandals, or even slippers are preferred.

Socks: Socks worn closest to your skin should *not* be made of cotton. Cotton absorbs perspiration and holds it, producing blisters. A sock made of a hydrophobic synthetic will wick sweat away and keep your feet drier. When purchasing hiking boots, be sure to wear the type of socks you will wear on the trail.

Outerwear: A Polartec-type jacket is essential for walking or sight-seeing in the Alps, and remember, it gets chilly in mountain villages at night. Rain protection is best provided by a waterproof poncho, large enough to fit over your backpack, or a waterproof jacket with a hood. Don't let a light rain cancel your walking plans.

HINT: Rain gear should be stored in your backpack until needed. Don't let a sudden mountain storm catch you unprepared.

Hat: A hat with a brim provides protection from sun as well as rain and should always be worn.

Pants: Hiking knickers for both men and women are worn with high socks which protect the legs but can be rolled down in warmer weather. They can be bought in most sporting goods stores in the Alps. In warmer weather, hiking shorts, also worn with high socks, are a good alternative.

Sweaters: A medium-weight sweater is essential for cool evenings in the mountains, even in summer.

Sweatshirts: A medium-weight sweatshirt can be layered over shirts for hiking.

Shirts: A cotton/polyester blend can be used for ease of laundering. Short-sleeved knit shirts, along with long-sleeved shirts and turtlenecks, are essential for layering under sweaters or sweatshirts, for both day and evening.

Backpacks: Every *Easy Walker* should carry a lightweight backpack with wide, adjustable, foam-padded shoulder straps. Roomy, outside zipper compartments will organize daily hiking essentials.

Waist Pack: Use a roomy, comfortable waist pack to carry money, passports, etc.

Walking Stick: Walking sticks are an indispensable aid to balance when hiking downhill or on rocky terrain. They come in many sizes and styles and can be bought in the United States or in an alpine village sporting goods store. The newest and best sticks telescope to fit into your backpack when not in use. We think this item is a must for all *Easy Walkers.*

RULES OF THE TRAIL

Alpine trails are generally well signed and marked. Signs may indicate the time it takes to walk to the next destination—1 std. indicates one hour—std. being the abbreviation for the German *stunde,* or hour. Most *Easy Walkers* should allow about 25 percent more time than the signpost estimates.

In Switzerland, yellow, diamond-shaped signs represent *wanderwege,* lower level paths over easy hills and lower mountain slopes. Red and white signs and blazes denote higher level *bergwege*—narrower, rockier mountain trails.

1. Plan the route by checking this book and local hiking maps before beginning each walk. Always carry a local hiking map with you.
2. Ask about local weather conditions and adjust the day's activities accordingly.
3. Tell someone about your planned route, either a friend or one of the hotel staff.
4. Take your time, especially at higher altitudes.
5. *Never* leave the marked trail.

6. Turning back is not a disgrace if you feel the trail is too difficult or the weather looks threatening. Return on the same path or check the nearest public transportation.

7. Be sure your hiking boots are in good shape and your backpack holds the needed items, plus a snack in case you are delayed. Always carry bottled water in your backpack and stop frequently to drink. Longer and more strenuous hikes require more water.

8. Never start a hike without stowing a special energy treat in your backpack. We prefer one or two f the many varieties of "**Ritter Sport**" chocolate bars.

9. In case of an accident, send for help. If this is not possible, use the standard alpine distress signal with your whistle. Make six signals spaced evenly within one minute, pause for one minute, then repeat. Of course, a **Cell Phone** will help.

10. Appreciate the beauty of the wildflowers but do not pick them.

11. Do not litter. Take out what you bring in.

12. Alpine meadow gates work in wondrous ways—some are turnstiles, some have spring-attached hooks, some feature sliding boards, and others are meant to be ducked under or stepped over. Whichever the case, be sure you leave the gate the way you approached it—closed.

13. Always check current timetables when using public transportation.

14. Sunscreen and sunglasses are very important, especially at high altitudes and on glacier walks.

The purpose of any walking trip is to have fun. Tuck a copy of *Walking Easy* in your backpack and take a hike…**you can do it!**

SWITZERLAND—THE MATTERHORN

SWITZERLAND

Modern Switzerland is a federation of more than 3,000 communes. Years ago, neighboring communes formed twenty-three cantons, each with its own constitution, laws, and government, leaving only foreign policy, national defense, economic policy, etc., to the federal parliament. Although Switzerland is a small country, it has four official languages: German, spoken by 65 percent of the population, French, 18 percent, Italian, 12 percent, and Romansch, spoken by only 1 percent of the people in the southeastern mountains. The German language of the native Swiss is called *Schwyzer Deutsch*, a dialect different in vocabulary, pronunciation, and grammer from classical German. However, English is usually spoken in even the smallest village. Tourist information offices in Switzerland are designated by an **i** (tourist information office) sign and are a valuable friend to the hiker. You'll usually find them on the village main street and the personnel are multilingual and friendly.

From high panoramic trails at the foot of the snowcapped peaks to peaceful rambles around lakes and through pastures, the Swiss Alps offer *Walking Easy* at its best.

BERNESE OBERLAND

LAUTERBRUNNEN/WENGEN
(GRINDELWALD, MURREN, MEIRINGEN)

The Bernese Oberland villages of Lauterbrunnen, Wengen, Grindelwald, Murren and Meiringen form the hub of some of the finest hiking in Switzerland. Lauterbrunnen and Wengen, the preferred *Easy Walker* base villages, welcome you with the snow-capped peaks of the Bernese Oberland's famous mountains towering over a deep glacial valley.

Lauterbrunnen, at 2625 ft. (800 m.), sits in the middle of a picturesque valley, near convenient rail connections that can take *Easy Walkers* throughout pocket-sized Switzerland. The Lauterbrunnen train station is a great jumping off place—for a shopping visit to Lucerne, to Interlaken and a steamer outing on Lake Thun or Brienz, to Wilderswil for a cog-wheel railway ride to scenic Schynige Platte, or to the medieval arcades and bear pits of Bern.

Car-free **Wengen**, at 4160 ft. (1275 m.), Lauterbrunnen's upstairs neighbor, is perched on a sunny plateau with enchanting views of some of the Bernese Oberland's most imposing peaks—the Eiger, the Monch, and the Jungfrau.

Neighboring **Grindelwald**, also boasting a myriad of hiking trails for *Easy Walkers* to enjoy, is easily reached by train or gondola from Wengen and Lauterbrunnen. A car-free hamlet with a population of 350, **Murren** is perched on a sheltered, sunny terrace above the Lauterbrunnen Valley, facing the Jungfrau massif. At 5400 ft. (1646 m.), it is the highest village in the Bernese Oberland. **Meiringen**, home of Reichenbach Falls, where famous fictional detective Sherlock Holmes plunged to his death along with evil Professor Moriarty, is the center of several not-to-be-missed hikes.

TRANSPORTATION

By Train—To arrive in Lauterbrunnen, take the train to Interlaken Ost and change to the Lauterbrunnen train. To continue to Wengen, change trains in Lauterbrunnen for the 20-minute trip by cog railway.

By Car—Drive towards Interlaken and pick up the local road through Wilderswil, into Lauterbrunnen. To Wengen, park your car in the garage at the Lauterbrunnen station and continue the trip to Wengen by train.

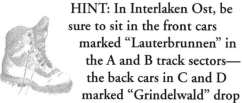

HINT: In Interlaken Ost, be sure to sit in the front cars marked "Lauterbrunnen" in the A and B track sectors— the back cars in C and D marked "Grindelwald" drop off in the village of Zweilutschinen for the trip to Grindelwald.

FAVORITE *WALKING EASY* HOTEL

HOTEL SILBERHORN

Three-Star, Owners—Familie Christian von Allmen
CH 3822 Lauterbrunnen; **Tel:** 33 85 2210 **Fax:** 33 855 42 13
Internet: www.silberhorn.com
Email: info@silberhorn.com

A breathtaking view of the Lauterbrunnen Valley and Staubach Falls can be seen from the balconies of many rooms, as well as the newly renovated dining room. A full Swiss buffet breakfast is served, along with a salad bar and excellent regional cooking at dinner. The Silberhorn caters to walkers of all ages and nationalities, and it is a convenient and comfortable jumping-off place for hiking and sight-seeing in the Bernese Oberland.

EXCURSIONS

The Lauterbrunnen Tourist Information Office is across from the train station ...
Internet: http://www.lauterbrunnen.ch
E-mail: info@lauterbrunnen.ch

A Jungfrau train and cable car pass (**Jungfraubahnen Pass**), available at tourist offices and train stations, is valid for unlimited use of most trains and lifts in the Jungfrau area, including Interlaken, Grindelwald, Murren and Wengen/Lauterbrunnen. This pass also offers a reduction on the excursion to the Jungfraujoch from Kleine Scheidegg.

1. **Trummelbach Falls (Trummelbachfalle)**—The ten glacier-fed waterfalls, cascading inside a mountain, have been made accessible by a Swiss engineering miracle … Remember, it's cold and damp inside the mountain, so dress warmly.
   Directions: *Take the bus to the falls at the Lauterbrunnen train station, or walk through town and follow walking signs to the falls.*
2. **The Schilthorn**—A cable car ascends to 9750 ft. (2972 m.) to an incredible panorama. (See Walk #1.)
3. **The Jungfraujoch**—The "top of Europe" is reached by the highest rack railway (and probably the most expensive) on the continent, climbing to an ice wonderworld at 11,333 ft. (3454 m.).
   (See Walk #3.)
4. **Schynige Platte**—At 6500 ft. (1981 m.), the Schynige Platte's remarkable panorama overlooks both mountains and lakes from Grindelwald to Interlaken.
   Directions: *Take the train from to Wilderswil. Change for to the Schynige Platte Railway for the 50-minute scenic ride up the mountain.*
5. **Grindelwald**—This tourist mecca lies at the foot of several imposing mountains and serves as a central point for many walks. (See Walks # 6 and 8.)
6. **Interlaken**—Named for its location between Lake Thun and Lake Brienz, Interlaken is a busy tourist center, surrounded by a superb mountain panorama. The Hohweg *is a* a wide main street bustling with stores and restaurants Lake steamer excursions can be boarded from Interlaken to Lake Thun or Lake Brienz—the piers are only a minute's walk from either the Interlaken Ost or the Interlaken West train stations.
   A) Heimwehfluh—The Heimwehfluh funicular's top station, a five-minute walk from the Interlaken West station, features an elaborate scale-model railroad.
   B) Harder Kulm—The top of Harder Kulm is reached by a 15-minute funicular ride, a few minute's walk from the Interlaken Ost station.
   Directions to Interlaken: *Take the train to Interlaken Ost and change for Interlaken West, a three-minute ride.*
7. **Meiringen**—A visit to **Reichenbach Falls** strikes right at the heart of the mystique surrounding Meiringen. Take the funicular up to the falls to view the place where Holmes and Moriarty fell to their death. The **Sherlock Holmes Museum** is located on the main street, with the first authentic replica of Holmes' front room at 221b, Baker Street. The **Aareschlucht**, just outside of Meiringen, is a natural wonder, with towering rock walls lining both sides of the gorge.
   Directions: *Take the train to Interlaken Ost and change for the train towards Lucerne, exiting at Meiringen.*

AN EASY WALKING TRAIL

8. **Brienz**—If you interested in woodcarving or violin-making, be sure to visit Brienz, a lake village offering local artisans' work.
   Directions: *Take the train to Interlaken Ost and change for the train to Brienz. An alternate means of transportation is by steamer. The dock in both Interlaken Ost and Brienz is just outside the railroad stations.*
9. **Swiss Open-Air Museum in Ballenberg**—This beautifully landscaped area provides fascinating insights into Swiss lifestyles of the past.
   Directions: *Take the train to Interlaken Ost and change for the train toward Lucerne, exiting in Brienz. Take the connecting bus to Ballenberg at the Brienz station.*
10. **Thun**—(See Kandersteg, Excursion #3.)
    Directions: *Take the train to Interlaken Ost and change for the train to Thun.*
11. **Bern**—The capital of Switzerland is a delightful city of medieval arches, fountains and towers. (See "Kandersteg," Excursion #4.)
    Directions: *Take the train from Lauterbrunnen to Interlaken Ost and change for the train to Bern—a two-hour trip from Wengen.*

LAUTERBRUNNEN/WENGEN
(Grindelwald, Meiringen, Murren) **WALKS**

Recommended Maps:
1) Wanderkarte—Lauterbrunnental Jungfrau Region
2) Wanderkare—Grindelwald Jungfrau-Region
3) Wanderkarte—Oberhasli, Meiringen-Hasliberg, Haslital

Walk #1: Introductory Walk—Lauterbrunnen to Stechelberg, Murren to Grutschalp (Excursion to the Schilthorn)
Walking Easy Time: 2 1/2 hours
Rating: Gentle

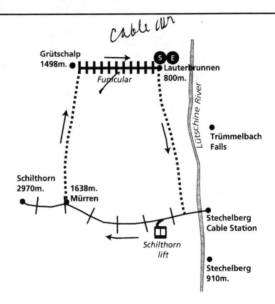

Today's walk introduces *Easy Walkers* to the lovely Lauterbrunnen Valley. The level path parallels the Lutschine River, and in summer the surrounding fields are ablaze with wild flowers, a perfect foil for the snow-capped mountains above—leading past Staubbach and Trummelbach Falls At Stechelberg, take the cable car to Murren and, if the weather is clear, to the Schilthorn. Return to Murren and continue on the last part of this walk, the gentle path from Murren to Grutschalp, taking the funicular back to Lauterbrunnen.

Start: Walk through Lauterbrunnen, toward Staubbach Falls, ahead and on the right. Follow a paved path signed "Stechelberg-1 hr., 15 min." As you approach Staubbach, note the sign "Zum Staubbachfall" and a path ascending up to the base of the falls—take this detour for a closer look.

Continuing to the hamlet of Buchen, a bridge crosses the river to Trummelbach Falls. (See Excursion #1.) Today however, continue ahead on the main path. You soon arrive at a small bridge leading to the lift station. Cross the bridge and walk to the Schilthorn lift. Buy a ticket from Stechelberg to the Schilthorn, with a return to **Murren only**. This cable car runs frequently and, after changes in Gimmelwald, Murren and Birg, lifts you to the *Piz Gloria* restaurant of James Bond fame. Visit the sun-terrace with its incomparable views and when ready, take the cable car down to Murren to explore this tiny hamlet. Mürren is car-free and perched on a hillside high above the valley.

When ready, follow the sign to Grutschalp, the gentle mountain trail paralleling the railroad tracks. Don't be tempted by signs pointing directly to Lauterbrunnen, these paths are usually steep. You may encounter friendly cows, sheep or goats along the path, and the typically alpine sound of their echoing bells is a fitting accompaniment to the spectacular mountain scenery. At the Grutschalp funicular station, return to Lauterbrunnen.

Walk #2: Allmendhubel to Grutschalp
Walking Easy Time: 2 1/2 hours
Rating: Comfortable

Today's outing will take you by funicular to Allmendhubel 6257 ft. (1907 m.), above the charming village of Murren 5374 ft. (1638 m.), with outstanding views of the peaks that make this Bernese Oberland area so famous. As you walk from Allmenhubel toward Grutschalp on the Hohenweg or high trail, the panorama includes the Jungfrau, the Eiger, the Monch, Mannlichen above the village of Wengen, and all the way to the Schynige Platte.

At Grutschalp, you will take the funicular down to Lauterbrunnen.

Directions: *Take the Grutschalp funicular to the top and board the little mountain train to Murren. At Murren, follow the sign to the Allmendhubel funicular—riding it to the top.*

Start: After exiting, follow the sign "Grutschalp-1 hr. 20 min." The trail—with spectacular views of the snow-capped Eiger, Monch and Jungfrau—rises to the top of a hill and descends quickly. You will meander on this red and white blazed mountain *bergweg* through the *alp*, always following signs to Gryutschalp. After about 75 minutes, you can turn down the mountain to Murren at Pletschenalp. if necessary. Descend the mountain following signs to the Grutschalp funicular. As you walk to Grutschalp, this path becomes a bit steep, but manageable. At the road, turn left toward the station, taking the funicular down to Lauterbrunnen.

STAUBACH FALLS AND
THE LAUTERBRUNNEN VALLEY

Walk #3: Mannlichen Top Station to Mannlichen Gipfel to Kleine Scheidegg to Wengen (Optional Walk to Lauterbrunnen)
Walking Easy Time: 3 to 4 1/2 hours
Rating: Comfortable

This walk, one of the most popular in the Bernese Oberland, begins in the shadow of some of Switzerland's most famous mountains—including the Eiger, the Monch and the Jungfrau.

Directions: *If starting from Lauterbrunnen, take the train to Wengen. The Wengen-Mannlichen cableway is a short walk . Follow signs on the main street. Buy a one-way ticket to the top station. This plateau is at 7313 ft. (2229 m.) and offers many options, such as riding on the four-mile long Mannlichen/Grindelwald gondola, the longest in Europe*

Start: From Mannlichen Top Station, follow the sign to "Mannlichen Gipfel-20 min."—the Mannlichen peak—clearly visible up on the hill to your left. The short climb to the top is worth the effort. You'll be able to see Interlaken, the Schynige Platte, and the surrounding mountains and glaciers of the Bernese Oberland. When ready, return to the cable station and follow the sign "Kleine Scheidegg-1hr., 20 min." (There may be a few signs that vary a bit in walking time—don't be put off—*follow the main path to Kleine Scheidegg*.)

As you walk towards the Eiger, the mountain used by Trevanian for the setting of his best selling book and movie *The Eiger Sanction*, you are hiking on one of the most traveled paths in the Bernese Oberland. Grindelwald is on the left in the distant valley, as you walk easily down towards Kleine Scheidegg and its railroad stop, bustling with hikers, climbers, and tourists changing for the train to and from the Jungfraujoch.) See walk # 4)

Cross the railroad tracks at Kleine Scheidegg to the sign "Wengen-1 hr., 45 min." **NOTE:**

Two trails at this point lead to Wengenernalp and Wengen, one taking about 2 1/2 hours to Wengen via Stalden. You have the option here of taking the longer way to Wengen or following the trail closest to the railroad tracks.

If you choose the shorter option, Wengernalp is an easy, 30-minute walk from Kleine Scheidegg with the railroad tracks on your right, and the Jungfrau peak on your left. At Wengernalp, walk past the station and follow signs to Wengen.

If you wish to take the longer, more interesting route signed "Wengen-2 1/2 hrs.," this path leads through the meadow and forest towards Stalden at 5515 ft. (1681 m.), with exceptional views of the Lauterbrunnen Valley. At Stalden, take the middle path towards Wengen, eventually meeting the railroad and the main path above Schiltwald at Allmend. Turn left and follow the path into Wengen.

Easy Walkers can continue down to Lauterbrunnen, by following the signs marked "Lauterbrunnen." This walk will take another 1 1/2 hours. Or, take the short train ride from Wengen to Lauterbrunnen.

Walk #4: Excursion to the Jungfraujoch, Walk to Monchjochhutte and Return (Optional Walk Eigergletscher Station to Kleine Scheidegg)
Walking Easy Time: 2 to 3 1/2 hours
Rating: More Challenging

Reserve the better part of a clear day, making an early start, for a visit to Europe's highest altitude railway station. You will find that the Jungfraujoch train station is more than a stop on the rail line. It houses a high-altitude weather observatory and research station, several restaurants, a post office, a busy souvenir shop, an Ice Palace, and a snow-field where visitors can ski, take a sleigh ride pulled by huskies, bask in the sun and take a two-hour round-trip hike to the Monchjochhutte across a snow-field.

The Jungfraujoch rail station is at 11,333 ft. (3454 m.) between the imposing peaks of the Monch at 13,449 ft. (4099 m.) and the Jungfrau at 13,642 ft. (4158 m.). This ice-world features a multitude of glaciers tucked in between these jagged, snow-covered peaks, in a pristine and dazzling, environment that defies the imagination.

HINT: Be sure you bring sun-glasses and protective sun lotions, as well as cold weather gear.

Directions: Take the train from Lauterbrunnen or Wengen to Kleine Scheidegg and change for the special Jungfrau train. After station Eigergletscher at 5524 ft. (2320 m.), the train enters a mountain tunnel, with stops at Eigerwand and Eismeer, where viewing windows have been cut into the face of the mountain. At the Jungfraujoch station, signs direct you to all the possible activities.

Start: After taking in all the sights, walk on the wide, well-signed snow trail for about an hour, ascending to the Monchjochhutte, along with hundreds of other hikers, and return along the same path. At the beginning of the snow trail it is possible to ride on a sleigh pulled by a team of huskies.

HINT: This is an expensive trip but tickets can be purchased in several ways. For current specifics, check at the Tourist Office or train station.

When ready, walk back to the complex. NOTE: The return train stops at Eigergletscher, one stop before Kleine Scheidegg. You can take a one-hour hike down to Kleine Scheidegg where you pick up the train again.

Walk #5: The Eiger Trail—Eigergletscher Station to Alpiglen
Walking Easy Time—2 3/4 hours
Rating: Comfortable

One of the major attractions in the Jungfrau Region of the Bernese Oberland, is the notorious north face of the Eiger, site of many climbing expeditions. Close-up views of this awesome mountain face are now available from the new Eiger Trail, which begins at the Eigergletscher station—where the Jungfrau Railway enters a tunnel on its way to the Jungfraujoch. The trail meanders past fascinating rock formations and over small streams to Alpiglen—all in keeping with the surrounding alpine environment. While this hike can be taken in either direction, we feel that *Easy Walkers* may prefer beginning at the Eigergletscher station, ending at Alpiglen.

Directions: *Take the train to Kleine Scheidegg and change trains, getting off at Eigergletscher, the first stop on the train to the Jungfraujoch.*

Start: Cross the railroad tracks, following the sign "Eiger Trail," leading up past the stone house and on to the well-blazed *bergweg.* After a short ascent, the trail reaches a vantage point with an imposing view of the north wall of the Eiger. This trail, winding along the mountain's base, provides views from Kleine Scheidegg and Mannlichen down through the meadows and peaks above Grindelwald. You ascend and descend over scree and alp, first to the "cow line," then down to the tree line. The final half hour descent through the forest can be steep and muddy—take it slowly and soon the restaurant at Alpiglen appears. At Alpiglen you have a number of options, depending on the time:

1) Follow the signs to Grindelwald and walk 1 1/2 hours to town, returning by train to Lauterbrunnen or Wengen.

2) Take the train from Alpiglen to Grindelwald, returning by train to Lauterbrunnen or Wengen via Zweilutschinen.

3) Take the train from Alpiglen to Kleine Scheidegg, returning by train to Lauterbrunnen or Wengen.

4) Take the train to Kleine Scheidegg and walk to Wengen (1 3/4 hour by the shorter path by the railroad tracks, as in Walk #3).

Walk #6: Grindwald "First" Top Station to Grosse Scheidegg (Excursion to Grindelwald)
Walking Easy Time: 1 1/2 hours
Rating: Comfortable

Today's excursion is particularly interesting because it includes a visit to the famous town of Grindelwald, with a hike on its surrounding mountains. This walk provides excellent views of the Wetterhorn, whose dark cliffs seem to loom directly above tiny Grosse Scheidegg, your trail destination.

Directions: Take the train from Lauterbrunnen to Zweilutschinen and change for the connecting train to Grindelwald. Walk through town, following the signs "First," and buy a one-way ticket to the top.

Start: Follow the sign indicating "Grosse Scheidegg-11/2 hrs." This trail is entirely in the open, with nothing to block the magnificent views. A sign directs you ahead and slightly up to the left on Panoramaweg.

This trail brings you directly to Grosse Scheidegg. Check the bus schedule outside the restaurant for the return to Grindelwald. The bus ride, on a steep, narrow, winding road, offers incredible views—an appropriate ending to a magnificent day. Take time to explore Grindelwald before returning to Lauterbrunnen and/or Wengen, via a change of train in Zweilutschinen.

Walk #7: Mannlichen Top Station to Grindelwald
Walking Easy Time: 4 hours
Rating: Comfortable

Today's hike begins in Wengen, ascending to Mannlichen by cable car. The downhill walk to Grindelwald through alpine meadows and pine forests is in the shadow of the great Bernese Oberland mountain peaks

Directions: *Follow the signs through Wengen to the Mannlichen cable station and by a one-way ticket to the top.*

Start: As you leave the lift station, take the path marked "Grindelwald-3 hrs., 10 min.," but plan on four hours to complete this hike. Begin walking on a paved, descending road, under the Grindelwald-Mannlichen Gondolas. The path is blazed in red and white, and a red and white marker takes you to the right, from the paved path to a grassy trail across a meadow.

The trail criss-crosses the paved path—always follow the red and white blazes. Since you are walking through pastures, be cautious about where you step—the cows graze throughout the meadows. Follow signs and blazes to Grindelwald and Holenstein, the mid-station on the Grindelwald-Mannlichen Gondolas. In about 90 minutes you will have walked down 2000 feet (610 meters) on a scenic meadow path to the Middle Station where you have the option of proceeding to Grindelwald by gondola—or continuing the walk (about two and a half more hours.)

To continue, at Holenstein follow the signs to the right to Grindelwald Grund and Grindelwald Dorf. In about ten minutes you'll reach a paved road. Turn left and you'll see another paved road. Facing you, on a barn in a small pasture, is a Grindelwald *wanderweg* sign. Follow this sign on to a forest path. As you get closer to Grindelwald, follow signs to Grindelwald Dorf and the main railroad station. If you prefer not to walk up the hill to the main train station at Grindelwald Dorf, walk down to Grindelwald Grund and wait for the next train or bus leaving for the main station. At the main station, take the train to Zweilutschinen and change for the train to Lauterbrunnen and/or Wengen.

Walk #8: Pfingstegg Top Station to Stieregg to Pfingstegg to Cafe Milchbach to Hotel Wetterhorn—A Double Glacier Visit (Optional Walk to Grindelwald)
Walking Easy Time: 4 to 5 hours
Rating: More Challenging

There is a double treat in store for *Easy Walkers* today. After taking the cable car from Grindelwald to Pfingstegg, the trail will ascend 984 ft. (300 m.) to Stieregg at 5577 ft. (1700 m.), for a close look at the Unterer Grindelwaldgletscher. After returning to Pfingstegg, the path descends 1500 ft. (457 m.) to Cafe Milchbach and the Oberer Grindelwaldgletscher—the second glacier to be visited—with the possibility of walking into the glacier's ice caves. The hike ends with a walk to the Hotel Wetterhorn and a bus ride back to the Grindelwald station, or another hour's pleasant hike into Grindelwald from the hotel.

Directions: *Take the train to Grindelwald (with a change in Zweilutschinen) and walk up the main shopping street, following the sign "Pfingstegg Bahn." Purchase a one-way ticket to the 4564 ft. (1391 m.) Pfingstegg station.*

Start: Follow "Stieregg-1 hr." to the right, heading towards the glacier, the trail blazed in red and white. The leading edge of the glacier becomes visible and Mannlichen can be seen on top of the mountain to the right. Within ninety minutes you'll reach the plateau overlooking the glacier, and then descend to Restaurant Stieregg, completing the first part of today's double glacier hike.

Return by retracing your steps to Pfingstegg and continue by following signs to Milchbach and Hotel Wetterhorn. The rest of today's hike is mostly downhill, except for a short rise before reaching the Café Milchbach. This path to Milchbach and Grindelwald is highlighted by rock formations revealing deposits representing a time span of 80 million years.

Follow directions to the Milchbach, with a sun-terrace overlooking the glacier. From the cafe you can walk down to the Hotel Wetterhorn in 20 minutes by way of the Blue Grotto Ice Caves. The small admission charge allows you to walk through man-made tunnels into the glacier itself, with its brilliant blue color.

Continue on the path to the Hotel Wetterhorn, crossing a wide gravel auto road leading into the parking area across from the hotel. Buy a bus ticket for the short ride back to the Grindelwald station. Or, if you still feel fit, walk through the parking area to your left and follow a sign directing you through meadow and forest for a pleasant, one-hour walk back to Grindelwald.

Walk #9: Grosse Scheidegg to Schwarzwaldalp to Rosenlui to Zwirgi to Reichenbaach Falls (Excursion to Gletscherschlucht Rosenlui and Reichenbach Falls)
Walking Easy Time: 4½ hours (including a forty-five minute gorge walk and excursion to Reichenbach Falls)
Rating: Comfortable

Meiringen (home of the *merinque*) is not only rich in history, culture, and great walks, it also boasts the spectacular gorge at Rosenlui and Reichenbach Falls, made famous as the spot where the evil Professor Moriarity "done in" Scherlock Holmes. Get and early start for today's excursion and hike because of the transportation involved on both ends of the trip. **NOTE: Check all train and bus schedules carefully and coordinate times before leaving. This trip is worth the extra effort involved.**

    Directions: *Take the train to Grindelwald (changing in Zweilutschninen). Walk 1 block from the train station to the bus bahnhof and take the bus to Grosse Scheidegg, and exciting ascent on a winding mountain road.*

THE TRAIL ABOVE WENGEN

Start: Follow the path with signs pointing through the meadow to Schwarzwaldalp, then to Rosenlui—first on the road, then through a wide meadow along the Reichen River. Today's walk is particularly pretty in early summer, when the meadows are filled with wildflowers and gently meandering herds of bell-clanging cows. A half-hour from Schwarzwaldalp you'll arrive at Gletscherschlucht Rosenlui. The gorge walk begins at 4430 ft. (1350m.) and rises over the torrent on stone steps through dark, cave-like tunnels, close to the wild and stormy rush of the glacial waters—climbing to 4922 ft. (1500 m.) at the top—and followed by a fifteen-minute descent.

Resume the walk down the road, reaching the old Rosenlui Hotel, with a sign pointing toward KALTENBRUNNEN-35 MIN. At Kaltenbrunnen, with a small restaurant, you have two choices:

Take the bus to the Meiringen train station.

1. Take the the bus to the Meiringen train station …

2. Walk on to Zwirgi, where you can descend to the top of Reichenbach Falls for a visit, then take the ancient funicular down to Meiringen, where you follow signs to the *bahnhof.* Either way, take the train to Interlaken Ost and change for the train to Lauterbrunnen and Wengen.

Walk #10: Planplatten Top Station to Balmeregghorn to Tannenalp to Engstlenalp
Walking Easy Time: 4 hours
Rating: More Challenging

HINT: Plan a full day for this hike—it will be necessary to get an early start if you are coming from the base villages of Lauterbrunnen or Wengen. Make bus reservations for your return from Engstlenalp to Meiringen at the bus *bahnhof* in Meiringen (at the Meiringen train station), upon arrival.

Use the Meiringen hiking map today. One of the most popular, high-level walks in the Meiringen area—and a favorite of ours—is from Planplatten to Engstlenalp. You will leave Meiringen on the Meiringen-Hasliberg lift, changing for the lift to the Planplatten peak at 7366 ft. (2245 m.). You will walk along the spine of the mountain, crossing over the Balmeregghorn, past the Melchsee and the Tannensee, down to Engstlenalp at 6070 ft. (1850 m.), where you will return to Meiringen by bus.

Directions: *Take the train to Interlaken Ost and change for the train to Meiringen. At the Meiringen bus station, make a **reservation** for the return from Engstlenalp to Meiringen. Walk up the main street to the Sherlock Holmes Hotel, turn* *left to the lift station and take the cable car to Reuti, transfering to a gondola through Bidme to Magisalp. Exit the station at Magisalp, and take the chairlift for the breathtaking, 20-minute ride to Planplatten, where the walk begins.*

Start: A sign directs you left—"Engstlenalp-3 hrs." Be careful **not** to follow the sign to Engstlenalp Steiler Absteig—a lengthy, steep trail. The views from this path are exceptionally beautiful and, after about 40 minutes, you will arrive at the Balmeregghorn for a climb to the peak—taking between 30 and 60 minutes—depending on your pace. Walk down the other side of the peak, following signs to Engstlenalp and Tannenalp. When the path divides, take the mountain path up to your right, as the wider path continues down to Melchsee. The trail continues to be blazed white and red as you walk along the spine of the mountain. Follow the main trail to the right and down towards the Tannensee. Reaching the main path, make a right turn to the restaurant at Tannenalp, following a sign indicating "Engstlenalp-35 min." The rocky trail descends to Engstlenalp at 6070 ft. (1850 m.). The bus stop is past the hotel. **When you see the crowd at the bus stop you will be delighted you made reservations.**

MANNLICHEN TO GRINDELWALD

Walk #11 Lauterbrunnen to Zweilutschinen to Wilderswil to Interlaken (Excursion to Interlaken)
Walking Easy Time: 3 1/2 hours
Rating: Gentle

This walk can be reserved for a day when clouds or drizzle are not conducive to high-altitude exploration. The trail begins at the Lauterbrunnen train station. Walk down the station steps, turn right under the tracks, and follow the yellow *wanderweg* signs. The gentle path passes through the villages of Zweilutschinen, Gsteigwiler and Wilderswil, then into Interlaken for an excursion. (See Excursion #6). The appeal of todays low level walk is that it can be shortened or extended at each train station, depending on the weather.

LENK

Lenk, at 3543 ft. (1080 m.) is nestled near the end of the bucolic Simmental or Simmen Valley, surrounded by lush, undulating alps filled with placidly grazing *Milka* cows, a special breed of cattle. The area is interlaced with comfortable paths in the shadow of snow-covered peaks, including the 10,640 ft. (3243 m.) Wildstrubel, with lifts bringing hikers to scenic mid-and high-level trails. Zweissimen, the small village at the entrance to the Simmental, is headquarters for the Rinderberg lift, the beginning of a sensational high-level trek to Schönried, a neighbor of fashionable Gstaad. The hike from Iffigenalp to dramatic Iffigfall, through meadow and forest to Lenk, is another not to be missed experience for *Easy Walkers*.

Lenk is off the beaten path, yet close enough to public transportation for day-excursions to the castles at Spiez and Thun, steamer rides on Lake Thun, and shopping trips to Bern and Interlaken, along with panoramic rail excursions to Gstaad, les Diablerets, Gruyeres and Montreux. If you appreciate good walking we recommend Lenk, a village far from main roads and exhaust fumes, a beautiful corner of Switzerland.

FAVORITE *WALKLING EASY* HOTELS

Hotel Kreuz
Three-Star, Director—Familie Ischi-Michel
Internet: www.kreuzlenk.ch
E-mail: info@kreuzklenk.ch
> The outstanding, three-star hotel, located in the heart of the peaceful village of Lenk, is a charming, chalet-style hotel with large, modern guest rooms and public sitting rooms. The hotel boasts several dining rooms, and half-board guests have the choice of many menus.

TRANSPORTATION

By Train—You **always** change in Zweisimmen for the local train to Lenk.

By Car—From western Switzerland, drive east to Zweisimmen. Turn south on the local road, driving through the Simmental to Lenk. From eastern Switzerland or the Bernese Oberland near Interlaken, drive to Spiez, then to Zweisimmen, picking up the local road into Lenk.

EXCURSIONS

The Lenk Tourist Information Office is located in the middle of town, between the train station and the Hotel Kreuz.

Internet: http://www.lenk.ch
e-mail: info@lenk.ch

1. **Gstaad**—At an altitude of 3543 ft. (1080 m.), the chic village of Gstaad lies at the junction of four valleys. The area around Gstaad is called Saanenland, with a 200 mile (322 km.) network of hiking trails and a variety of cable lifts. (See Gstaad section.)
   Directions: Take a train from Lenk to Zweisimmen and change for the train to Gstaad—about an hour trip.

2. **Spiez**—This charming town on the shore of Lake Thun boasts a medieval castle overlooking the lake and vineyards. (See "Kandersteg," Excursion #2.)
   Directions: Take a train from Lenk to Zweissimen and change for the train to Spiez—about a one-hour trip.

3. **Thun**—The medieval city of Thun, with its cobblestone streets and famous castle, lies at the northern end of Lake Thun—a center for a number of walks around the lake. (See "Kandersteg," Walk 8.)
   Directions: Take a train to Zweisimmen, changing for the train to Spiez. Change again in Spiez for the train to Thun (one stop towards Bern).

4. **Interlaken**—Interlaken is a busy tourist center, surrounded by a superb mountain panorama. (See "Lauterbrunnen," Excursion #6.)
   Directions: Take a train to Zweisimmen, changing for the train to Spiez. In Spiez, change for the train to Interlaken West—a trip of less than two hours.

LENK WALKS

Recommended Map: Lenk Wanderkarte Trail Map

Walk #1: Introductory Walk—Lenk to the Lenkersee along the Obersimmentaler Hausweg to Simmenfalle to Metsch Lift, Metsch Mid-Station to Lenk
Walking Easy Time: 3 to 3 1/2 hours
Rating: Comfortable

If you arrive in Lenk early enough to spend about three hours on a low-to mid-level walk on your first day, this is a good introduction to the region. You will walk past the Lenkersee (the tiny lake outside of central Lenk), to the hamlet of Ey (Oey), all the way to Simmenfalle and its cascading waterfall, passing old, wooden farmhouses, some dating back to the 17th century—along the

Obersimmentaler Hausweg. The Tourist Office can provide an English description of these landmark buildings. You'll then walk to the Metschbahn and take the cable car up to Metsch mid-station for the hike back to Lenk.

Start: Walk past the church, following the Obersimmentaler Hausweg sign. A wide path leads past tiny Lenkersee on your left, a breeding ground for birds and waterfowl and continues around the end of the lake. Turn right, following the signs for Hausweg. After passing through tiny Ey, proceed on the Hausweg path along the rapids of the Simme, through the forest. After walking about 90 minutes you will reach the Hotel Simmenfalle. Walk past the hotel to the viewpoint overlooking the falls.

When ready, return to the hotel and walk for a half hour on the small, paved auto road, through Oberried, passing other houses on the Hausweg, all the way to the Metschbahn. Buy a one-way ticket to the Metsch mid-station at 4856 ft. (1480 m.), and on exiting, turn left, following the sign to Lenk. After about ten minutes, a sign directs you to Lenk through the forest on a somewhat steep trail. We prefer to pass this trail; walk straight ahead on the road for open views of the Simmental and note the sign reading "Lenk-50 min." After walking a half hour from Metsch, pass a sign indicating BRAND-HUBEL 1295 m., and continue walking on the road. At the sign FUSSGANGER (footpath), turn left, then right, down the steps in the direction of the red and white arrow. Take the *bergwanderweg*, shortcutting the road through the meadows and forest, eventually leading to a wagon path. This descending path brings you into the center of Lenk.

Walk #2: Iffigenalp to Iffigfall to Schroand to Ey to Lenk
Walking Easy Time: 2 1/2 hours
Rating: Comfortable

This fabulous hike should not be missed by *Easy Walkers*. Part of the fun is the bus ride from Lenk on a steep, winding mountain road, to the start of the walk at Iffigenalp at 5197 ft. (1584 m.), then descending on a forest trail to Iffigfall at 4397 ft. (1340 m.) and hiking down along the waterfall. This hike is a favorite, offering many kinds of trails with views of the rolling alps of the Simmental and a bonus of dramatic Iffig Falls.

Directions: *Take the private bus across from the bahnhof to Iffigenalp. Purchase your one-way bus ticket at the train station. The bus ascends 1693 ft. (516 m.) on a winding, narrow mountain road to Iffigenalp.*

Start: Several hikes begin at this location. More adventurous walkers can continue up from Iffigenalp at 5197 ft. (1584 m.) to the Iffigsee at 6844 ft. (2086 m.), returning back to Iffigenalp (a four-hour round-trip hike) for the walk back to Lenk by way of the falls. Another hike that can be taken by *Easy Walkers* is the popular three-and-a-half-hour mountain hike to Simmenfälle. (See Walk #3.)

Today, *Easy Walkers* will follow the sign IFFIGFALL-40 min., passing a trail on the right marked SIMMENFALLE, and walking ahead on the little auto road. About ten minutes from Iffigenalp, follow a *wanderweg* sign directing you down steps to the right, into the forest. This trail takes you along the river on your right, crossing the road several times—always continue on the marked *wanderweg*.

At one point, after crossing the road, you pass in front of a 600-year old farmhouse. Stay on the main trail, walking past the bus stop sign, descending into the forest and crossing the bridge for a view of the falls. Follow the trail to the left, to a sign to Poschenried at 3937 ft. (1200 m.), where it is possible to depart from the trail to the Alpenrosli Restaurant and bus stop, if the weather turns bad. Return to, or stay on the main trail, following the sign LENK 1 hr. 10 min. The trail narrows and ascends through a meadow, then enters the forest for the final descent into Ey. At the road, follow signs past the Lenkersee into Lenk.

OLD SWISS BARNS

Walk #3: Iffigenalp to Langermatte to Rezliberg/Sibe Brünne to Simmenfälle
Walking Easy Time: 3 1/2 to 4 hours
Rating: More Challenging

Another popular walk from Iffigenalp, reached by bus as in Walk #2, is the hike that ascends from Iffigenalp at 5197 ft. (1584 m.), along the Langermatte at 6090 ft. (1856 m.), descending somewhat steeply to Rezliberg/Sibe Brünne at 4610 ft. (1405 m.) along the Simme River, to the bus stop at SimmenfAlle at 3616 ft. (1102 m.).

Directions: See Walk #2.

Start: After exiting the bus at Iffigenalp, walk down the road for a few minutes to the sign directing you right, to SimmenfAlle. The first 90 minutes ascends steadily from 5197 to 6090 ft. (1584 to 1856 m.), a rise of 892 ft. (272 m.), to Langermatte. This portion of the hike, under the Oberlaubhorn, should be taken slowly until you reach Langermatte, the high point of today's hike.

At this point the trail descends, somewhat steeply in areas, to the Rezliberg mountain restaurant at 4610 ft. (1405 m.), along the Simme rapids. A short diversion to Sibe Brunne, the source of the Simme River, is a worthwhile stop. As you continue to descend, walk in the signed direction of Simmenfalle. At the falls, take the path down to the hotel, restaurant and bus stop at Simmenfalle, for the ride back to Lenk. If you feel fit, pick up the gentle path to Lenk behind the restaurant.

Walk #4: Zweisimmen/Rinderberg Top Station to Parwengen to Horneggli, Lift down to Schönried (Excursion to Gstaad)
Walking Easy Time: 2 1/2 hours
Rating: Comfortable

Be sure to reserve the better part of a beautiful day for this lovely hike and excursion to the famous resort of Gstaad—this is one of the most scenic walks in the Bernese Oberland. You will take the train from Lenk to Zweisimmen, ascend by gondola to Rinderberg at 6575 ft. (2004 m.), and hike up to an exciting viewpoint for an incredible panorama. The hike continues on a comfortable trail along the spine of the mountain to Parwengen, where you will walk in the direction of the next valley, home of the sophisticated mountain resort of Gstaad. The hike ends at the Horneggli chairlift for a descent to the Schönried train station and the short train ride to Gstaad. After visiting Gstaad, you will return to Lenk by train via Zweisimmen.

Directions: *Take a morning train to Zweisimmen and exit the train station, following signs to the Rinderberg Gondelbahn. Buy a one-way ticket to top station Rinderberg.*

Start: See Gstaad, Walk #5

Walk #5: Leiterli Top Station to Stublenipass to Leiterli to Stoss Mid-Station
Walking Easy Time: 4 hours
Rating: Comfortable

After taking the Betelberg lift to the Leiterli top station at 6431 ft. (1960 m.), you will continue ahead to the Stüblenipass 6562 ft. (2000 m.), and return via the same trail to the Leiterli lift station

Although it is possible to take the gondola back down to Lenk at Leiterli, you might enjoy continuing the hike to the Stoss mid-station at 5361 ft. (1634 m.), then taking the lift down to Lenk.

Directions: *At the church, follow signs to the Betelberg lift, about a ten-minute walk. Purchase a one-way ticket to the Leiterli top station.*

Start: After exiting at Leiterli, walk ahead following the sign STURLENIPASS-1 hr., 15 min. (Flower lovers might wish to detour to the Alpenblumenweg, a signed alpine garden trail.) The trail winds comfortably around the mountain and passes a "geologically protected" area below, on the right. This marshland was formed millenia ago, and is one of 87 protected marsh areas in Switzerland. An ancient sea, it is now the highest marsh area in the Alps. Views are spectacular, with remote dairy farms dotting the alpine landscape above the tree line. There are some splinter paths along the way, stay on the main *bergweg* all the way to the pass at Stübleni. Here, *Easy Walkers* can continue as far as they wish, and then continue back on the same path to the Leiterli lift station. At Leiterl, you have a couple of options:

1) Continue the walk down to the mid-station by following signs to Stoss, taking the gondola to Lenk from there.
2) Take the gondola from Leiterli all the way down to Lenk.

Walk #6: The Luchs (Lynx) Trail—Leiterli to Wallegg to Lenk
Walking Easy Time: 3½ hours
Rating: Comfortable

Two Lynx were caught near the Betelberg cable car and were fitted with transmitters in order to trace their activities. These shy, elegant animals choose only the most attractive areas for their home. Today's Lynx Walk is along a similar trail, and six lifelike fake lynx have been hidden close by. They are well camouflaged—

so look carefully and see if you can spot them! You'll take the *Betelberg Lift and return to Lenk through Siten and Walleg.*

Directions: *Walk past the church, following signs to the Betelberg Lift, and purchase a one-way ticket to Leiterli Top Station, at 6375 ft. (1943 m.)*

Start: After exiting the lift, walk down in the direction you came from toward LENK, WALLEG—2 1/2 HRS. Follow red-and-white posts left, through the meadows to a small farmhouse and the sign *bergwandereg*. Pass the farmhouse and walk on a little jeep road toward Siten and Lenk.

After passing siten, walk down the steps toward Wallegg and Lenk. After crossing the ridge over the gorge, continue left along the gorge to the Hotel Wallegg, 4331 ft. (1320 m.) (closed on Wednesday). At the restaurant you have several options.

1. Take the bus back to Lenk
2. Take the *schlucht* trail alongside the gorge to Lenk.
3. Continue down the road to see the sign BUEL, LENK, and turn right, into the forest on a mountain *bergweg*. Return to Lenk by following the LENK BAHNHOF signs.

Walk #7: Metschberg Top Station to Hahnenmoospass to Buhlberg to Simmenfalle to Lenk
Walking Easy Time: 2 to 5 hours
Rating: Comfortable

Today you will visit the heights over the Simmental by taking the Metsch lifts to the top station at Metschberg 6198 ft. (1889 m.), hiking to the Hahnenmoospass and continuing down to Bühlberg at 5443 ft. (1659 m.). From Bühlberg there are several options to return to Lenk.

Directions: Take the private bus from back of the *bahnhof* to the Metsch lift station. Buy a one-way ticket to the top and take the cable car to the mid-station, transferring to the purple *Milka* chairlift.

Start: After taking in the views, follow HAHNENMOOSPASS—30 MIN, directing you on a mountain path to the left … More adventurous walkers might wish to hike up to Metschstand and continue on to Hahnenmoospass by the high, ridge route—a bit more challenging. The lower route offers views of the soft, green alps overlooking the Simmental, while the high route to Hahnenmoospass gives you a 360-degree panorama.

There is a mountain hotel at Hahnenmoospass and a gondola descending the mountain in the direction of Adelboden. Today however, follow the sign BUHLBERG—45 MIN. At Buhlberg, you can exercise any one of three options:

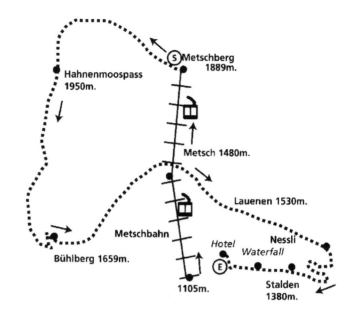

1. Continue walking 45 minutes from Buhlberg to the Metsch Mid-Station, taking the lift down to the base station for a gentle, half-hour valley walk back to Lenk. Or, if you wish, there is always the bus.

2. Continue to walk three hours from Bulberg to Simmenfalle—through Metsch, Nessli and Stalden—taking the bus back to Lenk.

3. Continue from Buhlberg to Mid-Station Metsch and return to Lenk, walking gently down the mountain, as described in Walk #1, another one and three-quarter hours from Buhlberg. We recommend option #2—the hike from Buhlberg to Simmenfalle—an additional three hours of more challenging, downhill walking. Follow the signs to Simmenfalle, continuing ahead at the cut-off to the mid-station of the Metsch Lift. At the Simmenfalle bus stop near the hotel, take the bus back to Lenk.

KANDERSTEG (ADELBODEN, LOTSCHENTAL)

The village of Kandersteg has everything going for it—a central location in Switzerland's majestic Bernese Oberland, a profusion of quality hiking trails, and proximity to the Lotschberg Tunnel for quick access to southern Switzerland's impressive mountains, glaciers and centuries-old villages. The charming lakeside towns of Thun, Interlaken and Spiez are only a short train ride away, with Zermatt—home of the Matterhorn—an easy day-excursion.

Kandersteg, at 3793 ft. (1156 m.) sits in a narrow valley, sandwiched between towering mountain peaks. Hiking from Kandersteg includes a large network of trails—a gentle walk to the remarkable Blausee, a small, crystal-clear lake; hike on the heights around Kandersteg, with views of the snow-covered Blumlisalp mountain range; ramble through the Kander Gorge along the raging Kander torrent; and marvel at the unspoiled beauty of the Gasterntal (Gastern Valley). The mountain trails above Kandersteg lead from the Gemini Pass down to the spa village of Leukerbad or up to Oeschinensee, a glacial lake set under high cliff walls. Walkers return year after year to comfortable hotels and breathtaking scenery around Kandersteg—a hiker's paradise and a perfect setting for *Walking Easy in the Swiss and Austrian Alps.*

TRANSPORTATION

By Train—From Zurich and the Zurich airport there are a few direct trains to Kandersteg. From points south of Kandersteg, such as Zermatt or Saas-Fee, involves a change of train in Brig and a ride north though the Lotschberg Tunnel.

By Car—From the north, drive to Spiez and follow signs south to Kandersteg. From the south, follow signs north to Goppenstein, where the car-train leaves every 30 minutes through the Lotschberg Tunnel. You will remain in your car for the 9 1/2 mile (15km.) trip, detraining in Kandersteg.

FAVORITE *WALKING EASY* HOTEL

Hotel Adler
Three-Star; Owners—Familie Fetzer
Email: info@chalethotel.ch
Internet www.chalethotel.ch
The hotel, under the caring eyes of Familie Fetzer, has been constantly renovated and offers many amenities and comfortable rooms. The kitchen serves regional food, with a salad bar at dinner and a Swiss buffet at breakfast. The

Hotel Adler is always busy, so make reservations in advance. Ask for a quiet room in the rear.

EXCURSIONS IN AND AROUND KANDERSTEG

The Kandersteg Tourist Office is located diagonally across the street from the Hotel Adler.

Internet: www.kandersteg.ch
e-mail: info@kandersteg.ch

1. **Blausee (Blue Lake)**—The translucent, azure color of the Blausee is exceptionally beautiful, and this small lake sits amid a network of paths winding though the surrounding forests. (See Walk #2.)
2. **Spiez**—This charming town on the shore of Lake Thun boasts a medieval castle, now a museum, overlooks the lake and nearby vineyards. Paths take walkers along Lake Thun, with a lovely waterside trail from Spiez to Faulensee, where you catch the boat back to Thun or Spiez, or ahead to Interlaken West.
   Directions: *Trains to Spiez run hourly from Kandersteg.*
3. **Thun**—The medieval city of Thun, with its cobblestone streets and famous castle, lies at the northern end of Lake Thun.
   Directions: *Take the train to Thun through Spiez.*
4. **Bern**—The capital of Switzerland is a delightful city, declared a "world landmark" by the United Nations. The Bern Tourist Office, inside the railroad station, can supply you with maps and sightseeing suggestions. Walk into the Old Town or *altstadt,* 3 1/2 miles (10km.) of ancient arcades, fountains, towers and shops. Visit Theaterplatz and the Clock Tower (Zytgloggeturm), Kornhousplatz and its much-photographed Ogre Fountain, and of course, the famous Bear Pits for which the city is named.
   Directions: *Trains to Bern leave hourly for the one-hour ride.*
5. **Interlaken**—Interlaken, named for its location between Lake Thun and Lake Brienz, is a bus tourist center, surrounded by a superb mountain panorama. (See Lauterbrunnen/Wengen, Excursion #6.)
   Directions: *Take the train to Spiez and change for the train to Interlaken West.*
6. **Zermatt**—Zermatt is a tourist and hiking mecca encompassing some of the world's most magnificent scenery, including the mighty Matterhorn. (See Zermatt section.)
   Directions: *Trains leave hourly from Kandersteg to connect in Brig with the train to Zermatt.*

KANDERSTEG WALKS

Recommended Maps
1) Kandersteg Wanderkarte—Blausee, Leukerbad mit Qschintal, Gemmigebiet, Gasterntal, Oeschinensee, Hohturlipass
2) Kummerly+Fry Wanderkarte—Lotschental
3) Kummerly+Fry—Adelboden

Walk #1: Selden to Heimritz to Selden to Waldhaus to Kandersteg—Through the Gasterntal
Walking Easy Time: 3 to 4 hours
Rating: Comfortable

The Gasterntal or Gastern Valley, was formed millenia ago, well before Walt Disney created his Magic Kingdom, but it surely must mean that Mr. Disney visited this dream valley for creative inspiration. The magic kingdom you will visit today ends at the leading edge of a great glacier, the source of the Kander River, which flows into Lake Thun. After arriving at Selden you'll walk into the valley to Heimritz, with its tiny *gasthaus* and views of the glacier. You'll return to Kandersteg, walking though forests and over meadows, never far from the rushing Kander River, the Kander Waterfall and the spectacular Kander Gorge.

A CHURCH IN KANDERSTEG

Directions: *A day before this trip is planned, make reservations though your hotel with the mini-bus for riding to Selden and walking back to Kandersteg. We recommend the 9:30 am mini-bus across from the Kandersteg railroad station. Exit the bus in front of the Hotel Steinbock, after a ride on a narrow, one-way mountain road.*

Start: Follow the sign to Heimritz, leading towards the distant mountains, gradually ascending from 5043 to 5364 ft. The view on the right is of the Kander River, with high mountains on either side of a long, narrow, fertile valley. Continue to Heimritz on the main path, and within twenty–five minutes you'll reach Gasthaus Gletscher Heimritz. Walk past the *gasthaus* and around the bend for a magnificent view of the Alpetligletscher. NOTE: If you wish, continue along the trail towards Kanderfirn and the glacier, remembering to leave enough time for the return walk to Kandersteg.

When ready, retrace your steps to Selden for the two-and-a half-hour hike to Kandersteg. Begin walking on the car road, but after fifteen minutes, follow signs pointing left towards Eggenschwand, Waldhaus and Kandersteg, on a *wanderweg,* blazed with a yellow diamond. The trail descends through the forest and empties on to a path signed KANDERSTEG AND WALDHAUS to the left. Crossing the river on a small bridge as directed, follow the path through an open meadow, passing though a sea of larch trees. The Balmhorn is on the left, with high, jagged peaks reflecting the sun and casting dancing images across the valley floor. Continue through the valley, passing a statue of a Swiss climber pointing to the Balmhornhutte, up on the mountain. Follow the signs to Waldhaus and Kandersteg, and within ninety minutes from from Selden you'll reach the Hotel Waldhaus at 4456 ft. A refreshment stop here is a must; the beer is cold, the *kuehen* is tempting, and the views are unforgettable.

Continue on the trail behind the hotel, towards Kandersteg. Reenter the forest, follow *wanderweg* blazes, with an offshoot of the river on your left. Walk with the now raging Kander River on your right, and after 15 minutes of descending, the rocky path recrosses the river as you enter the Kander Gorge. Walk on the auto road for a few minutes, but as the road turns left to enter a tunnel, follow signs to Eggenschwand and Kandersteg and turn right on a descending mountain path. This is an exciting part of the trail—traversing the gorge, feeling the power and the spray of the torrent. The path is rocky, so watch your step as you descend, and the tranquil, green valley beyond Eggeschwand soon appears.

Cross the bridge to the right, and turn left, as the path becomes a car road and enters the parking area of the Sunnbuel cable car. *Easy Walkers* have the option of returning to Kandersteg by bus, or continuing on a half-hour stroll to the village.

Walk #2: Kandersteg to Blausee to Kandergrund (Excursion to Blausee)
Walking Easy Time: 2 1/2 hours
Rating: Comfortable

The hike to Blausee from Kandersteg is a gentle walk along the Kander River, leaving Kandersteg at 3858 ft. and walking easily down to the beautiful Blue Lake at 2910 ft. About 15,000 years ago an avalanche shook the Kander Valley and enormous chunks of ice thundered down the mountain. These ice blocks left crevices in the rocks and resulting hollows filled with water as the ice melted, forming tiny Blausee, or Blue Lake—famous for its trout.

Start: Walk to the railroad station and follow the sign marked BLAUSEE., 15 mm., though the parking area. As you head north in the direction of Blausee and Frntigen, the Kander River is on the right. In about ten minutes the path splits—stay on the right path, along the river. Continue on this *wanderweg*, walking under the railroad tracks, past the power station, still along the river, following signs to Blausee. Continuing ahead on the main path, turn right as directed, and follow the trail to Blausee, leaving the path continuing on to Frntigen. Crossing over the river, you reach the main auto road, with signs pointing to Blausee across the highway and left. Within ten minutes, note the sign announcing BLAUSEE—THE BLUE LAKE, back across the road to the left.

Pay an admission fee entitling you to visit the trout nursery and take a boat ride. You should plan to spend an hour or two visiting this lovely park—enjoying your picnic lunch and wandering on some of the forest paths.

Leave Blausee by the Rock Path and walk back to the road. Turn left on the sidewalk and continue down the hill towards Kandergrnnd. A few minutes after passing the Zoo Tierpark, a sign across the road points to Wanderweg Kandergrnnd. Take this *wanderweg*, walking through the meadow, in the direction of Inner Kandergrnnd Kirche. As you pass the church and arrive at intersecting paths, walk up the hill to the right, following the sign FRUTIGEN, SPITZRUTELI, AND KANDERGRUND.

This trail ascends into the forest, with spectacular views of the valley below. Follow the KANDERGRUND STATION—20 MIN. sign and turn sharply left on a narrow, meadow path. This path continues to be blazed with the *wanderweg* diamond and enters the forest, descending the mountain to Kandergrnnd. This trail takes you through a turnstile, and soon meets an auto road. Turn left through a tunnel, where the road enters the area of the rarely-used Kandergrnnd railroad station. Follow the sign pointing down a paved, zig-zagging path, to the Kandergrnnd bus stop. Cross the road to wait for the bus to Kandersteg.

WALK # 3: Kandersteg to Höhwald to Kandersteg (Excursion to Ailmenalp)
Walking Easy Time: 2 1/2 hours
Rating: Comfortable

Today's walk entices *Easy Walkers* with some of the dramatic scenery surrounding the village of Kandersteg. You will take the gondola up to Allmenalp, a plateau under the Bundespitz with a cheese-making dairy and restaurant—a favorite jumping off place for paragliders. After returning by gondola to the valley floor, the walk will continue on the *hohweg* (high trail), along the Kandersteg heights.

Start: Facing the Kandersteg station, turn left and walk through the tunnel under the tracks. Turn left again, so you are walking with the tracks on your left. This signed path goes directly to the Allmenalp *luftseilbah* (cable car). Buy a round trip ticket. At the top, visit the cheesemaking dairy and walk to the lookout point for spectacular views of the Kander Valley, all the way to the Oeschinensee. Return by gondola to continue walking along the heights bordering Kandersteg.

Leave the base station and retrace your steps on the paved road. Make a left turn on the first road, marked PRIVAT STRASSE. Proceed though the meadow, passing the Waldrand Ski lift on the right, walking in the direction of the waterfall. The road empties into a small parking area with a large, flower bedecked house inscribed BUDDIST KLOSTER, DHAMMAPALA. This charming, weathered *kloster* (monastery) is run by Buddhist monks.

A path enters the forest on the left side of the *kloster,* marked with a sign HOH PANORAMAWEG.

After ascending through the forest, the trail breaks out of the woods, passing a small wooden barn. Continue walking to an intersection and turn left to the Hoh Panoramaweg. Within a few minutes, the mountain ranges that give this valley its special flavor come into view—including the jagged peak of the Doldenhorn up on the right, overlooking the valley. The trail continues through the alp.

Take a narrow mountain trail to the left, marked HOH and GOLITSCHENALP. Walk around a farmhouse and up the hill on a narrow trail leading to a high point, for all-encompassing views. Follow this *wanderweg,* a grassy path though the meadow, passing though several wooden gates, crossing from one pasture to another.

Take the path down to the right marked KANDERSTER WAALDWEG—30 MIN. Cross the wagon road, and pass to the right of a small cabin, entering into a forest area. Within a minute, the yellow, diamond-blazed trail splits. Take the left trail for a ten-minute descent though the forest to the road below. Turn left on the road in the signed direction of Buhl and Kandersteg. The road winds around the mountain, and at a major intersection marked KANDERSTEG to the right and BLAUSEE to the left, turn left, as if walking to Blausee, then make an immediate right turn. Walk though the power station and tunnel, under the highway, continuing on the path back to Kandersteg.

A GENTLE WALKING EASY TRAIL

Walk #4: Kandersteg to Eggeschwand, Sunnbuel to Spittehnatte to Schwarenbach to Sunnbuel
Walking Easy Time: 3 1/2 hours
Rating: Comfortable

Your first part of the trip is the 30-minute walk from Kandersteg toEggeschwand, where you will board the cable car for the ride up to the 6345 ft. (1934 in.)Sunnbuel station. You will walk though the Spittelmatte meadows, and then ascend to Schwarenbach at 6759 ft. (2060 m.) with a restaurant and facilities, returning to the lift station on a new path.

Directions: Follow the sign "Stock Gemini," walking past the Hotel Schweizerhof to Eggeschwand. Buy a round trip ticket.

Start: Walk ahead, following the sign SCHWARENBACH-1HR., 15 MIN. Proceed down and though the Spittelmatte meadow, as if walking though the center of a large punchbowl. After about 40 minutes, you can picnic at the working dairy farm on your right, with a snack of fresh milk and cheese.

The path ascends, with directions "Hotel Schwarenbach-30 mm." painted on a rock. Don't believe it! 50 minutes is more realistic for *Easy Walkers,* as this path ascends more steeply to reach Schwarenbach at 6759 ft. (2060 m.)

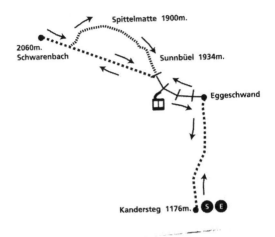

Take the same path back towards Spittalmatte and the lift station, but just before the dairy farm you passed earlier in the day, note the sign pointing left to Arvenseeli. This *bergweg* is blazed red and white and meanders around the Arvenwald and its small lake (Arvenseeli—usually dry in late summer), ending at the lift station. Of course, you can also stay on the main path all the way to the lift station. The Sunnbuel cable car descends to Eggeschwand, and you can walk back to Kandersteg or take the bus outside the lift station.

NOTE: Another version of this walk is an exciting and rewarding full day's excursion and 3 1/2 hour hike over the Gemini Pass, from Leukerad. You would not want to do both walks—just one or the other. This alternate version starts from Leukerbad, taking the lift up to the Gemini Pass, walking past the Daubensee to Schwarenbach and then to the Sunnbuel lift. It's best to take this version on a Saturday or Sunday, when a morning bus goes directly to Leukerbad from the train station at Goppenstein, one stop south of Kandersteg.

Walk #5: Schwandfeldspitz Top Station to Adelboden (Excursion to Adelboden)
Walking Easy Time: 2 hours
Rating: Comfortable

(Use the Adelboden map.) Today's hike is a good way to become acquainted with Adelboden, a resort in the Bernese Oberland. You will take a lift to the top of the Schwandfeldspitz, then proceed along Tschenten Alp. The trail follows the

Hornliweg and, at Hornli you will descend on a comfortable wagon path into Adelboden for the bus ride back to Frntigen and the return train to Kandersteg.

Directions: *Take a morning train one stop from Kandersteg to Frntigen. You'll arrive in time to catch the connecting bus outside the Frntigen train station for the 30-minute, scenic ride to Adelboden. Arriving in Adelboden, exit the bus station, turn right and walk towards the center of town. The Tourist Office is on the left side of the main street. Locate the Hotel Kreuz, diagonally across from the i where a sign directs you to the Schwandfeldspitz Lift. Purchase a one-way ticket for this gondola, rising to 6400 ft. (1951 m.)*

Start: Outside the top lift station, follow the signs, "Tschentenegg-15 min.," "Hornli-50 min." and "Adelboden-l h., 50 min." Walk to the right, up and over a small grassy meadow, following the trail down the ridge of Tschentenegg. After about 20 minutes, ignore a sign indicating "Adelboden-l hr." Do not take this steep trail, but walk ahead following "Hornli-30 min., Adelboden-1 hr." You are now at Tschentenegg and, within a short time you'll arrive at a split in the path—the left marked Lechterweg and the right marked Steilerweg. *Steiler* means steep in German, and while we have descended this trail, we recommend taking the easier path to the left. Both forest trails eventually lead to a small grassy plain, the entire valley visible in front of you. The level of descent eases on a path now marked not only with the familiar *wanderweg* diamond but, in rockier spots, with white and red blazes. You'll soon reach an overlook with benches and signs pointing to Adelboden.

Turn right and follow the sign "Adelboden-30 mm., Unter Hornli"—meaning "to Adelboden by the lower trail." This blazed path descends gently though the forest, eventually reaching the meadows and suburbs around Adelboden. Within another ten minutes you'll reach the bottom of the road. Turn right for the bus station and the return to Frntigen, where you catch the train to Kandersteg.

Walk #6: **Lauchernalp Top Station to Weissenreid to Blatten—Through the Lotschental**
Walking Easy Time: 3 hours
Rating: Comfortable

The day we took our hike, the little, handmade weather sign at the Kandersteg train station ticket office showed a happy, sunny face in *die Lotschental—the Lotschen Valley*—while the weather in Kandersteg was marginal, with low, ominous clouds. You too, may find this a great opportunity to visit the other side of the mountains. The Lotschental appears to be lifted from another century. In fact, it was isolated for centuries, until roads and the Lotschberg Railway were built in the early 1900s. Each small village has managed to maintain much of the culture and character of the region, including many of the old, wooden barns—some in the traditional Valaisian *mazot* style.

Today you will depart from the more traditional trail walks in order to wander by road through one of these old mountain villages, filled with centuries-old barns and homes. The walk begins at the Lauchernalp top station, winds up and around on the Hohenweg, though meadow, forest, and small alpine villages to Tellialp. Here you will take a mountain road through the charming, old hamlet of Weissenried and continue down to Blatten, another small, traditional village.

Directions: *Catch the morning train (before 9:30 am) from Kandersteg to Goppenstein, the first stop after a short ride though the Lotschberg Tunnel. Leave the station, following signs to the Lotschental-Lauchernalp bus, and take the bus marked LAUCHERNALP-WILER to Wiler, where you take the Lauchernalp cable car. Buy a one-way ticket to the top.*

Start: At the top station at 6562 ft. (2000 m.) follow the signs towards "Fafleralp-2 hs. 30 mm." on the Lotschentaler Hohenweg. Look north to see the impressive Langgletscher, and the Lonza River flowing though the long, narrow valley below. Continue on an ascending, yellow-blazed trail as it turns and rises gently around the side of the mountain.

After you reach a high point of 6760 ft. (2060 m.) the path begins to descend for the remainder of the walk. It winds though the mountain town of Weritzalp, narrowing here and taking on more of the *bergweg* character of a traditional mountain trail. Enter onto a shaded forest path, rocky at times, and continue to descend along this trail towards Fafleralp. The blazes turn red and white, alerting walkers to be more cautious, as you proceed to Tellialp, easily recognized by a small bridge and a rushing waterfall. At Tellialp, a sign indicates the way to Fafleralp, up to the left, or to Blatten and Reid, descending to the right on a wagon path. *Easy Walkers* have two options at this point:

1) Walk on to Fafleralp, catching the bus to Goppenstein.

2) Walk down to Blatten though Weissenried, our suggestion for today. If you decide on Option #2, turn right and walk on the small road, rejecting a path going down the mountain on a trail to your left. Stay on the main wagon road to Weissenried—the reason we took you in this direction. Walk slowly though this tiny mountain hamlet, with its small chapel built in the 1700's. The village is filled with marvelous photographic opportunities—walking through Weissenried is like strolling through a small Swiss museum. When you're ready, follow signs to the picturesque village of Blatten, where you catch the bus back to Goppenstein, timed to meet the return train to Kandersteg.

Today was spent walking though one of the most beautiful and isolated valleys in Switzerland, with a tantalizing glimpse of the Switzerland that used to be—and still is—in many areas of *die Lotschental!*

Walk #7: Oeschinensee Lift Top Station to Oeschinensee to Kandersteg
(Excursion to Oeschinensee)
Walking Easy Time: 2 hours
Rating: Comfortable

Kandersteg is not only blessed with glaciers, snow-covered peaks and fabulous walking trails, it also boasts one of the prettiest mountain lakes in the Bernese Oberland. You will visit the Oeschinensee by taking a chairlift from Kandersteg to the top station at 5519 ft. (1682 m.) A 30-minute walk to the lake descends to 5177 ft. where you can boat, swim, picnic or *spazier* (ramble) before the return walk to Kandersteg. The lake is surrounded by the dramatic peaks of the Kandersteg area, including the Doldenhorn and Blumlisalp, and their glaciers.

Directions: *Walk past the Tourist Office to the second sign directing you to the Oeschinensee chairlift. Walk up through the meadow, following signs to the lift. Purchase a one-way ticket to the top station.*

Start: After leaving the lift station, follow the path to Oeschinensee. Shortly, the path forks, with both trails leading down to the lake. From the lake you can meander on trails on either side, rent a boat and enjoy the spectacular views.

When ready, walk up and around the Hotel Oeschinensee to a group of signs. Follow directions to Kanderesteg along the gravel path. After about five minutes, a *wanderweg* enters the forest on the right. You can continue on the road (the easier way down), or follow the *wanderweg* paths all the way into Kandersteg.

Walk #8: Excursion to Thun and Walk to the Lake Towns
Walking Easy Time: 1 to-3 hours
Rating: Gentle

The small city of Thun is an ideal location for a visit, not only when the weather is fair, but also when it is cloudy or drizzling—not conducive to high-level walking. Thun is the largest and most important town in the Bernese Oberland, situated on the beautiful Thunersee (Lake Thun), and easily reached by train. It has a delightful Old Town section, with a castle currently serving as a museum. While there are high altitude walks around Thun, we are bringing you there in less than ideal weather because the lakeside walks around Thun can help to brighten an otherwise dreary day.

Directions: Take *the train through Spiez to Thun. The Thun Tourist Office is located outside the train station and to the left. City maps are available.*

Start: As you leave the railroad station and enter the main shopping district, follow signs with a symbol of a castle. After a 15-minute walk, enter the castle area through ancient fortress walls dating back to the 12th century. The main center of attraction is the Knight's Hall, a large room paneled in tapestries, with a fine collection of 15th-century weapons.

After exploring the castle and Thun's many shops, walk down and around the hill, back towards the railroad station and the canal you crossed earlier. Note a group of signs with directions for walks along scenic Lake Thun. Turn left, in the direction of Oberhofen, and walk on the path along the canal, leaving the center of Thun. After walking 40 minutes, note the steamer stop at Hunibach., with several options, again depending on the weather:

1) You can follow the same lake path back to Thun and take the train back to Kandersteg.

2) On leaving Hunibach, walk in the direction of Hilterfingen where another castle awaits you—Castle Hunegg—more elaborate than Thun castle. It's situated in a park-like setting, with the small village and its mountains as a backdrop. From Hilterfingen, follow signs to Oberhofen and another medieval castle. Hunibach, Hilterfingen and Oberhofen are all regularly scheduled steamer stops for the return to Thun, where you change for the train to Kandersteg.

3) From any lake village, take the boat to Interlaken West and the train to Spiez, where you change for the Kandersteg train.

GSTAAD (SAANENLAND)

Sophisicated Gstaad, Switzerland's "Aspen of the Alps," enjoys a unique, world-wide reputation—the place-to-be for Europe's jet set. Situated in a quiet alpine location in southwestern Switzerland, Gstaad is close enough for one-day excursions to Montreux and its summer Jazz Festival on the shores of Lake Geneva, Lausanne with its Olympic Museum, the formidable peaks and glaciers of Les Diablerets at the Col du Pillon, and the picturesque, cheese producing village of Gruyères and its medievel castle.

Gstaad boasts exclusive shops, gourmet restaurants, two world-renowned five-star hotels, a well-maintained car-free walking street, and the Swiss Open Tennis tournament—usually held the second week in July. But, most important to *Easy Walkers* is the little-publicized fact that the Gstaad area has an outstanding network of lifts and over 185 miles (300 km.) of summer hiking trails tailored for all levels of ability.

Gstaad is recognized as the unofficial capital of Sannenland (the last outpost of the Bernese Oberland; the valley adjacent to the Sinmental and the *Walking Easy* base village of Lenk), and its traditional, villages of Saanen, Saanenmoser, Gsteig, Lauenen, Turbach, and Schonried, are all part of the impressive Swiss public transportation system—frequent trains and buses tied into the beginning and ending points of *Walking Easy* trails. Switzerland's alpine heritage is nurtured in Saanenland; its mountain farming, cheese-making, and chalet-style architecture still a way of life along with a lively music scene—a perfect combination for *Walking Easy.*

TRANSPORTATION

By Train—From Geneva (two and a half hours), take the train to Montreux and change for the train to Gstaad. From the Bernese Oberland area, take the train from Spiez to Zweisimmen and change for the train to Montreux, stopping in Gstaad.

By Car—From the north and Spiez, head southwest on Route 11. From the south you can pick up Route 11 outside of Aigle.

FAVORITE *WALKING EASY* HOTEL

Hotel Bernerhof
Four Star; Owners, Claudia and Thomas Frei
CH-3780 Gstaad; Tel: 33 748 88 44

E-mail: info@bernerhof-gstaad.ch
Internet: www.Bernerhof-gstaad.ch

The Hotel Bernerhof is located in the center of town on Gstaad's main walking street. All rooms and suites have private facilities, balconies, mini-bar, TV, and every guest has the use of a plush teny robe for use around the indoor pool, sauna, and steam rooms. Book with half-board as guests can choose from three excellent restaurants in the hotel, one of which offers outstanding Oriental specialities. The hotel is open year-round, and is geared to *Easy Walkers,* offering daily walking tours Many *Easy Walkers* will appreciate special discounts for senior guests.

EXCNRSIONS

The Gstaad Tourist Information Office is located on the main walking street.
E-mail: info@gstaad.ch
Internet: www.gstaad.ch

1. **Les Diablerets**—From the Col du Pillon, or Pillon Pass, cable cars transport visitors up to a spectacular panorama of ice and snow, with snow bus tours available on Glacier 3000.
   Directions: *Take the bus to Col du Pillon and the cable lifts to the top station*
2. **Montrenx**—Stretching along the shores of Lake Geneva in what is called the Vaud Riviera because of its exceptionally mild climate, Montreux is home to **Chillon Castle, made famous** by the poet Lord Byron. Above Montreux is Rochers-de-Naye, at 6700 ft. (2042m.) reached by rack railway. Montreux is also home to the world-famous Jazz Festival, beginning the first Friday in July and lasting two-and-a half weeks.
   Directions: *Take the train to Montreux—the Panoramic Express with its special windows and comfortable seats, if possible.*
3. **Gruyeres**—This tiny, fortified village is perched on a hillside dominated by a fifteenth-century castle. The cobblestone streets are lined with ancient houses and it is car-free between Easter and November. A model dairy, making the famed Gruyere cheese, is in operation at the entrance to the town, at the foot of a hill near the train station.
   Directions: *Take a morning train from Gstaad to Montbovon. Change/or the train to Gruyeres—about an hour and ten minute ride.*

Gstaad Walks
Recommended Map:
Wanderkarte Saanenland—Gstaad Saanenland:

Walk #1
Introdnctory Walk—The Menuhin Trail
Walking Easy Time: 1 to 2 hours
Rating: Comfortable

Today's short low-level walk from Gstaad to its neighboring village of Saanen, is a fine introduction to the Saanenland if you arrive too late in the day to attempt a longer and more strenuous hike. The return to Gstaad can be along the same path or by train. Lord Yehudi Menuhin was an integral part of the summer music community for many years, and is the commune's honorary citizen. This trail is dedicated to him—with panels in three languages reflecting the thoughts and philosophy of this famous musician.

At Alpenruhe, Yehudi Menuhin room where walkers can visit a Yehudi Menuhin room to view books, CDs and videos which reflect his philosophy and works. The walk ends in Saanen at the Mauritius Church, in which Lord Menuhin played and conducted many concerts.

Start: In Gstaad, leave the Kapalliplatz in the direction of Saanen. Pass the Atelier d'Artiste and walk under the train tracks. Continue towards Gschwend and follow the Saane River to the Bellerive restaurant where you pick up a pleasant, shady path that follows the river. Turn right to the Alpenrnhe, and visit the Menuhin Room. Walk across the area called Salzwasser as far as the Chouflisbach. By following this stream you reach the river again—head for Saanen and end the walk at the Saanen church. This path recalls the great artist and is intended to stimulate quiet reflection. To return to Gstaad, return on the same path, or take the train or bus at the *bahnhof*

Walk #2
Lanenensee to Gstaad
Walking Easy Time: 3 hours
Rating: Comfortable

Today you'll take a bus to the far end of the valley that rises easily from Gstaad, at 3416 ft. (1041 m.) to the Lauenensee, 4137 ft. (1261m.)and, after rambling around the lake, you'll walk back to Gstaad by way of Lauenen. The path is never far from the rushing Louisbach and is generally made up of a *wanderweg* through meadow and forest, close enough to the road and bus to Gstaad, if needed.

Directions: Take a morning bus from the Gstaad bus station next to the train station, to Lauenensee. (If you are using a Swiss Pass there is a small supplement from Lauenen to Lauenensee.)

Start: After exiting the bus at Lauenensee, follow the sign LAUENENSEE—5 MIN. As you pass the lake on your left, the path splits. Take the wider path ahead, marked HINTEREM SEE, and you will be walking to Lauenen. It takes about an hour to reach the outskirts of Lauenen, with the path emptying to the Hotel Alpenland and its wonderful restaurant, the Rosti Factory, offering many delicious variations of the famous Swiss national dish.

When ready, walk up on the gravel path next to the restaurant. Cross the little bridge and immediately take the trail on your right into the woods, following a sign marked *wanderweg* GSTAAD—2 STD. This path alternates between a *wanderweg* (always signed) and a small, country road. You can remain on the road, but it is more scenic following the yellow *wanderweg* arrows all the way to Gstaad.

Walk #3
Wispile Top Station to Gsteig
Walking Easy Time: 3 1/2 to 4 1/2 hours
Rating: Comfortable to More Challenging

This popular hike begins at the top station of the Wispile lift. The trail continues comfortably along the ridge of the Hohi Wispile to Chine Pass (Krinnenpass), where you have the option of descending three different ways. The views from the ridge trail are sensational—high mountain peaks in all directions. **NOTE: Try to take this hike during dry weather—these trails can be muddy and slippery.**

Directions: *Take a morning bus marked Gsteig from the bus bahnhof. Exit after a few minutes ride at the Wispile lift station. Remain in the gondola to the top station at 6267 ft.*

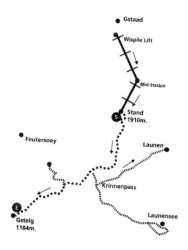

Start: Follow signs KRINNENPASS—1 HR., 20 MIN. (this may take *Easy Walkers* somewhat longer). You are now walking on the Meteopfad or Weather Trail, which rises to 6365 ft. (1940 **in.**) at the peak, where a group of photogenic llamas greet you. This is the high point of today's hike. Continue ahead, following the *wanderweg* and Krinnenpass signs.

The Meteopfad turns around to the left as you descend ahead. You eventually arrive at a narrow entry with a descent to the right signed to Gsteig, or a descent on the left trail to Krinnenpass, Lauenen, and the Lauenensee. This is where three options become available:

1. Follow the descending left trail to Krinnenpass, where the trail splits again. You can either hike down to Lauenen, a somewhat steep trail, with a bus return to Gstaad or,

2. Follow signs for a steep descent down to the Krinnenpass (Chrinepass). From the pass you climb about 330 ft. (100 **in.**) to reach a path which slopes gently down to the Lauenensee naturereserve.At Lauenensee, take the bus to Gstaad.

3. The forest trail descending to Gsteig is our option today, because we visited the Lauenensee in Walk #2.

With Option #3, descend through the forest in the direction of Gsteig uintil you arrive at signs to Gsteig and Feutersoey. Walk through the gate, following the trail marked GSTEIG, continuing to descend though the meadow to a small farm with a sign on the other side of the barn, pointing down to the right, along a wagon path, to the road below. Follow the yellow arrows on the road and the *wanderweg* signs, which shorten the descent by using forest trails cuffing off the mountain road. In Gsteig, take the bus to return to Gstaad.

Walk #4
Eggli Top Station to Vorder Eggli to Saanen
Walking Easy Time: 3 hours
Rating: Comfortable

Today's walk combines an interesting visit to a working dairy farm run by a friendly Swiss couple, with views of the rolling alps of Saanenland. At the farm you have the opportunity of tasting fresh milk and cheese made the old-fashioned way.

Directions: Walk, or take the bus stopping at the Eggli lift station. Buy a one-way ticket to the top.

Start: From the Eggli station, at 5118 ft. (1560m.), follow signs to Vorder Eggli, a rise of 330 ft. (100 m.). along a wagon path. Visit the friendly couple at the rustic dairy and cheese making cabin. They also serve fresh mountain products so don't forget to taste the cheese. At the dairy at Vorder Eggli, you have several options:

1. Continue ahead, with the wagon road becoming a descending, narrow, mountain auto road with little traffic. You'll walk through Chalberhoni (Kalberoni), all the way to Saanen, where you can take the train back to Gstaad, or pick up the river trail for an hour's stroll into Gstaad along the Menuhin Path.

2. Retrace your steps back toward the top station of the Eggli lift, where you can take the path down to Saanen (shorter than Option #1). In Saanen, take the train to Gstaad. As you descend the hill to Saanen, there is an option to walk directly back to Gstaad—just follow the signs.

Walk #5
Zweissimnmenl Rinderberg Top Station to Parwengen to Horneggli
Walking Easy Time: 2 1/2 hours
Rating: Comfortable

Reserve the better part of a beautiful day for one of the most scenic walks in the Bernese Oberland. You'll take the train from Gstaad to Zweisimmen, ascend by gondola to Rinderberg, at 6575 ft. (2004 m), and hike up to an exciting viewpoint. The hike continues on a comfortable trail along the spine of the mountain, ending at the Horneggli chairlift for a descent to Schonried and a train back to Gstaad.

Directions: Take a morning train to Zweissimmen and exit the train station, following signs to the Rinderberg Gondelbahn. Buy a one-way ticket to top station Rinderberg.

Start: Follow the large sign HOHENWEG NACH HORNEGGLI. Walk up to the *gipfel* (peak) at 6821 ft. (2079 m.) and check out the incredible panorama of the Bernese Oberland mountains. The trail continues—with minor ascents and descents, many of which are stepped for comfort—along Gandlouenengrat ridge to Parwengen, at 6024 ft. (1836 in.). Here, follow directions to Hornberg and the Horneggli lift. After passing two mountain restaurants at Hornberg, follow HORNEGGLI CHAIRLIFT—20 MIN. Walk through the meadow and down a mountain *bergweg* to the chairlift (buying your ticket at the bottom), and follow signs to the Schonried *bahnhof* for next train or bus to Gstaad.

Walk #6
Chatean-d'Oex/La Braye Top Station to Chatean-d'Oex (Excnrsion to Chatean-d'Oex)
Walking Easy Time: 2 hours
Rating: Comfortable

The French-speaking village of Chateau-d'Oex (pronounced "chateau day"), is in the Vaud canton, near the Bernese Oberland border. After walking in the lovely rolling countryside surrounding the village, where the famous l'Etivaz cheese is still produced in some 150 chalet dairies, pay a visit to the Musée du Vieux Pays d'Enhaut (Traditional Museum), located on three floors of an old chalet. At the end of the town is the eighteenth-century Etambeau Chalet (also part of the museum).

Directions: Take the train from Gstaad to Chateau-d'Oex, about a fifteen-minute ride in the direction of Montreux. In the village, follow signs for the five-minute walk to La Braye cable car. Exit at mid-station Pra-Perron, at 4003 ft. (1220 m.) and enter the covered chairlift for the ride to the top station, at 5414 ft.

Start: Exit and follow signs to the right reading PRA-PERRON—50 MIN., and CHATEAU D'OEX 1 STD., 40 MIN. The descent from the top is on a gentle wagon path with lovely views of the surrounding countryside, eventually turning into a small, paved, rarely-used mountain road. After about fifty minutes, a sign on a barn points though the meadows to the Pra-Perron mid-station and the cable down to the village. Or, continue walking into Chateau-d'Oex. With either option, pay a visit to the museum before returning by train to Gstaad.

Walk #7
Saanen to Unterbort to Rougemont
Walking Easy Time: 2 hours
Rating: Comfortable

Today's walk brings beautiful views of the surrounding Alpes Vaudoises, ending in a tiny village, home to a tenth-century church nestled under a huge, sloping roof The inside of the church is typically early Romanesque, but the adjoining sixteenth-century château was rebuilt in 1973. The church. ancient castle, and traditional chalets all contribute to Rougemont's unique, historical charm.

Directions: Take the train from Gstaad to Saanen.

Start: At the Saanen train station, cross the main road, walk past the church, at 3317 ft.

(1011 m.) and follow the street towards Unterbort. A well-kept path now leads to Point de la Scie, at 3599 ft., La Sausse at 3717 ft., and finally, Rougemont at 3304 ft.

In Rougemont, stop for a few minutes at the church before taking the train for the ten-minute ride to Gstaad.

VALAIS

SAAS-FEE (SAAS VALLEY)

Saas-Fee is a picturesque, traffic-free village of 1300 residents located high on a glacial ridge, at 5906 ft. (1800 m.) in the southern Valais region of Switzerland. One end of this alpine village narrows gently into serene pastures, ending abruptly as mountains and glaciers rise almost vertically, appearing to encircle and swallow tiny enclave Saas-Fee, the "Pearl of the Alps," sits beneath this giant, frozen wave of ice and snow.

Saas-Fee is ringed by more than a dozen mountains over 13,000 ft. (3962 m.) This charming resort attracts walkers of all ages, anxious to sample trails through woods filled with the aroma of pine needles, around gorges, and over rocks and ridges, surrounded by breathtaking panoramas. Saas-Fee is ringed by more than a dozen mountains over 13,000 ft. (3962 **m.**), including the Dom, the highest mountain entirely in Switzerland, and in the distance, the imposing Monte Rosa, the tallest mountain in Switzerland with its south face in Italy. The long narrow Saastal lies below the village of Saas-Fee, offering remarkable hiking options.

The village is dotted with centuries-old feed barns called *mazots,* cornered on four to six round, flat, chiseled stones that serve as elevated foundations, so feed for livestock can be stored safe from rodents. These remarkable landmark buildings serve as a reminder of earlier days, proudly standing along the streets and meadows of Saas-Fee.

Modern-day Saas-Fee has evolved from an ancient mule path into chic walking and shopping streets, a center for several international music festivals with almost 100 miles (280 km.) of well-signed trails beckoning to *Easy Walkers.*

TRANSPORTATION

By Train and Bus—Take the train to Brig and change for the bus to Saas-Fee, located outside the train station. The PTT bus is the only form of public transportation into Saas-Fee.

By Car—At Visp, head south to Stalden, where the road splits—take the left fork though the Saas Valley to Saas Grund, following signs and ascending into car-free Saas-Fee. Park in the car park at the entrance to the village and call your hotel for pickup in its electric cart. A discount on parking fees is available with your Guest Card and should be validated in the Tourist Office.

FAVORITE *WALKING EASY* HOTEL

Hotel Etoile
Three Star; Owners—Rolf and Daniela Bumann
CH-3906 Saas-Fee,
E-mail: info@hotel-etoile.ch
Internet: www.hotel-etoile.ch

The Etoile is located in a quiet area of Saas-Fee, with balcony rooms overlooking the glaciers. This family-operated hotel has twenty-two cozy rooms with modem bath facilities, TV, and mini-bar, and features regional Valais-style cuisine and typical Swiss buffet breakfasts. The large garden provides a quiet place to relax after a day of hiking. Rolf Bumann is an expert hiker and climber and arranges weekly hiking expeditions from the hotel. Evenings may feature a cookout with fun and games, inspired by Rolf's musical talent on the accordion. *Easy Walkers* will enjoy the home-like ambience at the Etoile, made possible by Rolf, Daniela, and their children.

EXCURSIONS

The Saas-Fee Tourist Information Office is located across the street from the bus terminal.
Internet: www.saas-fee ch,
E-Mail: to@saas-fee.ch

WALKING EASY TRAIL

From mid-June to mid-October, the **Seven-Day Saas Valley Hiking Pass**, available at cable stations, can be used for unrestricted use of all lifts in the Saas Valley, the PTT bus from Saas-Balen to Saas-Fee to the Mattmark Reservoir, free entry to the Ice Pavilion at Mittelallalin and the Saas Museum, and other activities. One passport-size photograph is necessary.

1. **Saas-Fee**—The **Saas Museum**, located near the church, is a typical Saas house, dating from 1732. Visit the world's largest **Ice Pavilion** on the Mittelallalin at 11,484 ft. (3500 **m.**) (See Walk #3.) Saas-Fee now hosts International **Music Festivals** during the summer .

2. **Zermatt**—Zermatt is a tourist and hiking mecca in the valley next to Saas-Fee. Its mountains and glaciers encompass superb scenery, including the mighty Matterhom. Zermatt section.)

    Directions: Take an early morning bus from Saas-Fee to Stal den, where you change to Zermatt (about a seventy-five minute trip).

Saas-Fee Walks
Recommended Maps:
Hiking Map of the Saas Valley
Panoramakarte Saas-Fee

Walk #1
Introductory Walk—Hannig to Hohnegg to Saas-Fee
Walking Easy Time: 2 hours
Rating: Comfortable

Today's walk serves as an introduction to Saas-Fee and its alpine surroundings, and it can be enjoyed your first afternoon in Saas-Fee. At the Hannig sun-terrace, look to the Fee glacier, dominating the panorama. The other cable lifts are visible—Plattjen directly across the valley, another lift to Spielboden and Langfluh, going directly up the center of the Fee glacier. A third lift, the Alpin Express, rises to Felskinn.

Direction: Follow signs in the village to PANORAMABAHN HANNIG. Purchase a one-way ticket to Hannig, at 7710 ft. (2350 m.).

Start: After admiring the view from the sun-terrace, follow the sign SAAS-FEE—1 STD., 20 MIN., walking to the right when facing the sign. The wide path descends easily, zigzagging down the mountain. Take the occasional foot-paths serving as shortcuts to the main path, and follow signs to Saas-Fee. The trail leads you to a main path, where you turn right in the direction of HOHNEGG-5 MIN.and SASS-FEE-25 MIN. Tiny Hohnegg consists of a few picturesque restaurants and chalets. The path continues to descend, now rnnning parallel to Saas-Fee, eventually bringing you to the outskirts of town. Your time is now free to explore the colorful streets of Saas-Fee.

Walk #2
Spielboden Lift Station to Saas-Fee (Excursion to Langfluh)
Walking Easy Time: 2 1/2 to 4 hours
Rating: Comfortable

The glacier formations on either side of Spielboden and Langfluh look like giant waves of ice. A narrow finger of land juts up as the foundation for these two lift stations, and on this small area, surrounded on three sides by glaciers, are much-traveled hiking trails.

Directions: *Walk down Saas-Fee's main street, past the church, toward the Fee glacier, following signs to LANGFLUH-SPIELBODEN LUFTSEILBAHNEN. Purchase a one-way ticket to Spielboden.*

Start: Your walk begins at the Spielboden stop, at 8039 ft. (2450 in.), above the tree line on a tongue of land surrounded by the Fee glacier. *Easy Walkers* can first ascend to Langfluh at 9417 ft. (2870 m.) on the cable car, or walk up on the trail marked LANGFLUH—I STD. (However, plan on a ninety-minute ascent)

Otherwise, meet and greet the marmots at Spielboden, waiting impatiently for your arrival. A walk to either side of this lift station brings you into view of the powerful Fee glacier, dominating the panorama around tiny Saas-Fee.

The trail down from Spielboden begins with a sign to Saas-Fee. Stay on the main trail, ignoring the little spin-offs, with marmot families coming out of their burrows to greet you and beg for food. Winding down the trail, note a fork in the trail next to a small stone house. Take the path to the left for a close-up view of the glacier—a scene worth a detour. Return to the main path and follow signs to Cafe Gletschergarten and then Saas-Fee.

Walk #3
Glacier Walk—Felskinn to Brittaniahütte—Return to Felskinn or Walk to Plattjen (Excursion to Mittelailalin and Ice Grotto)
Walking Easy Time: 3 to 4 hours
Rating: More Challenging/Can Be Dangerous

HINT: Check at the ticket office for the day's glacier walking conditions.

This glacier walk, at almost 10,000 ft. (3000 in.), emphasizes the grandeur and scope of the trails surrounding Saas-Fee. You'll travel by cable car to Felskinn, walk across the Fee and Chessjen glaciers to the Brittaniahutte, then walk back to Felskinn.

The excursion part of today's walk, a ride on the Metro-Alpin, the world's highest underground funicular, will bring you into the center of a glacial wilderness. Ride up for the unforgettable view and a visit to the Mittelalain Ice Pavilion.

Directions: *The Alpin Express is found by walking to the bus station and following lift signs. Buy a round-trip ticket to Mittelallalin. The ride up to Felskinn deposits Easy Walkers ready to begin an exciting glacier adventure. At Felskinn, you have the opportunity to change to the Metro-Alpin up to Mittelallin Ice Pavillion for a visit before or after the hike.*

Start: You can step off the Metro directly into the Ice Pavilion—a walk into the ice of the Fee glacier—the world's largest and highest ice grotto. The revolving restaurant at Mittelallin is the highest in the world, and a cafeteria with an exceptionally large sun-terrace is also available.

When ready, take the subway back down to Felskinn, where the hike begins. Leaving the Felskinn Lift station, follow signs to the Brittaniahutte walking over a snow field and on to the glacier. Enjoy the secenery and the fact that you're actually walking on a glacier! After about a half hour you'll come to a tiny ski lift at the Egginerjoch, between the two glaciers. The walk becomes more challenging at this point, so use your discretion to continue or turn back—many *Easy*

Walkers have told us that they "glacier walk" as far as the ski lift and then return to Felskinn and take the cable car down to Saas-Fee.

If you continue on to the Brittaniahutte, two options await you:

1. Walk back to the Felskinn cable car on the same path and take the cable car down to Saas-Fee.
2. Continue the hike by walking to the Plattjen cable car and riding it down to Saas-Fee.

Walk #4
Saas-Fee to Bideralp to Stafelalp to Saas-Fee
Walking Easy Time: 5 hours
Rating: More Challenging

Today's trails offer many types of alpine hiking—waterfall and stream crossings, rocky trails, pine-needled paths, and an altitude change of over 1000 feet (305 m.) At the beginning of the hike the path is gentle. In about an hour the ascent steepens and the trail becomes rocky. After the Biderbruche crossing, the trail rises, swings to the left, and meets the high-altitutde trail from Grachen. It then descends by way of Barenfalle, into the outskirts of Saas-Fee.

Start: Remember to: pack a picnic lunch and extra water—there are no restaurants on this trail.

Walk past the Hotel Etoile, away from the village. Passing the Alpen Hitte restaurant, follow signs to the right, to STAFELALP, BIDERALP, and SENGG, in the direction of the Hotel Fletschhorn. Walk through the hotel's sun-terrace and pick up the trail to Stafelalp, Bideralp, and Sengg. Follow this path but ingore the fact that it is marked STAFELALP—1 STD., 15 MIN.—it may take some *Easy Walkers* closer to two hours.

This *bergweg* passes though the hamlet of Sengg—enjoy the photographic possibilities in this area. Follow directions to Stafelalp. The trail begins to climb in the direction of Bideralp, at 6296 ft. (1919 m.) and Stafelalp, at 7028 ft. (2142 m.) crossing swiftly rnnning streams. As you ascend, follow signs to Bideralp. You'll cross the Biderbrnche on a small wooden bridge to Bideralp, with scenic opportunities for a picnic on its hillside. After Bideralp, be prepared to ascend 732 feet (223 meters). Walking past some wooden cabins, the trail buttonhooks to the left around Stafelalp to meet the high path from Grachen. *Note the trail caution above.* At the Grachen sign you are at the highest point of this walk, and from then on it's downhill into Saas-Fee, as you descend from a rocky mountain trail to a pine-needled forest path leading into Barenfalle and Saas-Fee.

If you leave your hotel by 10:00 a.m., you should be back before 5:00p.m.

Walk #5
Saas-Fee to Saas-Grund to Saas-Almagell (Excursion to Kreuzboden/Hohsaas)
Walking Easy Time: 4-5 hours
Rating: Comfortable

Plan a full day for today's walk and high-mountain excursion. The hike includes the Kappellenweg, or chapel path, to Saas-Gund. Fifteen tiny chapels-built from 1687 to 1709, representing the fifteen secrets of the rosary, were originally used as a pilgrimage route from Saas-Fee into the valley between Saas-Grund and Saas-Almagell. After walking down to Saas-Grund, you'll take the lift to Kreuzboden and Hohsaas. After returning to Saas-Grund, the walk continues through the valley to Saas-Almagell, where you catch a bus for the return to Saas-Fee.

Start: The path to Saas-Grund begins behind the bus **station and is** marked Kappellenweg. In some are the path descends on stone steps. Walk carefully. The descent is about 600 feet and before the hour is over, the end of the trail appears. A sign points to the right to Saas-Almagell, but turn left on the path and follow it along the river, past a campground. Cross the river on the first bridge, turning immediately left, and walk toward Saas-Grund. Follow lift signs to Kreuzboden. Buy a round trip ticket to Hohsaas, changing at Kreuzboden for the trip to the top station. After viewing the panorama, return to the Kreuzboden station with breathtaking views of the Saastal.

When ready, take the lift downs to Saas-Grund to begin the walk to Saas-Almagell. Retrace your steps to the end of the Kapellenweg and follow the sign SAAS-ALMAGELL. The bus stop is at the end of town. Check the posted schedule before exploring the town. Take the bus back to Saas-grund and change for the bus to Saas-Fee.

Walk #6
Around the Mattmark Reservoir (Optional Hike to Talliboden)
Walking Easy Time: 2 1/2 to 4 1/2 hours
Rating: Comfortable

Today you will walk around Mattmark, Europe's largest reservoir at 7244 ft. (2208 m.), on a comfortable trail with the option, at one end of the lake, to rise on a mountain *bergweg* to Talliboden.

Directions: *Take an early morning bus directly to Mattmark. (Check bus schedule.)*
Start: After exiting the bus at the Mattmark Restaurant, follow the sign SEERUNDGANG—2 1/4 STD.—the path around the lake. Take the right-hand path around the reservoir, staying on the lower path. After an hour you'll

reach Distelalp at 7139 ft. (2224 m.) and the other end of the lake, with signs to the Monte Moro Pass to Italy and Talliboden. Here you have a few options:

1. Take the mountain trail to Talliboden, a rise of some 800 feet. (244 meters),. Some strong hikers continue up to Monte Moro Pass, at 9220 ft. (2810 m.) for the trek into Italy. Other hikers will take the high route from Talliboden and descend on the Offental trail to the end of the reservoir. You can also return down the same trail to Distelalp and continue along the opposite side of the reservoir, toward the dam and bus stop.

2. Stay level and continue around the lake on the lower Seernndgang path to the dam and the bus stop.

Walk #7
Saas-Fee to Bodme to Saas-Amagell to Saas-Grund to Saas-Balen
Walking Easy Time: 2 to 4 hours
Rating: Comfortable

Today's lower level walk takes you from Saas-Fee, though the forest to Saas-Almagell, where you pick up the Saastal Valley path, walking to Saas-Grnnd or even Saas-Balen, with bus stops a short distance away on the main road.

Start: Walk past the Saas-Fee bus stop, crossing the river, following signs to BODME and then SAAS-ALMAGELL. This pleasant walk takes you into the forest, past the restaurant at Bodme, and into Saas-Almagell—about a one-hour stroll. In the village, look for signs to Saas-Grnnd and then Saas-Balen, walking along the river. Take the bus or walk back back to Saas-Fee whenever you are ready to end your Saastal walk.

ZERMATT

Zermatt, an all-season sports resort, nestled among alpine meadows and pine forests at 5315 ft. (1620 m.), encircled by many of Switzerland's tallest and most famous mountains. This *Walking Easy* base village is a hiker's paradise, with over 250 miles (400 km.) of marked paths, encompassing some of the world's most superb scenery and appealing walking trails. With a population that can burgeon into tens of thousands in summer and winter, this sophisticated town in the Valais region of Switzerland encompasses two contrasting areas. One section includes the main tourist street from the railroad station past the church—filled with day-trippers, skiers and hikers enjoying the crowded shops, bustling restaurants and old-world hotels. The second area reaches into the countryside, in the shadow of the Matterhorn, with typical Valasian chalets, *mazots* (preserved landmark barns), and a network of trails filling the needs of both occasional ramblers and experienced mountain climbers.

The Tasch railroad station car park in the valley below, holds the cars of the thousands who visit Zermatt and wander through quaint streets with only darting, electric mini-taxis and flower-bedecked horse-drawn carriages for local transportation.

Zermatt has become synonymous with the majestic Matterhorn; its silhouette and history are unique and instantly recognizable. *Easy Walkers* will enjoy Zermatt, boasting one of the finest networks of alpine trails in the Swiss Alps.

TRANSPORTATION

By Train—Take the train to Brig or Visp and always change to the Brig-Visp-Zermatt Railway, located outside the station. To be picked up, use the bank of telephones inside the station, directly connected to local hotels.

The **Glacier Express**, sometimes called the "slowest express train in the world," traverses the 167 miles (104 km.) between Zermatt and St. Moritz, with no change of train. This train is a panorama trip though the alpine heartland of Switzerland, and departs from Zermatt twice each morning, arriving in St. Moritz 7 1/2 hours later. Seat reservations are mandatory except for the Zermatt to Brig portion.

By Car—Drive to Visp, and head south to Tasch. Park and board the train for the last part of your trip to car-free Zermatt. Wheel your luggage cart directly onto the train. Call your hotel for electric cart pick-up.

FAVORITE *WALKING EASY* HOTEL

Hotel Antares
Four-Star, Owners-Familie Schnidrig und Holensein
CH-3920 Zermatt
Internet: www.zermatt.ch/antares
Email: antares@zermatt.ch

The quiet location of the Antares is ideal. This contemporary chalet-style hotel features paneled guest rooms with conveniences, handsome public area, spacious dining rooms, and an outdoor terrace, most rooms have a view of the Matterhorn. Dinner in outstanding and the breakfast buffet is sumptuous. When making reservations…ask for Monica.

EXCURSIONS IN AND AROUND ZERMATT

The Zermatt Tourist Office, located next to the railroad station, sponsors walking tours and many special events.

Internet: www.zermatt. ch
E-mail: info@zermatt.ch

1. **Zermatt**
   A) Check the **Alpine Musemn's** collection of documents verifying the first ascents of the mountains around Zermatt.
   B) **Alpine Cemetery**—This beautiful cemetery is located across from the church. It contains the graves of those killed while attempting to climb the Matterhorn.
   C) **Marmots' Fountain**—A sculpture by Swiss artist Edouard Marcel Sandoz stands in the center of Zermatt, across from the church.

2. **Saas-Fee**—Saas-Fee is a small, charming, car-free resort in the valley next to Zermatt. (See the "Saas-Fee" chapter.)
   Directions: Take the train from Zermatt to Stalden and board the PTT bus to Saas-Fee, outside the station, a total ride of about two hours.

ZERMATT WALKS
Recommended Maps:
   1) Wanderkarte—Zermatt—Cervina—Tasch
   2) Zermatt—Matterhorn Panorama Aerial Map

Walk # 1: Schwarzsee to Stafel to Furi to Zermatt (Excursion to the Klein Matterhorn and Glacier Walk)
Walking Easy Time: 3 to 4 hours
Rating: Comfortable

HINT: **Today's journey should be taken on your first clear day in Zermatt! Sunglasses, sunscreen and warm outerwear are necessary. Be prepared to spend the better part of the day on this excursion and hike.**

Today's trip includes an exciting adventure to the Klein Matterhom top station at 12,533 ft. (3829 **in.**), and an optional glacial, snowfield walk with close-up views of climbers ascending the Breithom. Enjoy the spectacular view from the top—this world of snow, ice and rock has not changed much since the glaciers of the ice age destroyed everything in their paths.

You will return to Furi by cablecar and chnge for the lifts to Schwarzee. Schwarzsee is at the foot of the Matterhom, an alpine lake below its northeast ridge.

You will leave Schwarzsee at 8472 ft. (2582 in.), descending comfortably to the Stafelalp mountain restaurant and sun-terrace at 7215 ft. (2199 in.). After taking in the views and outstanding *kaisersehnitte* at the restaurant, continue on a forest path—with views of the tiny mountain hamlet of Zmutt across the valley—to Fun, where you can walk or take the gondola down to Zermatt.

Directions: The Klein Matterhorn cable car is just past the Hotel Antares—follow signs from Zermatt. Buy a lift ticket from Zermatt to Klein Matterhorn, with a return to Schwarzsee. Fun is the first stop.

Start: After disembarking at the Klein Matterhorn station, move ahead through a long tunnel. On the left is small tunnel leading to an elevator that will take you to the *gipfel* or peak. Here you'll encounter a never-to-be-forgotten panorama—face-to-face with the Matterhorn!

When ready to leave, descend by elevator and continue though the tunnel to the glacial snowfield. Here you might see national ski teams training for the coming season, as well as hundreds of skiers and snow-boarders. Step out onto the snowfield if you wish, and walk as far as you feel comfortable along the ski lift, returning to the cable car station, when ready. **NOTE: Any extended hike in this area should be in the company of an experienced guide.**

To arrive at Schwarzsee, reverse the cable car procedure and return to Fun where you take the lift to Schwarzsee, via Furgg. At Schwarzsee, follow the sign to Stafelalp at the side of the sun-terrace of the Hotel Schwarzsee. After a while you'll come to an unsigned trail off to the right. Take it! This typical mountain *bergweg* leads to Stafelalp, and descends directly to the Stafelalp Restaurant at 7215 ft. (2199 m.). This part of the walk from Schwarzsee takes about an hour.

After taking your fill of the Matterhorn view, walk behind the sun-terrace, following signs to Fun. The path moves to the left down to the road, and after walking a few minutes, the road forks. Take the right fork to Fun on the wagon path into the forest, rather than staying on the road—although both meet eventually. Continue ahead, following signs to Fun. At the Fun lift station, follow the signed path down "Zermatt-1 hr." Or, climb aboard the Fun gondola for the quick descent to Zermatt.

MATTERHORN

Walk #2: Zermatt to Zmutt to Furi to Zermatt
Walking Easy Time: 3 to 4 hours
Rating: Comfortable

Today's hike is one of the most popular in the Zermatt area, and will take you on a trail comfortably ascending 1037 ft. (316 m.) to a tiny hamlet on the outskirts of town. Zmutt, at 6352 ft. (1936 m.), is a small cluster of buildings, with typical Valaisian slate roofs, set among hilly pastures. From Zmutt you will cross the river and walk to Fun, where you continue to Zermatt.

Start: At the village church and Marmots' Fountain, head up the main street towards the Matterhorn. After passing a newspaper stand on your right, note a sign indicating ZMUTT—1 HR. There are several ways to approach Zmutt—we prefer following this well-trodden path, although it may take *Easy Walkers* closer to 90 minutes. As you ascend on the trail, the river is on the left with the Matterhorn ahead. You'll pass old, wooden *mazots,* barns from the early years of Zermatt. Soon the asphalt ends, and the path ascends though woods and meadows.

THE MATTERHORN FROM STOCKHORN

After ascending for an hour, a sign indicates you have walked almost 1.9 miles (3 km.) from Zenmatt. Buttonhook up the trail and continue by walking though the terrace of a restaurant. Zmutt is now only a five-minute walk through the meadows—its miniature white-washed church, some old barns and houses in view. The pasture is covered with wild flowers from June through August, and is an idyllic place to enjoy a picnic lunch. From a vantage point in the high meadow, gaze down on the old slate roofs of Zmutt, the valley and the peak of the MatteRhonn. Ancient stories tell that these Zmutt meadows gave their name to the Matterhorn, which means "meadow—horn" in local dialect.

When ready, take the path into the center of Zmutt and follow a sign down the hill towards Furi and Stafelalp, walking through a pasture towards the hydro-electric plant, with the gorge on the left. Cross the bridge, walk up the hill to the road, and turn left towards Fun. Stay on this road and in another half hour the cable station at Fun can be seen. At Fun, you have two options:

1)   Continue the hike, following the sign "Zermatt-lhr."
2)   Take the cable can from Furi down to Zermatt.

Walk #3: Riffelberg and/or Riffelalp to Zermatt (Excursion to Gornergrat and Stockhorn)
Walking Easy Time: 1 1/2 to 2 1/2 hours
Rating: Comfortable

Although today's walk begins in Riffelbeng on Riffelalp and ends in Zermatt, we first include an excursion to Gornergnat and the Stockhorn—the unfolding mountain and glacier panorama is an awesome experience—and should be taken on a clear day.

From the Gornengnat station in Zenmatt, the train winds its way up the mountain; sit on the night side of the train for best views. The view from Gornengnat encompasses a spectacular panorama of 27 peaks higher than 12,000 ft. (3660 **in.**). Looming oven this frozen sea is Switzerland's highest mountain, the Monte Rosa at 15,203 ft. (4643 **in.**). From Gornengnat, a cable can brings you oven Hohtallignat at 10,781 ft. (3286 **in.**) andthento the Stockhornat 11,178 ft. (3407 **in.**), and an even closer view of the Monte Rosa and its surrounding glacial wilderness. You will return to the Gornengnat railway, taking it down to Riffelalp for the hike to Zenmatt. **NOTE: This hike can be extended by getting off the train at the high plateau of Riffelberg at 8472 ft. (2582 in.), with its 19th-century mountain hotel. You can then pick up the trail, descending 1181 ft. (360 in.) to Riffelalp, another hour of walking time.**

Directions: Walk to the Gornengnatbahn, across from the railroad station. Buy a round-trip ticket, Zenmatt to Stockhorn, with a return to Riffelberg/Riffelalp. The train makes four stops before arriving at Gornergrat, where you follow signs to board the Stockhorn cable can. Take the cable can back to Gonnergrat and its famous Kulm Hotel. You will remember this array of glaciers and snow-capped mountains long after you return home. When ready, neboard the train at Gornergnat and disembark at the Riffelalp station, the stop after Riffelberg. (Unless you have decided to walk the extra hour from Riffelberg to Riffelalp.)

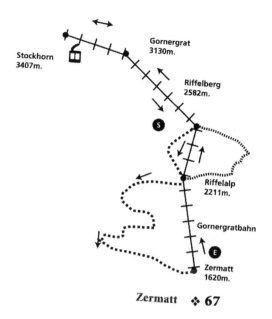

Stockhorn
3407m.

Gornergrat
3130m.

Riffelberg
2582m.

S

Riffelalp
2211m.

Gornergratbahn

E

Zermatt
1620m.

Zermatt ❖ **67**

Start: At the Riffelalp station, walk to the night, towards Zermatt and the Riffelalp Hotel.

Within a few minutes a sign points to Zenmatt. Do not take this path on the night—continue walking ahead on the main forrest path, and within five minutes the exquisite Hotel Riffelalp, with an unobstructed view of the Matterhorn, comes into view.

Passing the hotel, follow signs pointing night towards Zenmatt and Winkelmatten. This trail descends oven 1975 ft. (602 **in.**), so make sure your hiking boots are well-laced. The path divides at a restaurant—follow signs towards Zermatt and Winkelmatten until you reach a paved mountain bike path and road. Turn night to Zermatt. This road winds though the woods to the tiny hamlets of Moos and Winkelmatten. In Winkelmatten, walk ahead, continuing along the river into Zermatt.

THE MATERHORN FROM RIFFELALP

Walk #4 Sunnegga to Tuftern to Reid to Winkelmatten to Zermatt (Excursion to Blauherd and Unterrothern)
Walking Easy Time: 3 hours
Rating: Comfortable

Today's walk is on one of the many trails leading from the Sunnegga plateau—primarily a forest path with a comfortable 2231 ft. (680 **in.**) descent—and spectacular views of Zermatt and the Matterhonn. The underground Alpen-Metro funicular brings you to Sunnegga and to the edge of a plateau with a magnificent panorama. You can continue on the cable can to Blauherd and Unterrothern, for more extensive views.

   Directions: Follow signs to Sunnegga, and purchase a one way ticket to Sunnegga for the underground funicular. (On, to Unterrothorn if continuing to the top.). At Sunnegga, take the cable can to Blauherd and Untennothern for incredible views (if you have not already taken this excursion), but return to Sunnegga to begin today's hike.

Start: At Sunnegga, walk down to a plateau with a large cross, and follow the sign "Tuftern" to the night. After a few minutes, another sign directs you again to the night "Tuftern-30 mm." Remain on the main, wide jeep road (not descending on the grassy path).

The hamlet of Tuftern 7267 ft. (2215 m.), consists of a small group of picturesque old barns, houses and a restaurant with a fabulous view of the Matterhorn. Ignoring the high trail to the night (the Europaweg) to Grachen on Tasch, and the steep descent to Zermatt on the left, continue ahead on the well-marked trail to Reid. This path, a ski trail in winter, buttonhooks through the forest and alpine meadows, passing Othman's Hutte, a mountain restaurant. After a sun-terrace break, continue past another restaurant in Ried, and in about 25 minutes (some of which are on an auto road), follow the sign left indicating WINKEL-MATTEN-l/2 hr., taking you up, then winding evenly on a gentle mountain *bergweg*. This path by-passes Zermatt and leads comfortably to the church in Winkelmatten. At the church, walk halfway around, following a sign to Zermatt. This small road leads down to the Klein Mattenhorn cable station, where you turn night to your hotel.

Walk #5 Riffelalp to Grunsee to Findeln to Sunnegga
Walking Easy Time: 4 hours
Rating: More Challenging

Today's hike will take *Easy Walkers* on the Gornergrat Railway to Riffelalp for the start of the walk to Gnunsee, a tiny glacial lake. From there you will walk down through the forest, and then up to the tiny hamlet of Findeln, with its old wooden barns and houses. There are restaurants in Findeln, but a picnic lunch at the lake on in the meadows surrounding Findeln can also be a fine nest and relaxation stop. The walk continues on an ascending path from Findeln to the Leisee, and eventually up to Sunnegga, with a return to Zermatt via the underground funicular. While the walk to Grunsee is gentle, the last half of this walk requires some uphill hiking.

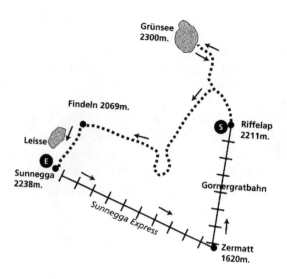

Grünsee
2300m.

Findeln 2069m.

Leisse

Riffelap
2211m.

Sunnegga
2238m.

Gornergratbahn

Sunnegga Express

Zermatt
1620m.

Directions: *Walk to the Gornergratbahn, across from the Zermatt train station. Buy a one-way ticket to Riffelalp and exit at the Riffelalp station.*

Start: Walk across the railroad tracks at the pedestrian crossing and follow the trail signed GRUNSEE 1 HR. This path is wide and well-marked, winding around the mountain and offering superb views of the tiny towns in the valley below. You are at 6500 ft. (1981 m.), and slowly approaching the tneeline. Note the Findelngletschen to the east and, up on the left, your destination at Sunnegga and the Blauherd-Unterrothorn lifts. Continuing, take the right trail fork up the hill to the lake. The Findeln Glacier and its surrounding peaks are now in front of you. Passing over a brook, follow signs to Grunsee.

After enjoying the panorama, return on the same trail, walking past the restaurant to a sign FINDELN ¾ HR on a night fork in the path. At this point you have two options:

1)   Take the left fork back to the Riffelalp station, the same way you walked to Grunsee, and return to Zermatt by train.

2).   Follow the trail to Findeln, winding though the forest, descending to the Findeln River. Reaching the gorge and the Findeln River, cross the bridge and walk up the steep path to Findeln at 6788 ft. (2069 **in.**), perched on the side of the gorge.

Continue on the ascending path, walking above the village to a junction. Turn left for a short, aggressive, uphill walk to the Leisee, noticing the Sunnegga lift station above, on the hill at 7546 ft. (2300 m.). From the lake, take either path leading to the top and the funicular subway which descends to Zermatt every 15 minutes. Buy a one-way, Sunnegga to Zermatt ticket.

Walk #6 Zermatt to Tasch
Walking Easy Time: 1 1/2 hours
Rating: Comfortable

If it is drizzling, clouds hanging low oven Zermatt and you cannot see the Matterhorn, you might wish to select a low-level hike. You can take the *wanderweg* mountain trail from Zermatt to the village of Tasch. On, if you prefer walking up rather than down, the hike can be taken in reverse, from Tasch to Zermatt. In either case, the altitude change is not significant, starting in Zermatt at 5315 ft. (1620 m.), and ending in Tasch at 4754 ft. (1449 m.)—a change of 548 ft. (167 m.). The walk is on a mountain trail, never fan from the train tracks and the rapidly flowing riven. You can take the train in either direction on walk the trail both ways. The following directions will take you from Zermatt to Tasch.

Start: Walk towards the Zermatt train station, past the *bahnhof* on a paved road to the Tasch sign. Turn left and walk up a concrete ramp, making a night turn on the unsigned but cleanly defined trail—towards Tasch. The trail rolls comfortably, but can be a bit rocky in places, as it parallels the train tracks though the valley. Do **not** be tempted by little trail offshoots now and then. Stay on the main, signed trail to Tasch. You might wish to take the train back from the Tasch station on return to Zermatt on the same *wanderweg* trail, depending on the weather.

Walk #7: Schwarzsee to Hermetji to Furi to Zermatt
Walking Easy Time: 3 1/2 to 4 1/2 hours
Rating: Comfortable

Today's walk begins in Schwarzsee, after taking the lifts to Furi and Fungg. You will visit the little lake and its tiny chapel. The hike is all downhill, offering enchanting views of Zenmatt and its surrounding high peaks.

Directions: *The lift to Schwarzsee is just past the Hotel Antares. Buy a ticket from Zermatt to Schwarzsee, and board the gondolas to Furi, where you change for the lifts to Fungg and Schwarzsee.*

Start: Pick up the descending trail to Furi, following signs "Henmettji" and "Zermatt," by the sun-terrace of the Hotel Schwarzsee. There are other ways to descend, but today we recommend staying on this trail—cleanly marked, rocky, but wide. At the first fork, take a left, following signs into Henmettji. At

Henmettji, follow signs to Fun. At the cable station in Furi, the following options are available:
1) Take the cable can from Furi to Zermatt.
2) Continue the walk down to Zenmatt by following the sign ZERMATT-1HR

VERBIER

The sports village of Verbier, at 4920 ft. (1500m.), is located in southwestern Switzerland in theValais, near the French and Italian borders, on a large, sunny plateau under the towering Mont-Fort and its 10,925 foot (3330 meters) glacier. The language of Verbier, the *cuisine,* the *mode* and the *attitude—are* all *tres Francais.* It is difficult to believe that this chic winter and summer mountain area has developed from its pastureland heritage, (mostly in the last quarter-century) into a year-round resort offering visitors a full range of modern services, including a cyber cafe for the internetters. Access to Verbier is quite different from other alpine villages; you can take a gondola from the rail station in Le Chable, directly toVerbier. You can use more traditional methods by driving up the scenic mountain road, or taking the post bus from the train station.

While Verbier is most famous in winter for its 250 miles (400 kin) of ski runs and dozens of lifts, summer in Verbier offers miles of paths for hikers of all capabilities. In addition to the higher, more challenging hiking trails, there are miles of comfortable, criss-crossing paths that cut back and forth along wide mountain ski slopes, all serviced by an operating network of summer lifts and free village bus service. The breathtaking views from the peaks at Mont-Fort, Attelas, Savaleyres, and Pierre d'Avoi, over to the Grand Combin and Mont Blanc massifs, are worth this trip up the mountain to the almost 5,000 foot village. And, with all that spectacular alpine scenery, Verbier is also home to an 18-hole, par 70 golf course located above the village, and is said to be the "Mecca of Paragliding" because of its exceptional flying sites.

If you enjoy a village with French atmosphere, lots of sports action, great hotels, and good summer *Walking Easy* in an exhilarating setting—try Verbier, in the mountains of southwestern Switzerland.

TRANSPORTATION

By Train—Take the train to Martigny and change for the Martigny-Le Chable line. Sit in the car marked Le Chable. In Le Chable, change to a post bus or, take the Le Chable-Verbier Cableway up to the village.

By Car—Drive to Martigny and take the Great-St-Bernard main road to Sembrancher. Turn left and drive into the Bagnes Valley, all the way to Le Chable and the ascending road to Verbier.

EXCNRSIONS

The Verbier/Val de Bagnes Tourist Office is located in the center of the village, on the main pedestrian and shopping street.

Internet: www.verbier.ch
E-mail: info@verbier.ch

1. **Verbier**—A highlight of the Swiss summer cultural season, the acclaimed **Verbier Festival and Academy is held** every year in July, featuring internationally famous soloists and orchestras. An 18-hole, par 70 Golf Conrse has been built at an altitude of 5250 ft.(1600 m.)

2. **Montrenx**—See Gstaad section, Excursion #2.
   Directions: *Take the bus or gondola from Verbier to Le Chable and the train to Sembrancher. Change for the train to Montreux. A bus to Chillon can be taken outside the train station.*

3. **Martigny**—Recognized world-wide for exhibits of such famous artists as Gauguin, Manet, Degas and Modigliani, **visit the Pierre Gianadda Foundation. This museum also houses a** collection of works by the masters, a sculpture park, a car museum and a Gaul-Roman museum.
   Directions: *Take the bus or cable car to Le Chable and take the train to Sembrancher. Change for the train to Martigny.*

4. **Aigle**—Dating from the thirteenth-century, **Aigle Castle is home to the Wine and Salt Museums.** Opposite the castle is the Maison de la Dime, which includes the International Museum of Labels, the "Pinte du Paradis," and the Cellar of Chablais, where you can sample wines of the region.
   Directions: *Take the bus or cable car to Le Chable and board the train/or Sembrancher.*
   Change/or the train towards Montreux, getting off in Aigle.

Verbier Walks

Recommended Map:
Val de Bagnes, Verbier—Carte de randonnées pédestres

The following hikes are just a few of those available in the Verbier area. *Easy Walkers* can wander about the many trails along the mountain side.

Walk # 1

Les Rninettes to La Chanx, Excnrsion to Mont-Fort, Lifts to La Chanx, Walk to Cabane de Mont-Fort to Les Ruinettes
Walking Easy Time—3 hours
Rating: Comfortable

Today's hike and excursion to Mont-Fort includes a short walk from Les Ruinettes at 7195 ft. (2193 m.) to LaChaux, at 7218 ft. (2200 m.) and the beginning of a fascinating cable car system. You will see summer skiers and snowboarders on the glacier at the Gentianes mid-station before continuing up to Mont-Fort, at 10,854 ft. (3308 m.) for unparalleled panoramic views. You will then descend back to the mid-station by cable car, where there is an additional lift system continuing to Tortin, Siviez, and further, if you wish. Today however, you will descend by cable to La Chaux for the hike up to the Cabane du Mont-Fort and the return to Les Ruinettes via a descending mountain path.

   Directions: *Walk or take the free shuffle bus to the Medran cable car. Take the lift to Les Ruinettes.*

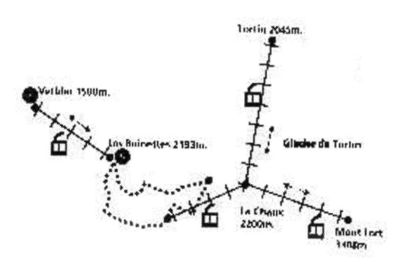

Start: After exiting, turn down to your right to the group of signs indicating LA CHAUX, where there are two options:

1. Walk along the wide, mountain road to La Chaux.
2. Descend a bit to the mountain *bergweg* just under the road towards La Chaux *(Bisse du Levron* on your map.) If you've chosen the *bergweg*, follow signs up to La Chaux for a forty-minute walk.

At La Chaux, take the large cable car (capacity of 150) to Mont-Fort, with a change at Gentiane at the base of the glacier. After taking in the views and noting the summer skiers on the glacier, descend to the mid-station, 9495 ft. (2894 m.). While it is possible to take another series of cable cars and lifts up to Tortin and Seviez, you might reserve that for another day.

Return by cable down to La Chaux, passing the Cabane du Mont-Fort on your right. At La Chaux, follow the signed trail for an hour hike up to the cabane. After rest and refreshments, you have some options:

1. Walk down the mountain directly to La Chaux for the walk back to Ruinettes and the lift down to Verbier.
2. Take the mountain trail just under the Cabane du Mont-Fort that descends directly to Les Ruinettes and the cable car return to Verbier.

Walk # 2
Savoleyres to Croix de Coenr to Les Ruinettes, Excnrsion to Attelas, Walk Les Rninettes to Verbier
Walking Easy Time: 1 3/4 to 3 1/2 hours
Rating: Comfortable

Today's walk gives *Easy Walkers* the opportunity to view the entire Verbier walking area—you'll see all the trails that cross the giant ski pistes around and above Verbier.

Directions: *Take the bus to Savoleyres Lift and ascend to the gondola to the top station, rising from 5217 to 7724 ft. (1590 to 2354 m.)*

Start: At Savoleyres, follow the sign down to Croix de Coeur, at 7133 ft. (2174 m.) There, turn into the wide path to Les Ruinettes, at 7195 ft. At Croix de Coeur, it is also possible to take other trails—make sure you take the wide path signed LES RUINETTES. Descend gently above the tree line, with fantastic views of Verbier and the Val des Bagnes. As you proceed, most of Verbier's hiking paths are visible. **NOTE: This path is also used by mountain bikers, so it's a good idea to stay to the right as you walk.**

About halfway, the path enters a short, mountain tunnel, and you'll then pass other trails rising up to Col des Mines and Attelas, and down to Les Planards. Continue walking to the lift at Les Ruinettes. There, if the weather is clear, you might wish to continue by gondola to Les Attelas at 8859 ft. (2700 m.) for panoramic views. We were considering the hike on the Tour du Val de Bagnes to the Cabane du Mont Fort, but July snow covered much of the trail, so instead we returned to Les Ruinettes by gondola and walked along the road down to Verbier. You can also take the Ruinettes lift down to Verbier.

Walk # 3
Savoleyres to Pierre d'Avoi to Savoleyres to Les Planards to Les Esserts to Verbier
Walking Easy Time: 3 to 5 hours
Rating: Comfortable

Today's hike, beginning at the top of the Savoleyres lift, offers views down to the other side of the Val des Bagnes to Mayens de Riddes, with additional views of the mountains of the Grand Combin. You'll walk to the jutting peak of Pierre d'Avoi, and ascend it if you desire, returning through Savoleyres to Croix de Coeur, to the restaurant at Les Planards, and then walking down though the meadows to the golf course at Les Esserts and Verbier.

Directions: *Take the Verbier shuttle bus to the Savoleyres Lift Station and take the gondola to the top.*

Start: After exiting the lift, take the mountain trail around the back of the lift station, in the direction of Pierre d'Avoi. After about ten minutes, the trail crosses the wide road. Continue ahead on the trail, *not* walking up to the right on the wide road. This comfortable trail leads directly to the base of Pierre d'Avoi in thirty minutes. You now have two options:

1. Hike up to Pierre d'Avoi, a steep ascent with railing help towards the top—and then hike back down on the same trail.
2. Admire the peak from its base.

With either option, return on the same trail to Savoleyres, walking on to Croix de Coeur, at 7133 ft. (2174 m.) At Croix de Coeur, follow the sign down to the restaurant at Les Planards, visible below. In the restaurant parking area, follow Chemin de Pedestre, a narrow, mountain trail descending steeply through Le Clou to the golf course at Les Esserts. Here you can walk or take the free shuttle bus back to Verbier.

Walk # 4
Les Rninettes to Les Planards to Chnte dn Bisse to Verbier
Walking Easy Time: 4 to 4/12 hours
Rating: Comfortable

The walk from Les Ruinettes to Chute du Bisse is mostly along the Bisse de Levron, through Les Planards. The *bisse* is a system of controlling and directing the mountain water for agricultural use, similar to the *waalwege* in Merano, Italy. From Chute du Bisse you'll return to Verbier though St. Christophe and Patier.

Directions: *Take the gondola from Medran and exit at the Les Ruinettes station.*

Start: Walk down to the right and follow signs to Les Planards and Chute du Bisse on the Bisse de Levron trail. In Les Planards, continue on the mountain trail along the *bisse* to Chute du Bisse. From Chute du Bisse, descend to Patier on the outskirts of Verbier—through the viewpoint at St. Christophe. At Patier you can either take the shuttle bus into Verbier or, walk fifteen minutes into the village.

NOTE: The following walks can be taken when the weather is not cooperating and you wish to stay low. These walks also give you an opportunity to discover the little villages down in the valley below Verbier, the Val des Bagnes.

Walk # 5
Val des Bagnes Walk—Le Chable to Charançon to Cries to Cotterg to Le Chable
Walking Easy Time: 3 hours
Rating: Comfortable

Directions: Take the Verbier/Medran gondola down to Le Chable.

Start: Walk around to the back of the lift station, cross the river on the little bridge, turn right on the road and left at the *boulangerie*. Make your first right turn into the village square with its town hall. Follow the sign to the path towards CharanCon and then Cries, continuing back towards Le Chable by way of Cotterg.

Walk # 6
Le Chable to Champsec
Walking Easy Time: 1 1/2 to 3 hours
Rating: Comfortable

Follow directions in Walk #5 to arrive at the center of Le Chable. Follow the sign to Champsec. There are two ways to walk to Champsec—the higher trail through Bruson, or on the lower trail (Promenade de la Dranse) through Prarriyer. We stayed on the lower trail because of the rain and caught the bus back from Champsec to Le Châble, where you can take a bus or gondola to Verbier. Or, if the weather remains okay, continue the circle-walk back to Le Chable by picking up the path from Champsec.

GRISONS

AROSA

The Rhatische Bahn or Rhaetian Railway, transports *Easy Walkers* from 2461 to 5742 ft. (750 to 1750 m.) via mountain ridges and sky-high trestles, through dense pine forests, across alpine meadows and near tiny mountain villages to the all-season resort of Arosa. The village lies in a sheltered hollow in the Graubunden (Grisons) canton, or state. This eastern region of Switzerland, home to the famous St. Moritz, Davos, and Klosters ski centers, is the largest and least developed of the Swiss Cantons—sparsely populated, mountainous, thickly forested, and with over 140spuare miles (363 square km.) of glaciers.

The main part of Arosa is built on the heights around two small lakes, the Untersee and the Obersee. Although parts of the village date from the fourteenth century, the predominantly modem architecture does not have that typical "Swiss chalet" feeling. However, Arosa does offer visitors a multitude of summer activities and an abundance of exciting day hikes, with over 125 miles (200 km.) of trails, and free bus service provided to all lifts and trailheads in the area.

Arosa's magnificent mountain scenery and excellent hiking attract an interesting mix of visitors. We hope more American walkers will sample Arosa's clear, invigorating air and its exciting, summer hiking trails.

TRANSPORTATION

By Train—To reach Arosa, *always* change trains in Chur to the narrow-gauge Rhatische Bahn, located outside the main station at the sign NACH AROSA (a one-hour trip).

By Car—Follow the 19-mile (31 km.) winding road from Chur to Arosa.

FAVORITE *WALKING EASY* HOTEL

Hotel Alpina
Three-Star CH-7050 Arosa; Tel: 81 377 16 58, Fax: 81 37737 52
Internet: www. alpine-arosa.ch
E-mail: info@alpine-arosa.ch

Created, cherished, and lovingly tended by Hans Eberhard (now retired), the Alpina is centrally located in this cool, high-altitude mountain resort. With chalet-style buildings, connected by a walkway, filled with Swiss memorabilia, the Alpina has comfortable rooms and apartments, most with balconies offering views of the surrounding lakes and mountains. The kitchen is just one of the reasons Alpina guests keep returning. Quality of service is warmly personal and the cooking is *hans gemaeht*. After-dinner drinks and coffee are served in a small, congenial bar area. The Alpina is exceptional when it comes to caring.

EXCURSIONS

The Arosa Tourist Information Office is located on the main street, across from the casino. Discount hiking passes are available for lifts and trains.
Fax: 81 378 70 21
Internet: www.arosa.ch
E-mail: arosa@arosa.ch

1. **Chur**—Chur is the oldest town in Switzerland, with archeological excavation dating back to 3,000 B.C. Although the city of 30,000 is now a large trade center, explore its colorful Old Town. The Tourist Information Office (follow the "i" signs outside the train station) provides walking maps of the Old Town area.
    Directions: *Trains leave hourly/or the one-hour ride to Chur.*

Arosa Walks

Recommended Maps:
Arosa Sommer-Wanderkarte
Arosa und Umgebung Wanderkarte

Walk #1
Introductory Walk—Arosa to Maran to Pratschli to LAW Middle Station to Tschuggenhutte to Arosa
Walking Easy Time: 2 hours
Rating: Comfortable

This walk is a pleasant introduction to the Arosa area. You'll take the Eichornliweg, the gently ascending forest path, to Maran, and walk on to Pratschli, then the LAW middle station oif the Weisshorn cable car. The path descends to Arosa past the Tschuggenhutte, with views of Innerarosa, the Weisshorn, and the Carmennahutte.

Start: Walk past the Hotel Alpina, up the road, to the path signed EICHORNLIWEG NACH MARAN. Turn right, walking through the forest. This path, the "Squirrel Way," lives up to its name, as the squirrels will greet you and beg for food. After a half hour you emerge at the Hof Maran Hotel and tennis courts. Turn left on the Pratschliweg, ascending on a meadow path. At Pratschli, turn right and follow signs indicating LAW MITTELSTATION—35 MIN. At the Weisshorn middle station, 6611 ft. (2015 m.). walk to the back following the sign WANDERWEG—5 MIN. This path leads to the Tschuggenhutte, at 6533 ft. (1991 m.) and the sign 15 MIN. TO AROSA, the path descending to Arosa's main street.

Walk #2
Hornlihutte Top Station to Alplisee to Schwelllsee to Innerarosa to Arosa
Walking Easy Time: 3 hours
Rating: Comfortable

Today you'll take the Hornli Express Lift from Innerosa to the Hornlihutte, at 8245 ft. (2513 m.) As you begin your descent to the Alplisee at 7189 ft. (2192 m.) look at the rocks to the right—marmots play and dart from their burrows. From Alplisee, the descent continues through Aroser Alp, past the Schwellisee, at 6342 ft. (1938 m.) with views up to the Weisshorn, Innerarosa, and the trail to Arosa.

Directions: *Take the bus to the Hornli Express lift and buy a one-way ticket to the top station.*

A WALKING EASY TRAIL

Start: After leaving the lift station, proceed down the mountain to the left, in the direction of Alplisee. After about an hour, the trail forks. Take the left fork and make an immediate right turn when the trail splits again. The Schwellisee is down on the left, and Alplisee is off to the right. Follow the left trail until you come to another intersection. Turn left again, following signs to Schwellisee and Innerarosa.

Stay on the left side of the lake, on a path carved into the lower part of the mountain, descending gradually to the Alpenblick Restaurant. Walk around the back of the restaurant and continue on the path marked Innerarosa. In a few minutes the path splits. Stay on the right path to Innerarosa. When you come to a fenced road walk sharply down to the right, past private homes, to the five-star Arosa Kulm Hotel. You can walk or take the free bus back to Arosa from here.

Walk #3
Hornlihutte Top Station o Tschiertschen (Optional Excursion To Chur))
Walking Easy Time: 3 hours
Rating Comfortable

The hike to Tschiertschen is a downhill, comfortable trek on the back side of Arosa Alp, the Weisshorn, and Ochsenalp. You'll pass the Urdensee, at 7376 ft. (2248 m.) and continue walking through Inner Urden, at 6477 ft. (1974 m.) and Oberwald, into Clus, ending in Tschiertschen, at 4430 ft. (1350 m.) Buses leave Tschiertschen for a thirty-minute ride and afternoon sightseeing visit to the ancient city of Chur.

Directions: *There are no restaurants on today's walk (although there are several in Tschiertschen), so be sure you've packed a picnic lunch and plenty of bottled water. Take the bus to the Hornli Express lift station and purchase a one-way ticket to the top.*
Start: Signs outside the station reading TSCHIERTSCHEN—2 1/4 STD. direct you down and to the left. However, this hike will probably take *Easy Walkers* closer to three hours. As you walk down the hill, take the right fork, following signs to Urdensee-Tschiertschen. The path is blazed red and white throughout the hike. You're still above the tree line as you approach Urdensee, an aqua lake down on the right. This path leads around to the left of the lake and bypasses it, dropping 1000 ft. (305 m.) Follow TSCHIERTSCHEN—2 STD.,as the path continues downhill to the right. It then swings around the mountain and becomes a wide, gravel path leading to the farm at Inner Urden. Another group of signs points to Tschiertschen. Be sure you take the lower path on your right, in the direction of the dairy farm. As you approach the farm, step over a small wire fence to continue (the fence is not for hikers but for cows). Walk around the right side of the barn, picking up the trail as you pass through a gate on the back side of the farm. A few more minutes brings you to a weathered, deserted barn. Follow a sign directing you to stay on the main path, now marked CLUS—TSCHIERTSCHEN. As you reach the tree line, the landscape softens and the path is less rocky. Note the signs saying CLUS-TSCHIERTSCHEN "straight ahead and FARWEG—TSCHIERTSCHEN to the right. Although both lead to the same destination, we reconmend the mountain path ahead, through the forest, blazed in red and white.
When you reach a paved road, the *bergweg* meets the/*arweg,* leading into Clus, where a sign directs you to Tschiertschen. Within fifteen minutes you'll enter this picturesque mountain village. Walk ahead to the church—to the right is the post office and bus stop, where you take the bus to Chur. The schedule is posted, and

if it's still early, pay the old city of Chur a visit. In Chur, take the Arosa train, outside and in front of the railroad station, signed "Nach Arosa."

Walk #4
Priitschli to Rot Tritt to Ochsenalp to Scheidegg to Pratschli
Walking Easy Time: 3 1/2 hours
Rating: Comfortable

A short bus ride from Arosa will take you to Pratschli, where the walk begins, ascending from 6234 to 6726 ft. (1900 to 2050 m.) The return hike leads up and over an alp, eventually down to Pratschli, where you catch the bus back to Arosa.

Directions: *Take the bus to Pratschli, the last stop.*

Start: Signs direct you toward Rot Tritt on a wide, paved path. Cows are grazing, farmers are haying, and you are surrounded by a tranquil, bucolic scene. Remain on the red and white blazed main trail to Rot Tritt.

Before the hour is up, you'll have turned around the mountain to reach Rot Tritt, a viewpoint and picnic tables at 6582 ft. (2006 m.) Following the sign OCHSENALP—35 MIN., you'll soon be on a shady path descending to Ochsenalp at 6352 ft. (1936 m.) After forty-five minutes a sign indicates an abrnpt change of direction. Walk up the hill to the left in the direction of Scheidegg. In about 20 minutes you will have ascended this grassy peak, on your way to the signed intersection MARAN, AROSA—1 HR. Walk through the gate, continuing in the direction of Maran and Arosa. From this point, it's downhill all the way. Follow the red and white blazing as there are branch trails going off in several directions. Cross a small gravel field, descending toward the main path back to Maran and Pratschli. The path is a bit rocky before you meet the paved path you walked up earlier this morning. Turn right, descending gradually to the bus stop at Pratschli.

Walk #5
Hörnlihütte Top Station to Carmennahütte to Weisshorn Mid-Station to Pratschli to Innerarosa to Arosa
Walking Easy Time: 3 hours
Rating: Comfortable

Our hike begins after taking the lift up to the Hornlihutte. You will descend to the Carmennahutte, continuing though the meadows to the Weisshorn Mid-station, then to Pratschli for a forest walk above Arosa to Innerarosa, where you continue into town.

Directions: Catch a bus to the Hornli lift station, and buy a one-way ticket to the top.

Start: Leaving the top station, follow the signs CARMENNAHUTTE—40 MIN. and LAW MITTELSTATION—1 1/4 STD. After arriving at the Carmennahutte, with a restaurant and sun-terrace, continue walking down the path to the middle station of the Weiusshorn cable car. At the mid-station, follow the sign PRATSCHLI—30 MIN, by making a half right turn on a red and white blazed path, winding down through the meadow, rather than staying on the road. After entering a forest area, the trail narrows. At a fork in the path, turn right and walk down through the meadow, following the trail under the Weisshorn lift lines. Reaching a gravel path, turn right, where signs direct you to Arosa. Turn right again on the Oberwald Promenade, ascending through the forest, over and around Arosa, to Innerarosa, and back to your hotel.

Walk #6
Weisshorn Mid-Station along the Arlenwaldweg to Pratschli to Rot Tritt through the Schafwald to Arosa (Excursion to the Weisshorn)
Walking Easy Time: 2 1/2 to 3 hours
Rating: Comfortable

You will enjoy the views from the Weisshorn, at 8705 ft. (2653 m.) although walking from the peak might be a little tough on the knees, so we'll bring you by return cable car to the mid-station for the start of today's hike.

From the Mittelstation you'll walk to Rot Tritt on a comfortable path. You visited Rot Tritt if you took Walk #4, but today, instead of walking up to Ochsenalp and Scheidegg, you will descend through meadow and forest to Arosa.

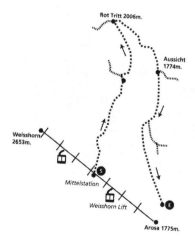

Directions: *Walk to the Weisshorn Aerial Cableway, near the train station and, if visibility is good, purchase a ticket to the top station, with a return to the mid-station. If visibility is questionable, buy a one-way ticket to the mid-station only.*

Start: After taking in the spectacular panorama from the *gipfel,* return by cable car to the LAW Mittelstation, and exit, following signs to the right to Rot Tritt. After a twenty-minute descent on a comfortable path, signs indicate Maran and Pratschli below—but follow the sign to Rot Tritt—a comfortable ascent from 6260 to 6582 ft. If you've taken Walk #4, Rot Tritt will be familiar but, instead of continuing ahead, descend from this point on the red and white blazed trail next to the picnic table. This descent though the meadow lasts for only ten minutes, until the trail empties onto a wagon road. Turn right, toward Arosa. Along the say, a sign indicates "Langwiesser Aussicht." Take the short detour to a scenic viewpoint of the villages in the valley below. Coming back to the main path, after about ten minutes, another sign directs you to your right, leaving the road. This comfortable forest strasse brings you to the Obersee in fifty-minutes, where it is a short walk back to your hotel.

SAMEDAN/ST. MORITZ (ENGADINE)

Simplicity, understated elegance and a feeling of antiquity characterize Samedan, a quiet Engadine village situated between its more famous sisters of St. Moritz and Pontresina. Samedan, our *Walking Easy* base village is situated at 5643 ft. (1720 m.), with excellent rail and bus service, a small airport (the highest in Europe), and the oldest 18-hole golf course in Europe.

The near-perfect weather of southern Switzerland is somewhat more reliable in summer than in other mountain regions, and there are dozens of trails at all levels accessible from Samedan. The well-preserved village of Samedan, with its ancient houses, appears to be lifted from a colorful history book of Switzerland, and the Engadine, in southeastern Switzerland, is probably the most interesting cultural and architectural area in the country. The Upper Engadine includes the famous resort towns of St. Moritz, Pontresina, Samedan and Zuoz, while the Lower Engadine is known for the mineral springs of Scuol and the wildlife preserve of the Swiss National Park. Visitors to the picturesque Engadine villages marvel at the distinctively ornamented *sgraffito* (two-tone designs in plaster) etched into the stately 16th-and 17th-century houses and the ancient Romansch language—spoken by many residents. Frequent trains and buses take hikers throughout the Engadine, from the Swiss-Italian border villages of Soglio and Castasegna, all the way to the unique villages of Zernez and Scuol.

St. Moritz is the commercial and social hub of this remarkably beautiful valley and the center of dozens of hikes along pristine lakes, into deep glacial valleys and on balcony trails—using the many lift systems to reach the area's snow-covered peaks.

TRANSPORTATION

By Train—Take the train to Chur, and change for the scenic, two-hour ride. Or, pick up the *Glacier Express* on one of its stops between Zermatt and Samedan. (See Zermatt Transportation, for information.)

By Car—Samedan is situated on Route 27, north of St. Moritz. From Chur, drive over the Julier Pass to Silvaplana, and north on 27. From southern Switzerland or northern Italy around Lake Como, drive through the Maloja Pass to St. Moritz and follow signs to Samedan.

FAVORITE *WALKING EASY* HOTEL

Golf-Hotel des Alpes
Three-Star, Owners-Familie Tarnuzzer
CH-7503 Samedan,
Internet: www.golf-hotel-des-alpes.ch
Email-info@golf-hotel-des-alpes.ch
 This cozy family hotel has been recently renovated and boasts an eighty-year tradition in Samedan. The hotel is located in a quiet secion of town, near public transportation. The rooms are comforable, equipped with all conveniences. In addition to a full Swiss Breakfast buffet, a salad buffet is featured at dinner, with owner Arnold Tarnuzzer, the talented chef, preparing excellent regional cooking.

EXCURSIONS IN AND AROUND SAMEDAN

The Samedan Tourist Information office is located on the main street across from the Hotel Bernina.
 Internet: www.samedan.ch
 Email: info@samedan.ch
1. **Samedan**—Visit the old parish church in the center of the village, built in 1771. The Planta House, also in the heart of town, is now a valued Romansch library.
2. **St. Moritz**—The resort of St. Moritz is a short, ten-minute train ride from Samedan. Situated at 6000 ft. (1829 **in.**) in a unique landscape of crystal-clear lakes, imposing glaciers and majestic mountains, St. Moritz also boasts five lifts for summer hikers to use. The St. Moritz Tourist Information Office is located at via Maistra 12, in the main square.
 Directions: *Trains and buses run frequently from Samedan to St. Moritz. A city bus runs* between St. Moritz Bad, the spa area, and St. Moritz Doff, the shopping and hotel area.
3. **Pontresina**—Near St. Moritz, at an altitude of 5821 ft. (1774 m.), Pontresina lies on a high, sunny terrace, surrounded by the Bernina mountains and imposing glaciers, with three area operating lift systems in summer. One is **at Diavolezza**, with summer skiing available at the glacier. The cable car rises to 9771 ft. (2978 **in.**), and a spectacular, glacial panorama. Take the train from Samedan to Pontresina and change for the train to Poschiavo, exiting at the Bernina-Diavolezza station. Because cable car **Lagalb** is only a few minute's train ride from Diavolezza, you might plan the day to visit both peaks.

4. **Zuoz**—Considered the best-preserved village in the Upper Engadine, Zuoz nestles at 5750 ft. (1753 **in.**) in lush, green meadows. Its Medieval Chapel of San Bastiaun contains some unusually fine murals. (See Walk #6.)
   Directions: *Trains leave Samedan hourly for Zuoz.*
5. **Celerina**—Lying between St. Moritz and Samedan at 5675 ft. (1862 m.), this small Engadine village is sometimes considered a suburb of glitzier St. Moritz. Celerina contains charming, Engadine houses, worth exploring on a walk from Samedan.
   Directions: *Trains and buses run frequently between Samedan and Celerina. However, it is a short walk from one village to the other.*
6. **Sils-Maria** and **Sils-Baselgia**—With a combined population of less than 500, these quiet, charming resorts in the Upper Engadine are situated at the beginning of the Inn (En) Valley. From 1881 to 1889, Sils-Maria was summer home to the philosopher Nietzsche, who wrote *Thus Spake Zarathustra* there, and his museum is located to the right of the main bus station. A Pferde Omnibus (horse and carriage) leaves every day from the Post Office in Sils-Maria for trips into the beautiful Fex Valley. Reservations are necessary. (See Walk #2.)
   Directions: *Take a morning train, arriving in St. Moritz to connect with the bus to Sils-Maria at the St. Moritz train station—a total trip of about an hour. To return to Samedan from Sils-Maria by bus, you must change at Schulhaus Platz in St. Moritz for the bus to Samedan through Celerina.*
7. **Scuol, Tarasp, Vulpera**—These tiny towns are enchanting—with their cobblestone streets and *sgraffito-decorated* houses. A bus from Scuol or Tarasp takes you to Schloss Tarasp, a restored castle still in use.
   Directions: *Trains leave Samedan regularly for the 75-minute ride to Scuol.*
8. **Poschiavo**—This small, Italian-speaking Swiss village, accessible by train through the Bernina Pass, offers a different style of architecture and surroundings from its Engadine neighbors—mixing German and Italian styles into its transalpine surroundings From July 1 through September 1, an open-air market is held every Wednesday in the town square.
   Directions: *Take the train from Samedan to Pontresina, and change for the Bernina Express to Tirano, stopping in Poschiavo.*
9. **Swiss National Park**—In this protected alpine sanctuary, plants and animals are allowed to develop without human intefference. The National Park House is in Zernez, and we recommend a stop before entering the park.
   Directions: *A mid-morning train arrives in Zernez from Samedan in about 45 minutes. Check with the tourist Office.*

SAMEDAN WALKS
Recommended Maps:
1) Wanderkarte—Oberengadin, Bergell, Nationalpark
2) Kunmerly+Frey Wanderkarte—Oberengadin, Bergell-Puschlav
3) Kleiner Wandeffuhrer der Engadiner Bergbahnen

Walk #1: Mnottas Mnragl Top Station to Alp Langnard Top Station
Walking Easy Time: 3 hours
Rating: Comfortable

You will take the short train ride from Samedan to Punt Muragl and the funicular to Muottas Muragl at 8048 ft. (2453 m.) The path *Easy Walkers* will take is a midlevel balcony trail at a comfortable 6600 ft. (2000 m.) towards Pontresina and the Alp Languard chairlift, under the famous Segantinihutte at 8960 ft. (2731 m.).

HINT: The views from this trail into the Val Roseg and its glacier, St. Moritz and its lakes, and the surrounding high peaks of the Engadine, are so compelling that we caution *Easy Walkers* to admire the views while taking a "scenery-break" rather than risking an accident while walking!

Directions: *Take a train towards Pontresina, one-stop to Punt Muragl. Buy a round-trip ticket—up to Muottas Muragl on the funicular and down on the Alp Languard chairlift.*

Start: On leaving the funicular, walk ahead though the turnstile and follow the sign "Alp Languard-2 3/4 hrs." This scenic hike speaks for itself—just continue to follow signs to Alp Languard—ignoring the side trails to Samedan and Pontresina.

After taking the chairlift down to Pontresina, follow signs for the 15 minute walk to the train station.

Walk #2—Furtschellas Top Station to Marmorê to Curtins/Fex Valley to Sils Maria
Walking Easy Time: 3 1/4 hours
Rating: Comfortable

Today's beautiful hike begins in Sils-Maria with the lift up to Furtschellas at 7,586 ft. (2312 m.)

You will hike to Marmorè, offering exceptional views over the lakes and through the valley to St. Moritz. The hike continues on a mountain *bergweg* to the village of Curtins in the Fex Valley, for the gentle walk back through Cresta and into the *schlucht* (gorge) to Sils-Maria and the bus.

*: Take a train from Samedan to St. Moritz, and pick up the bus to Sils-
? the train station. In Sils, follow signs to the Furtschellas lift station and
~~Duy~~ y ticket to the top station.

Start: On exiting, follow the path around the sun-terrace signed "Marmore-Val Fex-1 hr." Climb the hill for a few minutes till you reach a second sign directing you down the hill on a rocky path, eventually levelling, until you reach the viewpoint at Marmore.

After taking in the outstanding views, follow signs to Curtins on the lower path. As you descend, you will see the popular horse-drawn carriages of the Fex Valley. The trail can be steep and rocky, and sometimes slippery, so use normal caution while descending. The little village of Curtins, at the foot of the glacier, can be seen during your descent.

The *bergweg* ends at the road where you have two options:

1) Return to Sils via horse-drawn carriage.
2) Take the short walk along the road to Crasta and visit the famous Fex church with its ancient murals. Then follow "Schluchtweg, Sils-Maria" through the little village of Fex-Platta, and the gorge. In Sils-Maria, continue ahead for a few minutes to the bus stop. Exit the bus at the Schulhaus Platz stop in St. Moritz and change for the bus to Samedan.

Walk #3 Pontresina to Val Roseg (Optional Walk back to Pontresina)
Walking Easy Time: 2 to 4 hours
Rating: Gentle

This lovely valley walk will take *Easy Walkers* on a gently ascending forest trail from Pontresina to the foot of the Val Roseg Glacier—one of the most popular walks in the area. The path ascends comfortably from 5922 to 6562 ft. (1805 to 2000m.), and in two hours you'll reach the Restaurant Roseggletscher, with a buffet served on its sun-terrace. You can return by Pferde Omnibus or walk back on the same trail. Make reservations for the wagon ride in advance at your hotel.

Directions: *Take a train from Samedan, and in ten minutes you'll be at the bahnhof in Pontresina.*

Start: After leaving the station, turn right, and within a few feet note the standing area for the Pferde Omnibus. Since we suggest walking into the Val Roseg (Roseg Valley) and taking the horse and wagon back, follow the sign "Fussweg-Val Roseg 150 m.) and note "Val Roseg Fussweg" on your right, ascending gradually into the forest.

The path ascends easily and within 30 minutes, the snow-capped peaks of the Roseg range appear above the pine trees. When the path meets the road, take the trail to the left to avoid the bikers and horses and walk through the forest to the hotel. Check out the dessert buffet—no less than 30 varieties of homemade pies, cakes and fresh fruit—the rest is up to you (and your wallet)! After lunch, a walk around the restaurant will disclose signs to various destinations. Take the path towards the glacier on the restaurant side of the river and walk as long as you feel comfortable—enjoying the cool alpine air and the fantastic views of the Roseg glacier. Before taking any additional walks, make your decision as to whether to take that horse and wagon ride back to Pontresina or return on the same path you came on. The wagon ride takes about 50 minutes, while the return walk will take less than two hours.

Walk #4: Sils-Baselgia to Grevasalvas to Sils-Maria (Excnrsion to St. Moritz or Optional Walk to Maloja)
Walking Easy Time: 3 to 4 hours
Rating: Comfortable

Today's walk leads to the tiny alpine hamlet where the 1960 remake of *Heidi* was filmed. *Easy Walkers* will take the train to St. Moritz and change for the bus to Sils-Baselgia, where the trail begins. This high-level, mountain walk to Grevasalvas is on a path with unparalleled views of nearby Lej de Segl. After a steady ascent from 5900 to 6560 ft. (1798 to 2000 m.), you'll reach the heights overlooking Grevasalvas.

We're not sure Grandfather is around any more, but this wondrous little hamlet is still situated below a grassy alp, surrounded by grazing cows and craggy peaks. After conjuring up images of blonde braids, dirndl skirts and gentle, pipe-smoking grandpas, you will return on the same path, proceeding down the mountain towards Sils-Baselgia and Sils-Maria, or continue ahead on the same path to Maloja, set in a stunning mountain landscape, where you can take a bus to St. Moritz and Samedan.

Directions: *Catch a morning train to St. Moritz, in time to take a connecting bus to Sils-Baselgia, located outside the front of the station and to the left.*

Start: When you get off the bus in Sils-Baselgia, walk ahead, through the small village, toward the mountains. After crossing the road, follow the sign left, up a mountain path towards Grevasalvas. This stone-strewn trail is shaded by pine forests, and it gradually ascends 650 ft. (200 m.) Following the sign "Grevasalvas-1/2 hr.," you'll see wateffalls rush over rocky promontories on the right, as you step over streams, ascending on a narrow, rocky trail. Reaching the high point of 6562 ft. (2000 m.) the tiny hamlet of Grevasalvas is below and to the left. You can walk down a steep path to this hamlet of a dozen houses if you are going to continue on to Maloja, or remain on the hillside and enjoy lunch on a green-carpeted alp.

AN ALPINE TRAIL

There are options for your return:

1) Continue ahead and follow signs to Maloja, bringing you down from 6562 to 5955 ft. (2000 to 1815 m.) in about 11/2 hours. Buses leave regularly from Malojato St. Moritz, where you change at Schulhaus Platz for the bus to Samedan.

2) Or, retrace your steps along the same trail, passing through Sils-Baselgia, visiting Sils-Maria, taking the bus to St. Moritz and then to Samedan.

If you decide on Option #2, this reverse walk should take about 1 1/4 hours. At the base of the trail in Sils-Baselgia, cross the road and walk past a restaurant with sun-terrace and facilities. Continue to walk up the main street into Sils-Maria, taking the bus to the St. Moritz Schulhaus Platz stop, in the heart of the St. Moritz shopping area. This is a short block from the famous Hanselman's tea room and pastry shop, tempting weary travelers with some of the most delectable desserts in town (except on Tuesday when it is closed!). Check the bus schedule back to Samedan from Schulhaus Platz before exploring St. Moritz.

Walk #5: Marguns Top Station to Alp Mnntatsch via Alp Clavadasch to Samedan
Walking Easy Time: 3 1/2 to 4 hours
Rating: More Challenging

A quick train ride from Samedan will bring you to Celerina and the gondolas to Marguns where today's walk begins. The hike is mostly comfortable, except for a more challenging ascent during the first 45 minutes. *Easy Walkers* should be able to handle this—proceed slowly. The views from this mountain *bergweg* are sensational, the panorama including the lakes of St. Moritz, the mountains around Pontresina and the valley past Samedan, all the way to the Swiss National Park. Reserve the better part of a clear day for this hike. There are no restaurants or facilities along this trail.

Directions: *Take a train one stop to Celerina. As you exit the train, turn right and right again on a paved path to the lift station. Take the gondola to the top station, Marguns.*

Start: Although it is possible to take a chairlift up to Corviglia and eventually up to Piz Nair at 10,042 ft. (3057 m.) we suggest getting started on today's hike by turning left down the hill as you leave the Marguns lift station, following the sign to Alp Clavadasch. Just past the sign, enter the unsigned, red and white blazed path rising though the meadow. After ascending about 45 minutes on a mountain *bergweg*, you'll reach the high point of today's hike at 7358 ft. (2240 m.). Stay on the lower right path to Celerina and Samedan. This trail rambles along Alp Clavadasch in the direction of Alp Muntatsch. We do not recommend taking the steep paths that head down the mountain towards Samedan or Celerina. Stay on the trail towards Alp Muntatsch at 7181 ft. (2186 m.). After resting at the barn at Alp Muntatsch, follow the sign onto the jeep road, "Samedan train station-1/4 hrs."

Walk #6: Zuoz to Madnlain to La Pnnt to Bever to Samedan (Excnrsion to Zuoz)
Walking Easy Time: 3 hours
Rating: Gentle

Zuoz nestles in lush green meadows at 5742 ft. (1750 m.) far from the hustle and bustle of St. Moritz, and is considered to be the best-preserved village in the Upper Engadine. Today's excursion and walk brings *Easy Walkers* to this enchanting town, leaving time for sightseeing, photography and lunch. The afternoon will be made up of a low-level walk through the valley from Zuoz through the small and photogenic villages of Madulain, La Punt and Bever—largely through the meadows and close to the Inn River.

Directions: *Take a train to Zuoz, a 15-minute ride from Samedan.*

Start: Arriving in Zuoz, cross the tracks and walk up the hill to the town center. As you reach the main street, make a right turn, and within a few minutes you will reach the town square. Take an hour or so to explore the cobblestone streets and alleys and *sgrajitto*-decorated houses before beginning today's walk. The village has retained its original character, restoring its elegant 16th-and 17th-century houses. Most of its 1,200 inhabitants speak Romansch as well as Swiss-German. Visit Planta House, located on the main square of Zuoz, and the church with its heraldic symbol of the Planta family—a severed bear's paw. The church's modern stained glass windows were designed by famed sculptor Augusto Giacometti.

Leave Zuoz by retracing your steps to the railroad station. At the station turn right, walk through the long parking area to the end, picking up a path through a small tunnel underneath the railroad tracks. Walk past a restaurant, down to the river. Turn right along the river path, following the sign to Madulain, a tiny, quiet, well-preserved Engadine village.

After 25 minutes, the path veers up a hill to the right, where a sign points left to Madulain. This is the Zuoz-Madulain Innweg, a promenade between the two villages along the Inn River. As you proceed, Madulain comes into full view, and in the distance to the left is the village of Chamuesch-ch. Walk ahead through Madulain on its main road.

As you leave Madulain, the path crosses a major auto road. Do not cross. Walk across the little wooden bridge over the river on your left. Make a sharp right turn at the end of the bridge and walk down a flight of plank stairs, under the auto road, with the path spilling into the meadow on the other side. Continue to a four-way intersection and turn right to La Punt-Bever. La Punt lies directly ahead, and you'll soon be at the main road. At the Hotel Krone you have two options:

1)   Turn right and follow signs to the *stazione* for the next train back to Samedan.

2)   Cross the street behind the Hotel Krone and follow directions to Bever-Samedan-Pontresina. Cross a stream on a small wooden bridge to pick up a path alongside the river that leads directly into Bever and then Samedan.

Walk #7: Ospizio Bernina to Sassal Massone to Alp Grütn
Walking Easy Time: 2 1/2 hours
Rating: More Challenging

The Swiss area closest to the mountains separating Italy from Switzerland provides the setting for today's hike. All of the walking will be in the open, on and around mountains that are bare, craggy and rocky. You will take the train to Ospizio Bernina, the Rhaetian Railway's highest station, and hike to Sassal Massone and its restaurant at 7392 ft. (2253 m.). The walk will continue down the mountain to the 6860 ft. (2091 m.) railroad station at Alp Grum, a wonderful spot to admire the view across to the Palu Glacier and Puschlav, as far as the Bergamo Alps—before the train ride back to Samedan.

The train from Samedan to Ospizio Bernina brings you into the Italian-influenced region of Switzerland, and the signs and names are now in Italian, instead of German or Romansch. This change in atmosphere makes Switzerland even more appealing to visitors—as language, customs, cuisine, dress and living styles change dramatically the closer you get to the Italian border—see or lake, becomes *lago,* and *stunde* or hour, is now *ora.*

Directions: *We suggest a train leaving about 9:00 am to Pontresina, changing for the train to Ospizio Bernina and Tirano waiting on an adjacent platform. Sit on the right side for best views, and within 40 minutes you'll arrive at your destination— Ospizio Bernina.*

Start: At the end of the station, follow "Sassal Massone-1 1/4 hrs." Walk along the Lago Bianco reservoir and railroad tracks—below the Cambrena Glacier—on a white and red blazed path. At the end of the lake, the path forks. Take either path (they meet) for a short distance till you come to another fork in the road and a sign indicating "Sassal Massone" to the right. The left path stays lower and goes directly to the Alp Grum station. Turn right, proceeding up the mountain, bringing you to the Sassal Massone restaurant at 7392 ft. (2253m.), and a fabulous view of the glacier.

To return to Alp Grum, walk to the rear of the sun-terrace and proceed down a dirt path facing the glacier. This trail is a rocky, narrow, mountain *bergweg*, but well-marked, well-defined and well-used. There are many side trails—stay on the main path, blazed white and red. The trail buttonhooks and, instead of facing the glacier, turns towards the small train station of Alp Grum.

Within an hour you'll reach the bottom of the mountain. Turn right and walk up to the railroad tracks. Follow a sign pointing to a lower path along the tracks for the ten-minute walk to the Alp Grum station and its restaurant, inviting sun-terrace and facilities. Trains to Samedan (with a change in Pontresina) run hourly.

Walk #8: Signal Lift Station on the "via Engiadina" to Alp Snvretta to Orchas to Silvaplana
Walking Easy Time: 3 1/2 hours
Rating: More Challenging

As with all high-level walks in the Samedan/St. Moritz area, try to take this sensational hike on a clear, sunny day. You will take the cable car from St. Moritz Bad to the Signal station, where the hike begins. The first part is an delightful balcony walk along Alp Giop. At Alp Suvretta, the path becomes more of a mountain trail as it continues towards Silvaplana, though Orchas, with some "more challenging" ascents. This "via Engiadina" trail is well-signed and well-traveled and can be taken all the way to Maloja on a path above Lake Silvaplana and Lej da Segl. Today, however, *Easy Walkers* will depart the via Engiadina and descend to the little village of Silvaplana for the bus ride to St. Moritz.

Directions: *Take the bus from Samedan to the St. Moritz Bad Signal Lift stop. Buy a one-way ticket to Signal.*

SCENIC WALKING EASY TRAIL

Start: At the Signal lift station at 6989 ft. (2130 in.), follow signs left indicating "Alp Suvretta-45 mm.," picking up via Engiadina signs along the way. The path to Alp Suvretta is wide and gentle, and passes a mountain restaurant with sun-terrace and facilities. Within 45 minutes to an hour you will reach Alp Suvretta at 7254 ft. (2211m.) The path buttonhooks and descends, signed "via Engiadina," now on a typical *bergweg,* occasionally blazed red and white. The trail crosses a little wooden bridge to an unsigned fork in the trail. Stay on the lower left trail, still blazed red and white.

At a signed intersection, follow "via Engiadina" to the right, as the trai begins to ascend.

After about two hours, follow a large, red and white, unsigned, wooden arrow directing you sharply left, for a short descent to a group of signs, leaving the via Engiadina, which continues on to the right. Passing a large sign announcing an artillery position from World War I, the red and white blazed path continues to descend. The trail eventually buttonhooks down and around to the left at a via Engiadina sign, with a clear view of the road ahead.

Follow an arrow down to the auto road. Cross the road, turn left and walk on the road for about 100 yards to a sign indicating "Silvaplauna-IS mm." Shortly, enter a wagon path, blazed red and white on a fence. It descends through the forest, reaching a paved, rarely used mountain road, eventually emptying into an auto road. Turn right on the auto road. Cross the road and turn left where a sign indicates "Silvaplauna bus," entering the forest on a little winding, red and white blazed trail signed "Truoch Pignia." After a few minutes the trail empties into the village of Silvaplana. Wind down into the village, turn left on the main auto road and walk to the PTT bus station on the right.

Walk #9: Soglio to Castasegna (Excursion to the Val Bregaglia over the Maloja Pass) Walking Easy Time: 1 hour
Rating: Gentle

There are many opportunities for hiking in the Val Bregaglia or Bergell, the smallest of the southern Engadine valleys of the Graubunden/Grisons canton. Today however, you will descend gently through Europe's largest chestnut forest on the "Romantic Trail" from Soglio, an historic mountain hamlet, to the village of Castasegna at the Swiss-Italian border. This walk is only an hour, but we bring you on a bus ride over the exhilarating (hair-raising) Maloja Pass, so you can experience the gradual architectural and cultural change from Engadine Swiss to Engadine Italian, and ride through tiny hamlets that seem untouched by modern culture—the picturesque and unspoiled villages of the Val Bregaglia.

STONE HOUSE NEAR SOGLIO

Directions: *Please check bus and train schedules carefully—these times were in effect when we took this excursion—and may have changed. Take an early morning train from Samedan to St. Moritz. Walk outside the station to the bus terminal and take the connecting bus to Chiavenna area. This bus is non-stop to Soglio and, after a thrilling ride over the Maloja Pass and though the quaint mountain towns of the Bregell.*

Start: Take some time to explore this village where time stands still. The view from the church cemetery is breathtaking—glaciers and mountains in all directions—and the narrow streets are a photographer's paradise. When ready, walk back down the narrow road in the direction the bus came from. In about 20 minutes, turn into the forest on the right, following a sign "Castasegna on the

Historic Path." In five minutes, arriving at a lovely waterfall, follow the path though the mountain, under the falls, and continue through meadows filled with old log cabins, surrounded by chestnut trees, following signs to Castasegna. After about an hour, and just before Castasegna there is a tiny park with a picnic table.

Arriving at Castasegna's main street, turn left to La Posta and the bus for Schulhaus Platz in St. Moritz where you change for the bus to Samedan.

EASTERN SWITZERLAND

APPENZELL/APPENZELLERLAND

A first visit to Switzerland's Appenzellerland evoked a rush of excitement as the idyllic, rolling, velvety hills of the countryside embraced typical Appenzell farmhouses framed by the magnificent Alpstein mountain range—an ideal marriage for *Walking Easy* in an unforgettable landscape.

There are over 320 miles (515 km) of marked hiking trails in this area, and *Easy Walkers* will enjoy passing through verdant meadows and alps, past farms with herds of grazing cows, their milk used in the making of world-renowned Appenzeller cheese. One meadow walk features a unique *barfussweg*, a grassy path so soft that you are asked to remove your hiking boots as you cross the rolling fields. Other hikes wind through Stone Age caves at Wildkirchli and lead to a visit to Seealpsee, a picturesque mountain lake. A thrilling cable car excursion to the Säntis peak takes you from 4436 to 8209 ft. (1352 to 2502 m.), with far-reaching views into Switzerland, Germany, Austria and the Dolomites of Italy.

Historic Appenzell, with its brightly painted houses—now filled with busloads of day-trippers—is the political and economic center of Appenzellerland. Shops offer famous Appenzell lace, cheese, baked goods, chocolates, and primitive paintings by the area's artists. Choral and instrumental concerts featuring Appenzell string music and yodelling are frequent, as are folk festivals including traditional Appenzellerland costumes. Local bus and rail transportation brings hikers to and from the start of hikes, making sightseeing excursions to charming nearby villages easily accessible.

Once you've discovered the Appenzell trails you'll fall in love again—as we did.

TRANSPORTATION TO APPENZELL

By Train—Take the train to St. Gallen, and transfer to the local train to Appenzell.

By Car—Drive towards St. Gallen and follow signs to Appenzell.

FAVORITE *WALKLING EASY* HOTEL

Romantic Hotel Santis
Four-Star, Owner—Catriona and Stefan Heeb
CH 9050, Appenzell
Internet: www.saentis-appenzell.ch
Email: info@saentis-appenzell.ch
The romantic Hotel Santis is situated on the historic landsgemeideplatz, a famous square in the village of Appenzell. The hotel feattures traditional Appenzell architechture and design. Its rooms are quaintly yet elegantly furnished and have all the modern amenities expected in a four-star hotel. A recent renovation added six suites, a bar, a sauna, and a solarium. There are several top-quality restaurant in the hotel serving excellent Swiss and Continiental cuisine. Friday nights are reserved for a special buffet dinner. The Heeb family are always in attendance, creating special family atmosphere.

EXCURSIONS IN AND AROUND APPENZELL

The Appenzell Tourist Office, is located on the main street.
Internet: www.appenzell.ch
e-mail: info@appenzell.ch
1. **St. Gallen**—The largest city in northeast Switzerland, St. Gallen is the area's cultural and economic center and the highest city of its size in Europe. Also known for its embroidery and lace, its Old Town boasts medieval houses built in narrow, car-free alleys laid out during the Middle Ages.
   Directions: *The direct train from Appenzell arrives in St. Gallen in 45 minutes.*
2. **Stein**—This village is situated on a sunny hilltop and is famous for its Appenzell cheese. An Appenzell Showcase Cheese Dairy has been established here and visitors can watch the production of this famous cheese—from the milk delivery to its ripening.
   Directions: *Check with the Tourist Office for a bus excursion to Stein.*
3. **Zurich**—Switzerland's largest city, Zurich is located on Lake Zurich and bisected by the Limmat River. It is a center of international finance and its main street, Bahnhofstrasse, is lined with shops and banks. The Old Town however, boasts cobblestone streets and ancient squares.
   Directions: *Take a train from Appenzell to Zurich, changing in Herisau for the connecting train—a trip of about two hours.*

APPENZELL WALKS
Recommended Maps:
1) Wanderkarte—Säntis-Alpstein
2) Panorama-Wanderkarte-Appenzell/Alpsteingebiet
3) Wanderkarte—Obertoggenburg-Appenzell

Walk #1: Introductory Walk—Sammelplatz to Hutten to Hoch Hirschberg to Gais (Optional Walk to Appenzell)
Walking Easy Time: 2 to 3 hours
Rating: Comfortable

Today's walk can serve as an introduction to the tranquil green alps of Appenzellerland. If you arrive in Appenzell in the morning, this afternoon hike will acquaint you with the special qualities of the region. You will take a six-minute train ride from the Appenzell *bahnhof* to Sammelplatz and hike from 3042 ft. (927 m.) to Hutten at 3452 ft. (1052 m.), continuing up to Hoch Hirschberg at 3829 ft. (1167 m.) for refreshment and views of the surrounding alps and mountains. You will then descend to Gais 3061 ft. (933 m.) for the short train ride back to Appenzell. If it is early enough, you might want to return by walking to Appenzell.

Directions: *Take the train towards Gais at the Appenzell bahnhof. NOTE: Make sure that immediately after the train passes Hirschberg (where it may or may not stop), you press the halt button next to the train exit door, signalling the engineer to stop the train at Sammelplatz, an "on-request only stop station."*

Start: After exiting the train at Sammelplatz, cross the tracks and walk forward to the group of signs, following "Hoch Hirschberg Hohenweg-1 1/4 hrs." Walk up the paved path, passing the Gais/Guggeloch intersection, continuing to follow signs to the *hohenweg*. As you ascend through the meadow and arrive at an unmarked path to the right, **ahead, up the mountain on a beaten, grassy path**, all the way to the paved road. Turn left on the road and continue to follow it through the meadow, up to the house and barn. Turn left and walk past the barn. After about an hour of walking from Sammelplatz, you'll arrive at a four-way intersection at Hütten. Here, *Easy Walkers* have a few options:

1) Continue walking for another 30 minutes up to the country restaurant at Hoch Hirschberg for rest and refreshment, then walk down to Gais via Schachen.

2) Turn left at Hütten for the 40-minute walk to Gais.

At Gais you also have two options:
1) Take the train back to Appenzell.
2) Follow the *wanderweg* signs and walk from Gais to Sammelplatz to Guggerloch to Appenzell.

Walk #2: Ebenalp Top Station to Wildkirchli Caves to Ascher to Seealpsee to Wasserauen (Optional Walk to Schwendi, Weissbad and Appenzell)
Walking Easy Time: 3 to 5 hours
Rating: Comfortable

After ascending by cable car from the village of Wasserauen to Ebenalp at 5394 ft. (1644 m.) and viewing the soft green meadows of Appenzellerland framed by the Alpstein mountain range, you will descend to Wildkirchli and walk through its prehistoric caves. Stone Age bones and tools once used in this area are displayed in the hermit's dwelling just outside the cave exit. The unusual altar-cave is evidence of the religion practiced by hermits who lived in the caves for several hundered years, beginning in 1658.

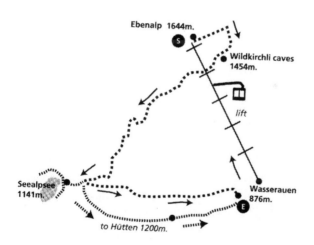

The path to Seealpsee is rocky and can be slippery. It descends rapidly, aided by natural steps, all the way to the lake at 3744 ft. (1141 m.). Here walkers can amble about the lake and/or have lunch on the sun-terrace of the Berggasthaus Forelle, overlooking this charming lake with the Säntis peak in the distance. You will then descend to Wasserauen, where you return by train or continue to walk towards Appenzell.

Directions: *Take a train from Appenzell to Wasserauen. Walk to the Ebenalp lift across the street and purchase a one-way ticket to the top.*

Start: At the Ebenalp top station, follow signs to Wildkirchli and Ascher, the trail looping to the right on a stepped path down the mountain. After about ten minutes, walk through the Wildkirchli caves, originally inhabited by Stone Age bears. On exiting the caves, stop at the hermit's hut, and continue past the altar-cave to the remarkable 150-year old Ascher Restaurant, built into the face of the sheer cliff. Walk through its sun-terrace, continuing down the rocky trail through the forest. The final ten-minute walk ascends to the right to Seealpsee. Turn left to the restaurant, where walkers can amble about the lake and/or eat lunch (we recommend the *bratwurst* and *rösti*).

When ready, return to the comfortable main trail towards Wasserauen. Here you have a few options:

1) Take the ten-minute train ride back to Appenzell.
2) Walk along pleasant meadow paths to Schwende, Weissbad, Steinegg and Appenzell. The walk from Wasserauen to Appenzell takes two hours, but it is possible to board the train at any of the above stations.

Walk #3: Wasserauen to Seealpsee to Hutten to Huttentobel to Wasserauen
Walking Easy Time: 3 to 5 hours
Rating: Comfortable

For those *Easy Walkers* who would prefer not to hike down from Ebenalp as in Walk#2, but would like to visit the beautiful lake at Seealp, this is the hike for you. After taking the train to Wasserauen, you will hike up to the lake from 2848 to 3744 ft. (868 to 1141 m.) on a paved path, and return by walking along the lake for a short distance to catch the path to Hutten at 4072 ft. (1241 m.). You will then hike down to Wasserauen on a mountain *bergweg*, more interesting and more demanding than the paved path you walked up on. At Wasserauen, take the train back to Appenzell or, continue the hike by following signs to Schwendi and Weissbad, all the way to Appenzell—with the option of taking the train at any of those stops.

Directions: *Take the train from Appenzell to Wasserauen.*

ALL DRESSED UP RETURNING FROM THE ALPS

Start: Exiting the train, follow signs to the left, walking up the path to Seealpsee. Turn left around the lake and left again at Resien, ascending up to Hutten. At this point the trail descends, partially through the forest to Wasserauen. Be a bit cautious with this descent, it can be a little slippery and steep at times. If you are concerned about a steep descent after wet weather, return to Wasserauen on the same path you came up on.

At Wasserauen, take the train back to Appenzell, or follow the trail for the two-hour hike from Wasserauen to Appenzell.

Walk #4: Gonten to Gontenbad to Appenzell on the Barefoot Trail (Excursion to Santis)
Walking Easy Time: 1 1/2 to 2 1/2 hours (not including Santis Excursion)
Rating: Comfortable

When skies are clear, plan an early start for today's excursion and hike. You will take the train to Ürnasch and board a bus to Schwagalp, the location of the Säntis cable car. We recommend the fabulous views from the *gipfel* (peak)—taking the lift up.

After descending by cable car to Schwagalp, you will return by bus to Urnasch to take the train to Gonten for the beginning of today's pleasant walk on the "Barefoot Trail." Most of this walk takes place on the soft, grassy meadows of Appenzellerland. Signs remind you to take off your hiking boots—inviting you to walk barefoot through the meadows to preserve the grassy paths rather than have them beaten by rugged hiking boots—and it can be fun. This particularly comfortable, scenic trail offers those special views of what Appenzellerland is all about—undulating, grassy alps filled with cows and dotted with the architectural details that make this area so distinctive.

Directions: *Take a morning train to Urnäsch and transfer to the post bus, located outside the train station, for the ride to Schwagalp. Purchase a round-trip lift ticket to Säntis. The cable car brings you from Schwagalp at 4436 ft. (1352 m.) to Säntis at 8209 ft. (2502 m.). This is a multi-tiered lift station, with restaurants, facilities, and a major weather and communications system at its peak. The views are spectacular, encompassing the peaks of Austria and Italy as well as those of Switzerland.*

When ready, descend by cable car to Schwagalp for the return bus ride to Urnäsch. Take the train to Gonten 2960 ft. (902 m.), where today's jaunt through the meadows begins.

Start: After leaving the Gonten train station, turn right, walking into the village and following the sign "Appenzell 1 1/2 hrs." The next sign reads *wanderweg*, directing you left and then right, between two small houses. Turn right again, along the fence, up a little grassy hill. Ascend gently to the farmhouse and note yellow arrows directing you past the left side of the house to a sign pointing to the right towards Gontenbad and Appenzell. Eventually you'll bear right at a little fork in the road, always following the *wanderweg* signs and blazes. This is Appenzellerland at its best—tranquil green hills dotted with barns, houses and friendly cows. The path switches between grassy meadow and jeep trail, and after about 40 minutes you'll reach Gontenbad at 2937 ft. (895 m.), where it is possible to make a right turn and walk to the *bahnhof* to take a train to Appenzell, if necessary. To continue, there are additional options:

1) If you wish to stay on a fairly level path, walk ahead following the *wanderweg* and Appenzell signs.

2) Or, you can turn left and walk up a narrow, grassy, yellow-blazed *bergweg*, following signs to Himmelberg. The ascent to Himmelberg takes you to 3609 ft. (1100 m.), where you follow signs across the meadows into Appenzell.

Walk #5 Hoher Kasten Top Station to Kamor-Rossberg to Brulisau
Walking Easy Time: 3 hours
Rating: Comfortable.

While we did not have the opportunity to complete this hike, it appears to be a comfortable, downhill walk from the peak of Hoher Kasten 5886 ft. (1794 m.) via the Kastensattel. The descent continues to Kamor, ending via Rossberg, in Brülisau at 3025 ft. (922 m.).

Directions: Take a train from Appenzell to Weissbad, and take the bus to Brulisau. Buy a one-way ticket to the top station at Hoher Kasten.

Start: Visit the easily accessible viewpoint that will acquaint you with most of Appenzellerland—past Appenzell all the way to the Alpstein massif and, if a clear day, to the mountains of Austria. After taking in the panorama, descend the mountain via Kastensattel 5506 ft. (1678 m.), towards Kamor 4488 ft. (1368 m.), winding around through Rossberg all the way to Brulisau. While it is possible to walk on the road before entering Brulisau, you might find it more interesting staying on the mountain trail.

At Brulisau, take the bus to Weissbad connecting with the train to Appenzell. NOTE: Please check all train and bus schedules before taking today's hike.

Walk #6
Kronberg top Station to Scheidegg to Kaubad o Eichen to Appenzell
Rating: Comfortable

For today's hike, you will take the train from Appenzell to Jakobsbad, where you take the Kronberg Lift to the top station. The views from the top are mesmirizing—the nearby Santis towering above the tranquil Appenzell alps. This walk descends Mount Kronberg to Scheidegg along trails with country inns located along the way—continuing to Kaubad and Eichen before retuning to Appenzell.

Directions: *Take the train to Jacobsbad. NOTE: Immediately after the train passes Gonten, press the halt button signaling the engineer to stop at Jacobsbad. Walk across to the Kronberg Lift Station, aand purchase a one-way ticket to the top.*

Start: There are several options from the Kronerg Top station. Today, follow the sign to Scheidegg, passing the little chapel at St. Jacob. In Scheidegg follow the signs to Kaubad and Eichen. Pass the restaurant, and follow the forest trail that cuts off to the right into Eichen. At Eichen follow signs to Appenzell.

CENTRAL SWITZERLAND

ENGELBERG

The picturesque village of Engelberg at 3281ft. (1000 m.) is tucked between mountain ranges in a fertile valley south of Lucerne, along the Aa river. Sunny, terraced meadows reach from the valley floor to high, green alps, filled in summer with grazing cows and criss-crossed by some of the most exciting combinations of lifts and trails in the Swiss Alps.

Engelberg's name and history are connected to its famous Benedictine *kloster* (monastery), located on the edge of the village. According to local legend, the builder of the *kloster* heard voices of angels from the peak of a nearby mountain instructing him to build where the monastery is now located; thus began Engel berg—town of angels!

Towering above Engelberg is Mt. Titlis, Central Switzerland (Zentralschweiz) canton's highest peak at 10,500 ft. (3200 m.). It's reached by a series of lifts, including an inovative, rotating "Rotair" cable car, the first in the world—operating from Stand to Klein Titlis, just below the summit. Imagine a rotating platform in a cable car, rising 2000 ft. (610 m.) to reach the top station. This ride takes visitors through many changes of scenery—from the green, flat valley floor up into the high, alpine glacier region with its spectacular views of crevasses and ice falls. A section of the Titlis lift from Engelberg takes hikers to Trübsee at 5893 ft. (1796m.), with another lift to the Jochpass at 7241 ft. (2207 m.), and trails that lead into the Bernese Oberland.

Surrounded by high mountains, icy glaciers and green alps, with a multitude of hiking trails for every level, and only an hour by train to enchanting Lucerne—Engelberg's magic is waiting to be discovered by *Easy Walkers*.

TRANSPORTATION TO ENGELBERG

By Train—From Zurich airport it's a 2 1/2 hour train ride to Engelberg, with a change in Lucerne. From the Bernese Oberland area, take the train from

Interlaken Ost to Lucerne, **always** changing in Hergiswil for the ride to Engelberg.

By Car—Take N2 south—the north/south Basel-Gotthard motorway—exiting at Stans-Süd for Engelberg.

EXCURSIONS IN AND AROUND ENGELBERG

The Engelberg Tourist Office is located in the Tourist Center, across from the *Coop* supermarket.

Internet: www.engelberg.ch

e-mail: tourist.center@engelberg.ch

Pick up a Guest Card at your hotel, allowing a reduction on local activities. The **Tell-Pass** for Central Switzerland's trains, buses, boats and cableways allows 5 days free travel in a 15-day period or 2 days free travel in a 7-day period, a 50% travel reduction the remainder of the time.

1. **Engelberg**—The **Valley Museum**, at Dorfstrasse 6, is located in an Engelberg farmhouse built in 1786 and provides insights into the history of this high alpine valley. The **Benedictine Monastery**, a **must** visit, was founded in 1120 and is still inhabited by monks of that order. The magnificent Baroque church, built in 1728, houses the largest pipe organ in Europe. Guided tours are given at 10:00 am and 4:00 pm, Monday through Saturday.

2. **Lucerne**—Once a simple fishing village, Lucerne is now a fashion mecca for shoppers, and sightseers throng its narrow, cobblestone streets lined with painted houses. (See Walk #5.)

   Directions: The direct train from Engelberg brings you to Lucerne in one hour.

3. **Mt. Pilatus**—Nine miles south of Lucerne, at 6995 ft. (2132 m.), Pilatus is a landmark of the area, with its distinctive rock pyramid at the top. From Kriens (12 minutes by bus from Lucerne), cable cars glide over meadows and forests to Fräkmüntegg, where an aerial cableway swings along the steep cliff, rising year-round to the peak. From May to November, the south side of the mountain at Alpnachstad boasts the steepest cog-wheel railway in the world. At the peak are hotels and restaurants with sun-terraces for viewing the incredible panorama.

   Directions: For a unique circle tour, from Engelberg take the train to Hergiswil, changing for the local train to Alpnachstad, where you take the old cog railway to Pilatus Kulm. Return to Kriens via the cable car and catch a bus for the short ride to Lucerne, taking the train back to Engelberg.

4. **Mt. Rigi**—At 5896 ft. (1797 m.), Rigi is located 15 miles (24 km.) east of Lucerne. Pilatus boasts the panoramic vistas, but the view from Rigi is con-

sidered more beautiful and the hiking trails more gentle—both Mark Twain and Queen Victoria stood at Rigi Kulm to watch the spectacular sunrise. **Directions:** *Take an early morning train from Engelberg to Lucerne, and just outside the bahnhof, catch the lake steamer to Vitznau, where you connect with the rack railway to Rigi-Kulm—the oldest cog railway in Europe. Taking an 8:45 am train from Engelberg, connecting with the boat and cog railway, brings you to Rigi Kulm at 12:15 pm. Confirm all transport schedules before you leave for Rigi.*

ENGELBERG WALKS
Recommended Maps:
1) Wanderkarte Engelberg, Central Switzerland
2) Panoramakarte-Engelberg
3) Wanderkarte Jochpass
4) Wandern im Herzen der Schweiz—Engelberg-Jochpass-Engstlenalp-Melchsee-Frutt-Hasliberg-Meiringen

---

Walk #1: Introductory Walk—Engelberg to Horbis/End der Welt to Engelberg (Excursion to Monastery)
Walking Easy Time: 2 hours
Rating: Comfortable

Today's get-acquainted walk brings you to the impressive Benedictine *kloster* for an hour tour, and a walk into the countryside to End der Welt or "End of the World," the narrow, closed-in valley behind Horbis and its 15th-century country church. The return walk to Engelberg is through the meadows and past the monastery. Benedictine monks have resided in this *kloster* since it was founded in 1120, and the imposing buildings dominate the landscape at the eastern end of town, both architecturally and culturally. The beautiful Baroque monastery church, built in 1728, houses one of the largest organs in Europe.

Start: Walk through town on the main, traffic-free, cobblestone shopping street to the *kloster*, situated at the end of the village. Tours are given Monday through Saturday at 10:00 am and 4:00 pm, so time your arrival for the morning visit or, hike early afternoon and take the 4:00 pm tour.

The walk begins at hiking signs on a wall before the monastery grounds. Follow the sign "End der Welt-55 min." Ascend the long flight of steps next to the school, and turn right at another sign leading through a green, fertile valley—the path rising gradually.

After about 40 minutes, cross the road and follow signs to Horbis and End der Welt. The little village of Horbis soon appears, with its small country church, originally built in 1489. After visiting the church, continue into town, to the

Restaurant Horbis End der Welt, with its sun-terrace and facilities. You can extend this walk a bit further. Locate the meadow path in back of the restaurant that leads to the massive mountain wall giving End der Welt its name. This path ends shortly, so retrace your steps back to the restaurant.

To return, walk back on the same path, but instead of turning right over the bridge, follow the sign pointing ahead to Engelberg. The path continues past a grass-processing plant (*grastrocknungsanlage*). You will then arrive at a small lake and picnic area. Proceed towards Engelberg along the small auto road. After the Eggliweg (a small road to the right), continue following the road over the river. At the gravel path, turn into the *kirchweg*, leading back to the monastery (St. Anna Haus will be on your left). This path splits—continue ahead on the upper path—spilling into the cemetery above the monastery and the flight of steps you climbed earlier in the day.

Walk #2: Trubsee Lift Station to Untertrübsee to Engelberg (Excursion to Mt. Titlis)
Walking Easy Time: 3 hours
Rating: Comfortable

Today you will take the series of aerial cableways from Engelberg to Mt. Titlis, the highest viewpoint in Central Switzerland at 9935 ft. (3028 m.), with spectacular views of glaciers and icefalls. The last part of the cableway, from Stand to Klein Titlis, will be in a cable car whose platform revolves as it rises to the summit station, with restaurant, facilities, sun-terrace, ice grotto, and glacier walks. After visiting the peak, you will descend to the Trubsee station for a walk around the lake, picking up the descending path to Engelberg.

Directions: *Walk through the Engelberg train station and, passing the Post Office, follow the sign to the right to "Titlis Rotair." Purchase a ticket to the top station with a return to Trubsee. Take the cable-way system to the top, staying in the gondola at Gerschnialp, changing in Trubsee and again in Stand, for the innovative cable car to the Titlis top station. After visiting the Glacier Grotto and the Panorama Restaurant, descend to Station Trubsee at 5893 ft. (1796 m.), where the walk begins.*

Start: Exit the Trubsee lift station and follow the path signed "Zum See," to the lovely, blue, glacial lake. Walk around the lake's left bank on a wide path, around the Alpstübli Restaurant, where you follow the sign to Huehutte at 5758 ft. (1755 m.). At Huehutte, turn left and walk down the path marked "Untertrübsee-50 min." and "Engelberg-1 1/2 hr." This white and red blazed trail narrows and becomes a descending, rocky *bergweg*. When the trail changes to a wagon road, follow the lift station sign. At the lift station, your options are:

1) Take the gondola down to Untertrubsee and continue walking to Engelberg.

2) Follow the red arrow pointing to the red and white blazed trail leading sharply down to the left. If you decide to walk, the next 15 minutes of descent is rocky and steep, but manageable. This trail meets another path to Untertrubsee, becoming an open ski path. Turn right, through the meadow to the Untertrubsee Restaurant. With either option, turn right again, down the hill, on a little-used auto road to Engelberg. After rounding the first bend, take a *wanderweg* trail on the left, through the meadow. Reaching a paved road, follow signs to Engelberg.

Walk #3: Gerschnialp Lift Station to Café Ritz (Vorder-Stafel) to Untertrubsee to Haltenhütte to Untertrubsee to Engelberg
Walking Easy Time: 3 hours
Rating: Comfortable

Today's mid-level walk, although glorious on a sunny day, can also be reserved for a cloudy day. You will take the Titlis gondola from Engelberg to the first stop at Gerschnialp at 4141 ft. (1262 m.) and walk on a level trail to Cafe Ritz at Vorder-Stafel. The path continues through the Gerschni Alp to the restaurant at Untertrubsee, then ascends gently through the meadows to Haltenhütte at the end of the valley, with the clanging of cow bells resounding in the cool alpine air. *Easy Walkers* will return to the Untertrubsee Restaurant along the same path, with fresh views of the snow-covered peaks rimming the valley, for the final descent to Engelberg.

Directions: *See Walk #2 and purchase a one-way ticket to Gerschnialp, the first stop on the Titlis lift system.*

Start: After exiting at Gerschnialp, turn left to CafeRitz, walking through forest and meadow—a short, 15-minute stroll. At the restaurant, walk around the sun-terrace to the parking area and follow the sign "Untertrubsee" on a *wanderweg*. This peaceful path, along a small mountain road, is through Gerschni Alp, a wide-open grassy meadow, filled with farms, old barns, and herds of grazing cows. Leaving the road, follow signs to Untertrubsee, ascending gently on a beaten, grassy path, eventually reaching a paved road and the Untertrübsee Restaurant. Pass the restaurant and continue along this road through the meadow, in the direction of Arnialp. After about 45 minutes, you will come to the end of the valley, the path turning right in the direction of Arnistalden. However, *Easy Walkers* will return on the same path to the Untertrubsee Restaurant where you have two options:

1) Walk past the restaurant on the road and, after the bend, take the *wanderweg* trail on the left, cutting down through the meadow. After reaching a gravel path, turn right and follow the road up to a group of signs directing you left to Engelberg-30 min. This mountain auto road goes down to the bottom Titlis lift station—about a 40-minute walk. It is possible to follow a *bergwanderweg* sign cutting through the forest, but this trail can be steep and slippery in places, and we recommend staying on the road until you reach Engelberg.

2) Retrace your steps to Cafe Ritz and take the Gerschnialp gondola down to Engelberg.

Walk #4: Engelberg to Alpenrossli to Engelberg (Optional Excursion to Furenalp)
Walking Easy Time: 4 hours
Rating: Comfortable

The restaurant at Alpenrosli is your destination today, and the walk through the valley, on the left side of the Aa River, ascends 847 ft. (258 m.) quite gradually. While the views are exhilarating, the *rösti* and desserts at the Alpenrosli Restaurant are your final reward. **Start:** Walk through the pedestrian shopping street of Engelberg to the monastery. Just before the gates, on the left, follow the sign "Alpenrosli-1 hr., 50 min." Walk up the steps and turn right at the Alpenrosli sign, leading through the cemetery, exiting on the other side onto a meadow path. The *kloster* is on your right as you walk. Cross the auto road, following signs to Alpenrosli. The path begins to ascend gently, and you soon pass by the Furenalp bottom lift station at 3557 ft. (1084 m.). (You can take the free Engelberg bus to this point if you wish.) If the weather is clear and sunny, take a ride to the top station and enjoy the views.

Return to the path towards Alpenrossli, which eventually splits, both paths going to the same destination. Stay to the left, as you ascend to the restaurant at 4128 ft. (1258 m.), famous for *rosti*, Switzerland's national dish.

To return, head back to Engelberg in the direction of the Furenalp lift.

Walk #5: Trubsee Lift, Walk to Jochpass Lift, Walk to Engstlenalp and Return
Walking Easy Time: 3 to 31/2 hours
Rating: Comfortable

This full-day, exciting Jochpass excursion and hike is an Engelberg favorite. You will take the Titlis lift to Trübsee 5896 ft. (1797 m.), and walk past the lake to the Jochpass chairlift at 5811 ft. (1771 m.), rising to the Jochpass at 7241 ft. (2207 m.), with sensational views of the glaciers above. You will then walk down past the Engstlensee to Engstlenalp at 6021 ft. (1834 m.), your destination for today. The return is by chairlift up to the Jochpass, then down to Trubsee and walking back to the lift station for the descent to Engelberg.

Directions: *See Walk #2. Buy a lift ticket to Trubsee and take the gondola to the second stop at Trubsee.*

Start: Follow signs to the Jochpass, walking around the left side of the lake to the Jochpass triple chairlift. Buy a round-trip ticket and ride up to the Jochpass at 7241 ft. (2207 m.). The hike down to Engstlenalp at 6021 ft. (1835 m.), begins at the top of the chairlift station. There are two paths to Engstlenalp. Take the lower path to the left, marked #3A B on your hiking map, signed "Engstlenalp-1 hr.," on a comfortable mountain *bergweg*. This trail descends to the lake and then to the restaurant at Engstlenalp. At Engstlenalp, you have a couple of options:

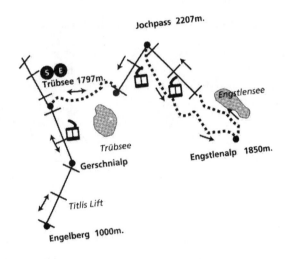

1) The longer way time-wise, but involving no hiking—take the bus to the Meiringen *bahnhof*, and take the train in the direction of Lucerne, changing in Hergiswil for the Engelberg train. **Check all bus and train timetables at the bus stop in Engstlenalp before choosing this option.**

2) Or, the option we prefer. Return on the same path, however, when the path splits at the lake, instead of following the sign to the Jochpass, walk ahead to the sessellift, (about 45 minutes from the restaurant). Take the double chairlift to the top (where your hike began), and change for the

chairlift down to Trubsee. Walk back to the Trübsee lift station and take the gondola down to Engelberg.

We left our hotel at 10:00 am to begin this day's exhilarating hike—from the canton of Central Switzerland over the Jochpass into the Bernese Oberland, and we returned to our hotel at 4:30 pm—a full day in the mountains of Switzerland and the best of *Walking Easy*!

Walk #6: Excursion to Lucerne and City Walk
Walking Easy Time: 2 1/2 hours
Rating: Gentle

This charming, old city is situated on Lake Lucerne. Its covered wooden bridges are still preserved, as are remains of the town's ancient fortifications. Lucerne is now a fashion mecca for shoppers, and sightseers throng its narrow, cobblestone streets lined with painted houses. Today's excursion features a 2 1/2 hour walk around Lucerne's lakeside quays and old squares.

HINT: It's a good idea to take your backpack with you on a city walking tour like this. You can stow raingear and a picnic lunch, which you can enjoy on one of the many benches along the lake.

Directions: *The train from Engelberg arrives in Lucerne in an hour.*

Start: Exit the train station. From Bahnhofplatz on the south bank of the river (at the train station), walk across the **Seebrucke** (bridge) directly in front of the *bahnhof.* At the first yellow-striped pedestrian crossing, cross the busy street to your left. You are now on **Schwanenplatz (Swan Square)**.

Walk ahead into the small square of **Kappelplatz**, with its colorful fountain and statue of a Swiss Guard on top. **St. Peter's Church**, built in 1178 and the oldest church in Lucerne, is on your left. Continue ahead on Kappellgasse, passing the church and entering another square, the **Kornmarkt** or **Grain Exchange**, the site of **Altes Rathaus (Old Town Hall)**, a Renaissance building dating from 1602. To the left of the Town Hall is a 17th-century building housing the **Picasso Sammlung (Picasso Museum)**. If you visit the museum, when you exit, make a right turn and a quick right again on Badergässli. Turn left at the river, walking past the outdoor cafes. Next, turn right, entering the famous Lucerne landmark, the **Kappellbrucke (Chapel Bridge)**, a covered, wooden footbridge crossing the Reuss River—the symbol of Lucerne. The original bridge, built in 1333, unfortunately burnt down in the 1990's, but was rebuilt within the year. After crossing the Chapel Bridge, turn right immediately and walk along the river, paying a visit to the large, beautiful Baroque **Jesuitenkirche (Jesuit Church)** on your left.

Recross the river on the covered **Spreuerbrucke (Spreuer Bridge)**, built in 1407 and restored in the 19th century. After crossing this bridge, make a sharp right turn and walk around to **Muhlenplatz (Mills Square)**. Turn left and walk diagonally through Muhlenplatz, bearing right on Kramgasse, with a quick left into **Weinmarkt (Wine Market)**, a lovely square with an old fountain. Note the ancient dwellings on this square. After passing the fountain, bear left to **Hirschenplatz (Stag Square)**, another square bordered with old, restored buildings.

From Hirschenplatz, turn right on to Weggisgasse, to Hertensteinstrasse. Walk on Hertensteinstrasse to its end, and bear left into Lowenplatz. Cross the street at the yellow pedestrian stripes to the 100-year old, circular building housing the **Bourbaki-Panorama**, a huge painting depicting the bloody retreat of the French army into Switzerland during the Franco-Prussian War. After exiting the Panorama, walk ahead up the narrow street, Denkmalstrasse, to the sign pointing to the right to the **Gletschergarten** and **Lowendenkmal**. View one of the most famous statues in Switzerland, the **Lowendenkmal** or **Lion Monument,** hewn out of natural rock and dedicated to the bravery of the Swiss Guards who died in Paris trying to save Marie Antionette.

Walk back to Lowenplatz and head down Lowenstrasse towards the trees and lake. On the left, pay a visit to the **Collegiate Church of St. Leodegar,** with its twin towers, wrought-iron work, carvings and famous pipe organ. Cross the road to the lake and enjoy a wonderful view—the Alps from Rigi to Pilatus. You can walk back to the *bahnhof* along the lake, take a relaxing boat ride, or turn back into the old town and visit some of the stores and cafés you passed earlier.

Walk #7: Ristis Lift Station to Schwand to Engelberg
Walking Easy Time: 2 1/2 hours
Rating: Gentle

Use the Engelberg Panorama Wanderkarte for this walk. You will take the Brunni cable car from Engelberg to Ristis at 5269 ft. (1606 m.) and walk on the country road to the restaurant at Schwand (marked #21 on the Panorama Wanderkarte). This is a gently descending mountain road with views over Engelberg. From Schwand you will take #18 on the Wanderkarte, passing through the heights over the valley and, eventually, to Engelberg's pedestrian street.

Directions: *Walk up the pedestrian street towards the kloster, turning left at the large "Brunni" sign. Purchase a one-way ticket to Ristis.*

Start: At Ristis, follow the sign left, "Restaurant Schrond-1 hr., 30. min." and eventually the sign "Engelberg-2 hrs., 30 min." Walk past the chairlift rising to the Brunnihütte and continue on the rarely used, small mountain auto road, all the way to Schwand. This path passes by working farms, old barns, and herds of cows, goats and sheep, with views of the dramatic mountains surrounding Engelberg. In 90 minutes you'll reach the restaurant at Schwand (Schroand), just after passing a tiny church. Turn left on the road below the restaurant, following the "Engelberg" sign. *Easy Walkers* now have two options:

1) If it hasn't been raining, you might wish to take the right fork just ahead, which goes through the meadow and forest, eventually joining the same auto road to Engelberg as in the second option.

2) Take the left fork, remaining on the road, all the way to the outskirts of Engelberg and the Hotel Waldegg. Just past the hotel, a small path called the "Sonnenweg" descends to the right, leading into the center of Engelberg.

A WALKING EASY TRAIL

AUSTRIA

AUSTRIA

Austria shares its borders with eight other countries—Germany, Italy, Switzerland, Hungary, The Czech Republic, Slovakia, Lichtenstein, and Slovenia- and each has had a dramatic cultural impact on Austrian lifestyle. Thes different ethnic groups contribute richly to Austrian cuisine, and *Easy Walkers* should be sure to sample local food specialties. Austrians take their dining and coffee enjoymjent seriously. In fact, the Viennese coffehouse is truly an institution. It is not nearly a place to savor coffee in venerable surroundings; it is also where one reads a newspaper, chats with friends, and, of course, enjoy mouthwatering Vienneses pastries.

Over seventy percent of Austrian's countryside is forest land in the shadow of dramatic snowcapped peak, and the hiking trails are well signed and well maintained. Hiking maps are available in local tourist offices, conveniently located in every base village and designated by an **i sign**. *Walking Easy* hotels are charming and offer some of the best values ion Europe. The warm and friendly Austrian welcome is almost as famous their apple strudle. Try it once—and you'll come back for seconds—and thirds.

TYROL

ALPBACH

(ALPBACHTAL)

Alpbach is probably the most charming Walking Easy base village in Austria. This Tyrolean resort, nestled on a sunny mountainside at 3281 ft. (1000m.), offers walkers a wide range of trails in the idyllic, picture-postcard landscape of the Alpbachtal (Alpbach Valley). Hikers have a choice of over 100miles (160 km.) of well marked trails. The Wiederbergerhorn gondola rises 5919 ft. (1804m.) and is the starting point of hikes with panoramic views of the Ziller and Inn valleys, the Stubai and Ziller glaciers, and the Karwendel mountain range.

The secret of Alpbach's charm is the standards established for restoration of old buildings and construction of new ones, making sure the village represents traditional Tyrolean architecture and atmosphere. Every balcony and window is adorned with colorful flowers, framing the old-style, wood-beamed construction. Considering there were no major roads into Alpbach until 1926, Alpbach has transformed itself from a sleepy farming community to a major Austrian Tourist destination very quickly. It is interesting to note that many mountain farms in the countryside around Alpbach still exist and function as they have for centuries.

Much of the hills surrounding Alpbach are grassy meadows, where walkers can stroll for hours on signed paths, all within sight of Alpbach's beautiful church steeple.

Walkers.can walk from village to village taking advantage of the bus service in the Alpbach valley.

Enjoy Alpbach—it's hiking, it's scenery, and it's flower-bedecked homes-a favorite *Walking Easy* setting.

TRANSPORTATION

By Train and Bus—Alpbach is reached from Brixlegg, a local train stop. From the west, always change trains in Innsbruck for the local train to Brixlegg. The bus from Brixlegg to Alpbach is located across the street from the train station. There are two bus stops in Alpbach; Tell the driver where you will be staying for the most convenient drop-off point.

By Car—Drive on the A 12 autobahn to Kramsach and pick up the local road to Brixlegg, Reith and then Alpbach.

FAVORITE *WALKING EASY* GUEST HOUSE

Haus Angelika
Three-Star; Owners—Sepp and Erna Steinlechner
A-6236 Alpach/Tirol TEL: 53 36/53 39
Internet: www.tiscover.at/angelika
Haus Angelika is lovely, flower bedecked guesthouse. Located on Alpbach's quiet main street, it offers fifteen comfortable rooms with balconies. The spacious front lawn provides a relaxing stop after a day of hiking. Breakfast is personally attended to by Mrs. Steinlechner, and Mr. Steinlechner is an accomplished hiker. While dinner is not served at the hotel, the Haus Elizabeth next door serves dinner in its Reblaus, located in front of the hotel, an outstanding restaurant specializing in Italian cuisine. We love the Angelika…It's like staying with Grandma and Grandpa.

EXCURSIONS

The Alpbach Tourist Information Office is located on the main street …
Internet: www.Alpbach.at
E-mail: info@alpach.at

1. **Alpbach—The Farmhouse Museum** is located in Inneralpbach, a hamlet near Alpbach. This mountain farmhouse was built in the dearly 1600's. (See walk # 3)
2. **Innsbruck**—See A Trail Of Three Cities—Innsbruck
   Directions: Take a morning bus from Alpbach to Brixlegg and the local train west to Innsbruck.
3. **Rattenberg**—The best–preserved medieval community in the Tyrol is noted for it's historic squares, narrow alleyways, frescoed houses, and the etching and the cutting of fine crystal. A must on your visit is the Augustinermuseum with collections displaying Tyrolean art treasures.

Directions: *Take the bus to Brixlegg and the train or bus to Rattenberg.*

4. **Kramsach**—Located in the village of the same name, next to Rattenberg, the Museum and Tyroler Bauernhof, or Farmhouse Museum, presents farms from different parts of the Tyrol, removed from their areas and rebuilt-an interesting way to see how people lived and worked in Old Tyrol.

   Directions: *See Rattenberg directions above.*

5. **Schwaz**—Known as the silver center of Europe, the mine railway takes sightseers through tunnels and stalactite formations.

   Directions: *Check for weekly excursions to Schwaz.*

6. **Wattens**—An opportunity to visit the Swarovski factory and retail store.

   Directions: *Take the morning train to Brixlegg and transfer to the local train to Wattens. Check for excursion busses.*

Alpbach Walks
Recommended Maps:
Mayr Wanderkarte #40—Alpbachal
Ortsplan—Street map

Walk # 1
Introductory Walk—Alpbach to Rossalm to Trat to Alpbach
Walking Easy Time: 1 1/2 to 2 hours
Rating: Comfortable

Today's walk can be taken on the afternoon of your arrival in Alpbach, introduc-ing you to this picturesque village, its flowered chalets, the Alpbach Valley, Inneralpbach, and the snow-covered Kitzbuehler Alps in the distance. After view-ing Alpbach from its surrounding heights, you'll walk through the upper part of the village, returning to the village center by descending to a forest path, ending at Alpbach's main street.

Start: Walk out of town along the side of the Hotel Post, on the paved road marked A2 on your hiking map. Continue on this road, passing a sign indicating the end of Alpbach city limits. Follow the auto road up and around until you reach a signed intersection. Make a right turn in the direction of Rossalm A2— 30 Min. The views across the valley are picture-postcard perfect.

Continue on the road, walking past Rossalm and the few houses that are Alsten. The paved road becomes a gravel wagon path, entering the forest for a few minutes. At the road, continue to the right, to the restaurant in Trat. Turn right and follow the descending path and road back to the Hotel Post. Walk through the upper part of the village passing the Hotel Bogler and the Kongresshaus. After walking past the Hotel Alphof, turn right on the first paved street, signed Alphof Rundgang, with a red fire hydrant. Walk down toward the tennis courts. Continue past the courts, over the bridge, and make a right turn onto a forest path signed Muhblach. Follow this trail along the stream until you arrive at a nar-row road. Turn right, walk up the hill, and in a few minutes you'll be in the cen-ter of Alpbach.

Walk # 2 Hornboden Top Station to Loderstein to Hechenblaikenalm to Kerschbaumer Sattel to Reithkogel Top Lift Station
Walking Easy Time: 4 ½ hours
Rating: More Challenging

This hike is made up of almost every kind of a trail. It's rated more challenging because of the rather lengthy downhill trail near the end of the walk. You'll travel to the Wiedesbergerhornbahn Base Station for the gondola ride to Hornboden Top Station. This is followed by a hike up to the panoramaweg partially around the mountain, picking up a spectacular trail along the spine of the mountain before descending through the forest to Hechenblaikenalm. The trail rises again to the Reithkogel Lift Station for the ride down to Reith. There are no restaurants between the Hornboden Station and the top station of the Reitherkogelbahn, so pack a picnic lunch and lots of water.

Directions: *Take an early morning bus (before 9:00 A.M.) to the Wiedersbergerhornbahn (A few minutes ride) and purchase a round-trip ticket. This ticket can be used at the Reith Lift at the end of the walk. Exit at the top station Hornboden.*

HINT: An early start is necessary for this hike. Before starting, confirm the closing time of the Reitherkogel gondola. If you miss it, you'll have to walk down the mountain to Reith.

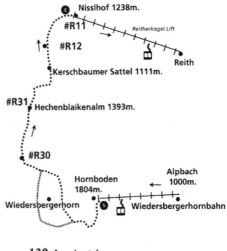

130 ❖ Austria

Start: Follow the sign up to the panoramaweg (do not take the lower path to the Reitherkogelobahn). At the panormaweg, take the path to the right to walk around the peak. After an hour, a sign directs you to the Zillertal. However, take the path R30 to the right along the ridge with spectacular views on either side. Continue along the spine ahead on R31 at a signed intersection. A well defined but steep and rocky trail takes you down to Hechenblaikenalm.

At the road, turn left and left again at a signed intersection to R16, Reitherkogelbahn Bergstation. You will descend tothe Kerschbaumer Sattel, at the road. Cross the road, following R12 up to the bergstation. Bear right at the fork in the direction of the Nisshof Gasthof and the lift down to Reith. Take the bus back to Alpbach.

Walk # 3 Alpbach to Thierberg to Zottahof to Rossmoos to Inneralpbach via the Oberer Hohenweg (Excursion to Farmhouse Museum)
Walking Easy Time: 4 hours
Rating: Comfortable

Reserve the day for this walk and excursion to the Farmhouse Museum in Inneralpbach.

You'll walk on the heights above Alpbach to visit the Zottahof, a country farmhouse restaurant, famous for kaiserschmarrn, a large, pancake-style omelet, made of eggs, milk, and flour, beaten and cooked in a large skillet until high, fluffy, and brown, then sprinkled with powdered sugar and served with homemade cranberry preserves. (You just have to try it) The next stop is the Farmhouse Museum in Inneralpach, originally built in the seventeenth century. After visiting the museum, you'll walk back to the main road for the bus ride back to Alpbach.

Start: Walk on Alpbach's upper town road with the church on your right, passing the Boglerhof on the left. Just past the hotel, turn left at the sign Thierberg A3. Ascend though the meadow, and at the top of the hill, turn right. Continue on the paved path, passing a gueshouse on the left, soon entering a grassy carriage trail marked Larchenweg A3.

A sign soon indicates that Zotterhof A3 is ahead, the first stop of the day. Turn right over the wooden bridge, following the path up to the auto road. Turn left and walk up the road to the Zottahof restaurant, around the turn at the top of the hill. Enjoy the kaiserschmarrn. It's worth the trip.

Walk back down the auto road and make a left turn at the intersection A8, following the sign to Rossmoos. Walk up the road, passing a little path to Alpbach. Stay on the Oberer Hohenweg across the bridge to the Buben chapel. Turn right on #721 on your map to the Restaurant Wiedergerhornhaus in Inneralpbach.

Here you can visit the Farmhouse Museum and when ready, walk back to the bus station for the short ride back to Alpbach.

Today's excursion to Reith is along a fairly level trail that darts in and out of the forest on pine needle-covered bergwege and wagon paths, all on signed path R20. You will walk on the Hohenweg to the Pinzgerhof Resaurant, with a terrace overlooking Reith and Brixlegg. It is then a forty-five minute descent along the road to the Reith church **square and the return bus to Alpbach.**

Start: Walk on the auto road alongside the Hotel Post, away from the village on A2. After about 30 minutes follow a group of signs indicating #R20 Hohenweg Reith to the left.

At an intersection where a paved road goes up to the right, watch carefully and take the little forest path signed #R20 Nach Reith, as it rises gently under tall pine trees. After a while, turn left on the wagon road to Hohenweg Reith R 20. After about 80 minutes of walking, the path, you will enter an open area. Arriving at an intersection, take the path up the hill. After walking between two wooden houses, take the road to the right marked Forest Strasse, and in a minute, a sign confirms your direction toward the Pinzgerhof Restaurant (closed on Tuesday)

When ready, follow the zigzagging auto road down the mountain. At a signed intersection, continue to the right following signs to Reith. The bus stop to Alpbach is 50 yards past the church and tourist Office.

Walk # 5
Alpbach Around the Graflspitz and Return to Alpbach
Walking Easy Time: 6 hours
Rating: More challenging

Although it is possible to hike up to the peak of the Graflspitz, at 6217 ft. (1895 m,.), it will probably be out of the comfort level of most *Easy Walkers*. We therefore suggest you walk around the back of the Graflspitz, mostly on a more comfortable jeep road. Leave Alpbach by way of the Larchenweg to Hosjoch, an ascent 3281—4872 ft. (1000 to 1485 m.), turning left on A20 via Kaiserbrunni to Holzalmhaus. Turn left on A18 to the Hauser Alm, leaving the road on A18 down to Bischoferalm, then down the road to Rossalm and Bischofen. Turn right, then left again, descending on the road to Alpbach.

Walk # 6 Hornboden Top Station to Panoramaweg around the Wiedersbergerhorn, Mid-Station Almhof to Alpbach

Take the Wiedersbergerhorn gondola to the Hornboden Top Station, at 5914 ft. (1804m.) for a popular two-hour panoramaweg hike around the peak. Descend by gondola to the Almhof—Mid-Station at 4416 ft. (1346 m.), for a gentle walk down to the base station along a zigzagging mountain road. The return bus to Alpbach stops at the base station.

KITZBUHEL

Kitzbuhel, the internationally famous ski resort, attracts summer hikers with dozens of well-marked trails, rustic mountain restaurants and scenic viewpoints—supported by cableways throughout the area. *Easy Walkers* can take valley walks to Schwarzsee, a resort lake only 30 minutes from Kitzbuhel, to the nearby village of Kirchberg and its imposing church; to the tiny chapel in Oberaurach; and on the rolling forest and meadow Bichlach paths. High-level treks on the Hahnenkamm and Kitzbuheler Horn mountains can be enjoyed by recreational walkers of all ages. Nearby valleys extend from the quaint village of St. Johann to Pass Thurn, adding a multitude of additional walks to the Kitzbuhel experience.

The Kitzbuhel Tourist Bureau offers a wide variety of daily activities, and the town's walking streets are lined with an eclectic collection of shops, hotels and restaurants, all housed in colorful Tyrolean-style buildings. Because of its location along an ancient trading route between Venice and Bavaria, Kitzbuhel achieved importance in the 13th century as a mining and merchant center. However, the Duke of Windsor's "discovery" of Kitzbuhel in the 1920s brought European wealth and royalty to the area, turning it into a fashionable year-round resort. *Easy Walkers* will enjoy Kitzbuhel's Tyrolean hospitality—its cool forests, sunny meadows, high mountains—and exciting hiking trails.

TRANSPORTATION

By Train—Always change in Worgl for the local train to the Kitzbuhel/Halnenkamm station (closest to most of the hotels and shops), or the main Kitzbuhel station, away from town center.

By Car—Take the A12 *autobahn,* exiting at Worgl Ost. Drive in the direction of St. Johann and then follow signs to Kitzbuhel.

EXCURSIONS IN AND AROUND KITZBUHEL

The Kitzbuhel Tourist Office is on Hinterstadt, one block from Vorderstadt, the main pedestrian and shopping street.

Internet: www.kizbuehel.com
E-mail: info@kitbuehel.com

Consider purchasing a Summer Holiday Pass for free use of all area lifts, the Bichlalm bus and the indoor swimming pool. A *stadtbus* operates around the environs of the town, with posted schedules.

1. **Kitzbuehel**—Open-air concerts are presented by the Kitzbuehel and Local Town Bands.

a) Churches—The Pfarrkirche (Parish **Church**), built in 1435, was renovated in Baroque style in the late 1700s and restored in 1951. The 13th-century Liebfrauenkirche (**Church of** our Lady), was renovated in the 18th century. Beween these two churches stands the **Olberkapelie** (**Olberg Chapel**), containing a Death Lantern from 1450 and frescoes dating from the late 16th century. **Katharinenkirche** (**St.** Catherine's Church) was consecrated in 1365 and restored in 1950, with a *glockenspiel* at the tower's top. The **Kapuzinerkloster** (**Capucine** Monastery) and its church were built outside Kitzbuehel about 1700.

b) Museums—The Heimatmuseum is located at Hinterstadt 34, featuring a chronicle of the town and its mining history. The **Cable Car Museum** at the top station of the Hahnenkamm lift provides a pictorial insight into the development of the cable car and the surrounding ski slopes.

c) Schwarzsee—This pretty lake outside Kitzbuhel offers swimming, boating, sunning, dining—and just relaxing. (See Walk #2.)

2. **Aurach Wildlife Park**—Located five miles from Kitzbuhel in Oberaurach, the park features 200 animals living at 3609 ft. (1100 in.) in the largest open-air enclosure in the Tyrol.
   Directions: *Take a local bus to Aurach.*

3. **Hohe Tauern (National Park) and Grossglockner Road**—There are 120 peaks over 9843 ft.
   (3000 m.) 169 glaciers, and thousands of waterfalls in Austria's National Park. (See "Kaprun/Zell am See," Walk #7.)
   Directions: Take an early morning local train at the Kitzbuhel/Hahnenkamm station for the hour ride to Zell am See. From the train station, walk across the street and take the next bus, which should get you to Kaiser-Franz-Josef-Hohe in the late morning.
   Directions: *Take a train from Kitzbuhel/Hahnenkamm to Zell am See.*

4. Innsbruck—See A Trail of Three Cities-Innsbruck.
   Directions: *Take the train to Worgl and change for a connecting train to Innsbruck (the ride takes 90 minutes.)*

5. Krimtnl Waterfall (Krimmler Wasserfillie)—Located near Mittersill, these shimmering falls are the highest in Europe, with a drop of 1250 ft. The second stage of the falls is a 15-minute walk from the lower level, with another five-minute walk to the third stage and trails leading even higher to the fourth and fifth stages. The sixth and seventh viewing areas overlook the middle part of the falls, but the most spectacular view is another 20-minute walk from the seventh stage, at Bergerblick. Pack raingear.
   Directions: *Check bus schedules carefully—there is limited service to the waterfall. If the Tourist Office sponsors a trip to the falls, it's the easiest way to go.*

KITZBUHEL WALKS

Recommended Maps:
1) Mayr Wander Karte #55—Kitzbuhel
2) Mayr Wander Karte—St. Johann in Tyrol
3) Kitzbuhel Wanderwege—Plan

Walk #1: Hahnenkamm Top Station to St. Bernhard's Chapel to Hochbrunn, Streitegg Chairlift to Steinbergkogel, Return Walk to Hahnenkamm
Walking **Easy Time:** 2 to 4 hours
Rating: Comfortable

This popular hike is one of many offering remarkable panoramas of this charming alpine town. The new Hahnenkamm gondolas ascend to 5473 ft. (1668 m.) gliding over cool forests and soft green meadows doffed with grazing cows. The top station offers new restaurants and facilities along with spectacular views. You will walk from the Hahnenkamm top station to the small Chapel of St. Bernhard on the *panoramaweg*. Here, you will continue around the mountain and take the Streitegg chairlift to the Steinbergkogelhaus at 5467 ft. (1971 m.) the high point of today's walk, where *Easy Walkers* have several options to return to the Hahnenkamm lift station. This walk should be taken when the weather is clear— to take advantage of the outstanding views across the valley.

    Directions: *Walk to the Hahnenkamm cable station, near the Kitzbuehel/Hahnenkamm local railroad station and purchase a round-trip ticket to the top.*

    Start: After exiting the cable car, savor the spectacular scenery, especially the Kitzbueheler Horn at 6549 ft. (1996 m.) Take the signed Panoramaweg, off to the right, leading to the tiny, whitewashed Chapel of St. Bernhard. At the chapel, follow signs to Hochbrnnn, Streitegg and Pengelstein, the path winding around the mountain, with the Fleckalm lift station above you on the right.

    Just before the Hochbrunn Restaurant, turn left to the Streiteck Chairlift and take it up to the high point of today's walk, the Steinbergkogelhaus, with its restaurant and facilities. From here you have the following options:

1) Return on the Streiteck chairlift to the bottom station and walk back to Hahnenkamm on the same trail.

2) From Steinbergkogel, follow the trail down towards Pengelstein, but turn right at the fork in the road to Hochbrunn, returning to Hahnenkamm on the same trail you came on. With either option, if you wish, at St. Bernhard's Chapel do not follow the Panoramaweg, but stay on the main path directly to the lift station. At the Hahnenkamm Top Station, take the gondolas down to Kitzbuehel.

Walk # 2: St. Johann/Harschbichl Top Station to Stanglalm to Steinbergalin to Haslach to Kitzbuehel via the Römerweg (Bauernmuseum Visit)
Walking Easy Time: 3 1/2 hours
Rating: Comfortable

(Use the St. Johann hiking map.) Today's hike begins at the charming village of St. Johann, reached by a short train ride from Kitzbuehel. You will take the lift to Harschbichl at 5263 ft. (1604 in.), then descend in the shadow of the Kitzbuheler Horn on a well-marked jeep road, all the way to Haslach. Just below Haslach you'll return to Kitzbuhel along the Romerweg, a peaceful, mid-level forest and meadow path, visiting the Bauernmuseum along the way.

Directions: Take the train or bus from Kitzbuehel to St. Johann, and from the train/bus station, walk in a southwesterly direction on Speckbacherstrasse, the main shopping street anchored by the church. Cross the railroad tracks and turn left on the Hornweg, walking to a large blue and white parking sign indicating the St. Johann Bergbahn. Buy a one-way ticket to Top Station Harschbichl.

Start: At the top, turn left on #1 Stanglalm. Stay on the wide path as it descends around the mountain, avoiding the temptation to climb up to the Kitzbueheler Horn peak, a steep rise of 1286 ft. Continue in the direction of Stanglalm. Turn left at the intersection, to visit the friendly, family-owned Stanglalm Restaurant, with a sun-terrrace, stunning views of the valley and delicious apple strndel. Continue down the zig-zagging road, passing Steinbergalm at 3957 ft. (1206 m.). Turn left at the intersection, on #34 on your map, to Haslach. At the church in Haslach, turn left again on #9, bearing right down the hill to Hintersteinerbach, at the intersection with the Romerweg, #2 on the map. Turn left, back in the direction of Kitzbuehel, all the way to the Bauernmuseum (Farmhouse Museum), for a must visit. This authentic farmhouse, dating from 1559, is open in summer only from 1:00 to 6:00 pm. Continue on the Romerweg, following signs into Kitzbuehel.

Walk # 3: Kitzbuehel to Schwarzsee to Munichau to Gieringer Weiher to Steuerberg to Kitzbuehel
Walking Easy Time: 3 1/4 hours
Rating: Comfortale

Today's mid-level walk from Kitzbuehel rolls gently on a trail through the Bichlach, a lovely forest and meadow area. There are many walking paths in the region north of Kitzbuehel, and this hike can be a full day's excursion, past

Schwarzsee, over the meadows to Munichau, around the small lake at Gieringer, to Steuerberg, then returning to Kitzbuehel.

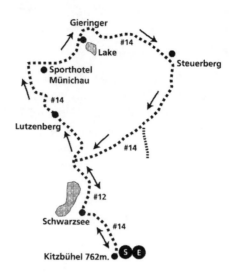

Start: The first part of this walk begins similarly to Walk #5. Begin at the church square, just outside the central Kitzbuehel shopping area. Just before the church walk down the steps to the left, past the *baekerei*. Follow the blue Schwarzsee sign to the right, picking up path Schwarzsee #1, next to the church. Turn right on the main auto road, towards Schwarzsee. At a fork in the road, cross the road and bear right on the Steuerberg road. After a few hundred yards, turn left onto meadow path #12, all the way to the Alpen Hotel and the lake.

When ready, walk to the back of the parking area and turn left on #12, the Seepromenade around Schwarzsee, walking around the end of the lake. Turn right at the intersection on "Bichlachweg #14" in the direction of Kirchberg and Reith. Walk past the camp grounds on the left and bear left on #14 and #39 to Munichau.

At the end of this path, just before the imposing Schloss Munichau hotel, turn right in the direction of Gieringer. Continue to follow signs to Gieringer Weiher until you come to the restaurant on your right which you walk through to get to the tiny lake—a nice spot for a picnic. When ready walk past the restaurant, still on #14, to a dead-end. Follow the sign right in the direction of Steuerberg, through the forest, all the way to a major road, just below the village of Steuerberg. Turn right, continuing now on #14 again, to the Seebichl Hotel.

Walk ahead, past the hotel, to meadow trail #12 you walked on earlier in the day. Turn left here and follow signs back to Kitzbuehel.

Walk # 4: Kitzbueheler Horn Top Station to Alpengarten to Alpenhaus to Adlerhütte Mid-Station
Walking **Easy Time:** 1 to 3 1/2 hours
Rating: Comfortable

Today's hike takes you from the center of Kitzbuehel to the Hornbahn. You will take the gondola to the Adlerhutte mid-station, continuing by cable car to the top. In 20 minutes you will arrive at the top station with its exciting 360-degree panorama from the peak of the Kitzbueheler Horn. After visiting the Alpengarten and continuing to the Alpenhaus at 5279 ft. (1609 im.) you have a number of options to return to Kitzbuehel.

Directions: *Walk on Vorderstadt towards the church. Turn right at the Hornbahn sign and walk down the steps and along the street until the road splits. Follow the Hornbahn Fussweg to the right, to the Hornbahn. Purchase a ticket to the peak (the return trip is included).*

Start: At the top station, take the path to Alpenhaus via the Alpenblumen Garten (Alpine Garden). The Alpine Garden is perched on the side of the mountain—a rocky landscape of cliffs and red-gray limestone. When leaving the garden use the exit at the bottom level, entering the path to the Alpenhaus. Excluding your alpine garden visit, plan on a leisurely 45-minute walk on a well-traveled, downhill path. You will soon understand why Kitzbuehel is a famous international ski resort—there are ski lifts in every direction. The Alpenhaus is at 5480 ft. (1646 m.) with a restaurant, large sun-terrace and facilities. There are a few options from this point:

1)   Continue walking down from the Alpenhaus to mid-station Adlerhutte at 4154 ft. (1266 in.), then ride down to Kitzbuehel. (The trail from the mid-station to Kitzbuehel is quite steep.)

2)   Take the gondola from the Alpenhaus to mid-station Adlerhutte and change for the gondola to Kitzbuehel—riding down the entire way. After arriving at the bottom, turn right and walk down the hill to Kitzbuehel.

Walk # 5: Kitzbuehel to Schwarzsee to Kirchberg
Walking **Easy Time:** 2 3/4 hours
Rating: Gentle

You might wish to take this excursion and low-level walk on a cloudy day when the weather is not conducive to high-altitude walking. A comfortable path brings you out of Kitzbuehel to Schwarzsee, a lovely resort lake 30 minutes from the center of the village, offering visitors many options. The walk continues past the lake and a golf course framed by jagged mountains in the distance, and on to Kirchberg, with its imposing hilltop church. While it is possible to walk back along the same path, a train or bus is available from Kirchberg back to Kitzbuehel.

Start: Begin at the Kirchplatz or church square, found by walking on the main street of Vorderstadt towards the church spire. Just before the church, walk down the steps to the left past the *baekerei*. At a fork in the road, follow the blue Schwarzsee sign to the right, picking up a path next to the church, marked with a walking sign to Schwarzsee. You are now on path #14 on your hiking map. After crossing the road at a signed split in the path, stay on the left, marked #12. Continue on #12, with the lake on your right. After walking through a parking area, take paths #10 and #39, next to the railroad tracks, to your first left—#10 Golfweg towards Kirchberg.on the Kitzbuehel Town Street Map. This path brings *Easy Walkers* alongside the golf course on the right.

The path narrows, leading to Kirchberg, with the towering steeple of its famous old church acting as a beacon. Pass through a tunnel and ascend steps to the left, which take you to town center. After visiting the church, return by train or bus to Kitzbuehel. A sign on the main street points to the *bahn* ho/for the short train ride. The bus stop is on the right.

Walk # 6: Kitzbuehel to Aumch to Oberaurach to Bichln to Kitzbuehel
Walking Easy Time: 3 to 4 hours
Rating: Comfortable

Today's low-level walk along the Ache River leads to Aurach, and the charming village of Oberaurach. You will return along the hills and meadows overlooking Kitzbuehel.

Start: Walk past the Hotel Maria Theresia. Bear right at the fork in the road at the Hotel Schwarzer Adler, walking on Ehrenbachgasse. Continue past private homes and through a small tunnel until you see Achenpromenade #1. Turn right, walking through a suburban area of Kitzbuehel with Tyrolean-style chalets.

As you proceed, the promenade alternates between a gravel path and a small auto road, with the river on the left. After about three miles, turn left and walk over a small bridge at Gasthof Auwirt. Cross the road and turn right. Just before the gas station turn left on a country path signed Oberaurach and Wildpark. After a few minutes you'll reach an intersection. Turn right and follow the sign to Wildpark, walking through rolling farmland and pasture until you reach an auto road. Turn left on the road and walk up the hill to the beautiful, onion-domed church, visible above the trees.

After visiting the beautifully restored church, continue to follow the ascending road for a few hundred feet. Cross over the brook on a small footbridge and follow a path across from the *Alterseheim* (residence for the elderly). In a minute you'll be at a mini-chapel built in 1867, still in use today. The grounds around this quiet chapel are shaded and its bench can provide a lovely spot for a picnic lunch.

When ready, return to the large church and walk down the auto road to the first signed right turn to Unteraurach. Follow this path, but at the same intersection you passed through earlier in the day, do not turn left, walk straight ahead. This small country road takes you to the tiny hamlet of Dorfmuhle. Follow signs to Kitzbuehel through the hamlets of Eichenheim and Mauringhof—marked #6 on the hiking map—below the Bichlalm Sesselbahn. At Mauringhof you have some options:

1) Continue ascending on #6, following signs to Bichln and the lift station, and catch an hourly bus back to Kitzbuehel.

2) At Mauringhof, continue through he forest following Kitzbuehel signs along the side of the golf course. At the tennis stadium, turn left into town.

3) Before reaching Mauringhof, this walk can be shortened by retracing your steps to the Gasthof Auwirt and catching the bus to KitzbuEhel on the main road.

NEUSTIFT

The Tyrolean village of Neustift fits snugly between high mountain peaks, reached via the narrow Stubai Valley road which winds though picturesque villages all the way to the impressive Stubai glacier at Mutterberg. Here a series of lifts takes over, bringing hikers and summer skiers up to Eisgrat at 9351 ft. (2850 m.) for a visit to the hub of all-season sporting activity, the Stubai glacier, which features skiing and glacier-walking in summer. Neustift's hiking is exceptional and improving every year. Eight mountain *hutte* (huts) encircle the Stubaital (Stubai Valley) with overnight facilities for hut-to-hut hikers. The Stubai Trail starts and finishes in Neustift, with 75 miles (120 km.) of high-level walking trails, most between 7218 and 8859 ft. (2200 and 2700 m.). But *Easy Walkers* should not be intimidated, as hut-to-hut walking is only one of the Neustift appeals.

A second feature, within the reach of most recreational walkers, are the trails to *alms* or pastures, located well below the higher-level huts, but above the valley floor. *Alms* offer rustic restaurants featuring local culinary *specialties—kaiser-schmarrn* (a fluffy omelette served with homemade preserves), soup with *knodl* (dumplings), *wurst* with sauerkraut, freshly made *kuchen,* beer and *schnapps.*

Finally, there is a network of low-and medium-level trails and paths, connecting *alms* with valley walks. Neustift's hiking infrastructure now includes the Besinnungsweg or Meditation Walk, a classic mountain hike featuring original sculpture, and the hike from Autenalm to Klamperbergalm. Most of the paths in the Neustift area are well-maintained and well-signed, helping first-time walkers feel comfortable on the trails, and it is interesting to note that every bus stop in the Stubaital is at the beginning and/or end of a hike.

TRANSPORTATION TO NEUSTIFT

By **Train and Bus**—Neustift is served only by the Bus Stubaital line from Innsbruck—a 50-minute ride. Arriving by train at the Innsbruck station, walk to the front of the *bahnhof* turn left and walk around to the *busbahnhof* (bus station). Look for the yellow and green Bus Stubaital sign closest to the main street.

By Car:—Drive on the A12 *autobahn* east or west towards Innsbruck and follow signs into the Stubaital and Neustift.

FAVORITE *WALKING EASY* HOTEL

Hotel Bellevue
Three-star—Owners—Familie Hofer
A-6167 Neustift/Stubai; Tel: 52 26 26 36 9

Internet: www.bellevue-tirol.at
E-mail: info@bellevue-tirol.at
Patti and Hans Hofer created there hotel in a quiet location outside the center of Neutsift, perfect for views for the Stubai Valley, yet close to shops. Rooms are very comfortable with balconies and modern conveniences. Hans Hofer is happy to share his hiking knowledge about the Stubai valley. Full breakfast buffet is included, and traditional Austrian specialties are served at dinner. If you arrive in Innsbuck by train or bus, the Hofers will pick you up at the station, with an advance call.

EXCURSIONS IN AND AROUND NEUSTIFT

The Tourist Information Office is located across from the church, with information about summer activities in the Stubaital.
Internet: www.neustift.at
E-mail: info@stubai.net

1. Neustift—The beautiful, Baroque Neustift church is the second largest country church in the Tyrol region. Note the magnificent Rococo side altar, contrasting with its Baroque interior. The church grounds, as is the custom in Austria, are devoted to an ornate cemetery, and most of the decorative iron-work headstones were crafted in nearby Fulpmes, a famous center for ornate metal-work.
2. Innsbruck—See "A Trail of Three Cities—Innsbruck."
    Directions: *Take the hourly bus from Neusift to Innsbruck*

A CHARMING AUSTRIAN RESTAURANT

NEUSTIFT WALKS
Recommended Map:
Kompass Wanderparadies—Stubaital

Walk # 1: Elfer Top Station to Pinnisalin to Issenanger Ahn to Neder to Neustift
Walking Easy Time: 3 1/2 hours
Rating: Comfortable

The hike to Pinnisalm, returning through the Pinnistal (Pinnis Valley), is one of our favorites. You will take the Elfer chairlift to the top station at 5886 ft. (1794 m.) for a superb view of the valley below. While there are a number of walks from this point, today you will walk down the back side of the Elferspitze, on a mountain trail to Pinnisalm at 5118 ft. (1560 m.) This busy little oasis is at the cross-section of several walks and after lunch you will continue back through the valley, past Issenanger Alm, along the Pinnisbach (Pinnis River), descending all the way into Neustift.

Directions: *At the Neustift church, walk down to the main road and turn left, walking to the Elfer Lift sign, which points across the road to the right. Follow the path to the lift station and buy a one-way ticket to the top.*

Start: At the top station, turn left and follow the sign to Pinnisalm on the carriage path, which soon becomes a narrow mountain trail. **NOTE: Make sure that you follow the sign to Pinnisalm rather than continuing on the road down the mountain.** The Pinnisalm trail leaves the road and continues into the forest. The rate of descent is not difficult, and after 1 1/4 hours, the restaurant in the Pinnisalm meadow appears though the trees. It is possible to lengthen this hike by walking deeper into the valley, ascending to the country restaurant at Karalm 5732 ft. (1747 m.) The route back to the restaurant at Pinnisalm is along the same path.

Either way, walk in the direction of Neustift on a wide, gravel jeep road with little traffic. After 45 minutes you'll arrive in Issenangeralm at 4528 ft. (1380 m.) and then Herzebenalm at 4390 ft.each with its own rustic restaurant. Make sure that you stay on the main road towards Neustift, eventually reaching Obergasse-Neustift. Turn left onto this mid-level panoramic trail with its views of the surrounding chalets and meadows. Descend into the village at the Neustift-Dorf sign.

Walk # 2: Elfer Top Station to Autenalm to Neustift (Optional Walks to Elferhutte and/or Klamperbergalm)
Walking Easy Time: 2 1/2 to 4 hours
Rating: Comfortable

Today's walk begins in Neustift, using the Elfer chairlift to the top station at 5886 ft. (1794 in.) where the walk begins. You will take a trail to Autenalm though the forest, with occasional glimpses of the valley below, descending from Autenalm to Neustift along a pleasant jeep road. The tiny mountain restaurant at Autenalm serves local specialties on a sun-terrace overlooking the spectacular Stubaital.

A more challenging option is to first climb to the Elferhutte at 6825 ft. (2080 m.)—a steep rise of 938 ft. (286 m.)—descending to Autenalm from there. Another option (taking 3 to 3 1/2 hours round-trip), is to continue the hike from Autenalm to Klamperbergalm at 5889 ft. (1795 in.), returning on the same path to Autenalm to begin the return hike to Neustift.

Directions: *See Walk # 1*

Start: At the top Elfer station, turn right and follow the "Autenalm" sign, marked #5B on your map, into the forest and onto a pleasant balcony trail, descending comfortably to Autenalm at 5440 ft. (1658 m.) in about an hour. As an option, strong walkers might wish to hike to Autenalm by first ascending for 45 minutes to the Elferhutte, on a steep trail to the right of the chairlift station, then descending on trail #5 on your map, directly to Autenalm from the *hutte.* After enjoying the spectacular views and refreshments at the Autenalm mountain cabin, it is possible to lengthen this hike by another 3 to 3 1/2 hours round-trip by following the sign to Klamperbergalm, returning to Autenalm on the same trail.

At Autenalm, return to Neustift by following the jeep road, considerably less steep than the Fussweg Neustift mountain trail. Stay on this comfortable jeep road, following signs to Neustift. After crossing back and forth under the chairlift, as you approach Neustift, turn onto the little path to the right marked Neustift Dorf, and follow signs into the village.

Walk # 3: Nurnberger Bus Stop to Bsuchalm and Return, Walk Ranalt to Falbeson to Volderau to Krossbach (Optional Walk to Neustift)
Walking Easy Time: 3 to 5 hours
Rating: More Challenging

After taking the bus from Neustift to the Nurnberger Hutte bus stop, you will climb along the Langanbach (Langan River) from 4298 to 5250 ft. (1310 to 1600 m.) through the woods to Bsuchalm. This walk is the first part of the climb for hikers continuing on to the Nurnberger Hutte. *Easy Walkers* can end their hike at the rustic restaurant at Bsuchalm, although stronger walkers may wish to continue on to the *hutte,* a steep climb to 7481 ft. (2280 m.)

You will return on the same route and take the bus to Ranalt at 4275 ft. (1303 m.) to resume walking—switching from side to side of the river, going though Falbeson, Volderau, Gasteig and finally Krossbach at 3612 ft. (1101 m.) This part of walk though the valley is gentle and can be shortened or lengthened at will, at bus stops marked with the yellow and green "H" signs. In fact, the walk can be continued on valley paths all the way into Neustift; there are restaurants, facilities and bus stops thoughout the valley.

Directions: *Take a bus towards Mutterberg and get off at the Nurnberger Hutte bus stop.* **Start**: After getting off the bus, cross the street and walk though the parking area and up to the right, on the trail marked Bsuchalm. (It may take Easy Walkers an hour for the walk to Bsuchalm, as the trail steepens.) Passing an impressive waterfall, continue on the ascending trail and note the sign Bsuchalm-15 min. The path levels off and veers to the right over a wooden bridge to the tiny, rustic restaurant.

You have walked up though the Langantal, where strong hikers can continue on to the *hutte*. It should be noted that each of the huts forming the Stubaital hiking infrastructure has an *alm* below it for hikers to enjoy. After lunch at the *alm,* retrace your steps down to the main road. Try to time your return to take the bus from the parking area to Ranalt. Exit the bus on the far side of Ranalt and take the fork on the left side of the road towards the Wald Cafe. Cross the road and follow path #1, a gentle trail all the way to Volderau. The path recrosses the road, passing Gasteig and leading into Krossbach at 3612 ft. (1101 m.) Please note that you may shorten or lengthen this walk towards Neustift by checking the bus schedules posted at each bus stop along the valley.

Walk # 4: Stubai Glacier Walk (Optional Walk to Mutterberg)
Walking Easy Time: 2 to 3 1/2 hours
Rating: More Challenging

Glacier walks are always exciting, and today you will travel though the narrowing Stubai Valley until the road ends at a giant winter sports arena, encircled by stark, towering mountains and the Stubai glacier. The bus leaves Neustift for a 30-minute ride, taking you from 3258 ft. (993 m.) to the Gletscherbahn Base Station at 5647 ft. (1721 m.) You will take the gondola to the Fernau mid-station at 7553 ft. (2302 m.) and continue on the same gondola over the barren, treeless landscape to Eisgrat at 9351 ft. (2850 m.).

The one-hour (each way) hike from Eisgrat at 9351 ft. on the Gletscherpfad (glacier trail), to 10,332 ft. (3149 m.) is well-marked, well-used and roped. The walk is not difficult, but it should be taken when the weather is clear enough to enjoy the views at the top—the Dolomites, the Bernina and Otztal Alps. After returning from the glacier, you will proceed by gondola back to the mid-station to visit the Dresdner Hutte, offering a cafeteria and facilities for hut-to-hut hikers. From this point, you can exercise the option of returning to the base station by gondola, or taking the rocky, steep trail down the front of the mountain. Buses leave for Neustift from the parking area at Mutterberg.

Directions: *Take a bus from Neustift to the Stubaier Gletscherbahn at Mutterberg, the last stop. Purchase a round-trip lift ticket to the top and hop on the gondola, staying in the same car as you glide by the mid-station to top station Eisgrat.*
Start: Depending on summer snow conditions, begin at the marked glacier trail for the hour-long hike onthe gletseherpfad to the kiosk at 10,335 ft. (3150 m.) Your descent will be on the same glacier trail. Skiers and snowboarders will be *schussing* down the glacial slopes, while sun-worshipers gather on the terrace of the Panorama Restaurant. When ready, take the gondola down to the mid-station where you can pay a visit to the Dresdner Hutte—bratwurst and sauerkraut might hit the spot. At the mid-station you have the following options:

1)   Hike down the steep, zig-zagging, rocky trail to the base station.

2)   Take the gondola down. If it is wet, snowy or slippery, or if you are a novice walker, we suggest you continue on the gondola, using the balance of your lift ticket. If it is clear and dry, and the view from the trail entices you, continue down by foot.

Walk # 5: Neustift to Kartnali to Forchach to Barenbad to Milders to Neustift
Walking Easy Time: 2 1/2 hours
Rating: More Challenging

We added this hike for those days when the weather is not conducive to high-level walking. Transportation is not necessary, as the hike starts and ends in Neustift. You will walk from the valley floor in Neustift at 3258 ft. to the heights above the valley and Kartnall at 4265 ft an increase of 984 ft. (300 m.) The hike continues up and around the mountain and then descends along a quiet road to Forchach. You will continue down to Milders at 3366 ft for the gentle valley return to Neustift.
Start: From the Hotel Bellevue, walk in the direction of the the village. Turn left, following signs to Kartnall, Forchach, Starkenburger Hutte and *schwim bad.* Walk up the road until you reach the *schwim bad* (swimming pool) parking area and turn left to Kartnall. Another sign directs you left again, up the gravel path towards Starkenburger Hutte and Kartnall. However, the Starkenburger trail branches off to the right as you walk ahead to the restaurant at Kartnall. After this climb, it might be time for a bowl of homemade *knoedl* soup and some *apfel strudel.* When ready, cotinue on the road, ascending to the high point at 4265 ft. (1300 m.). Descend past the restaurant at Forchach, meeting the road from Oberissalm. Turn left and walk down the road into Milders to the main auto road and bus stop. To walk back to Neustift—another half hour—turn left on the road, cross to the other side, and take the path though the fields to the church square in Neustift.

Walk # 6 : Kreuzjoch Top Station to Schlickeralm to Froneben Mid-Station to Vergor to Fulpmes to Grobenhof to Rastbichl to Rain to Neustift
Walking Easy Time: 5 to 5 1/2 hours
Rating: Comfortable

Today's walk begins at the Kreuzjoch Top Station, and you will walk through Schlickeralm to the Froneben Mid-Station of the Kreuzjoch lift, continuing though the forest on a pine-covered trail to the little hamlet of Vergor. After stunning views of the Stubaital, you will return to the base station of the Kreuzjoch lift for a low-level walk to Neustift.

In case of poor visibility this walk can be shortened by not taking the gondola to the Kreuzjoch top station. Instead, start the walk at the Froneben mid-station. It is also possible to begin the walk at the Kreuzjoch base station—not taking the lift at all.

Directions: *Take the bus from Neustift to Fulpmes, a 15-minute ride. In Fulpmes center, the bus stops in front of the i, inside a corner souvenir store across the street from the bus stop, where you can pick up a Fulpmes street map with directions to the Kreuzjoch Lift. Walk up the hill in front of the i to the end of the street. Turn right and continue uphill to your left, passing in front of the firehouse. Continue on this panoramaweg to the base station of the Kreuzjoch lift. Purchase a one-way ticket to the Kreuzjoch Top Station.*

Start: At the top lift station at 6890 ft. (2100 m.) follow directions to Schlicker Alm at 5391 ft. (1643 m.) and then Froneben mid-station at 4318 ft. (1316 m.) on a wide, comfortable path. At Froneben, pass the outside of the snack bar and pick up the mountain/forest trail marked "Vergor." This peaceful, pine-needled trail descends gently though the forest, eventually entering a sunny, open meadow with views throughout the Stubaital. At Vergor, just before an old barn, buttonhook left on a wide jeep road in the direction of Fulpmes and the base station of the Kreujoch lift. At the base station you have a pair of options:

1) Walk to Fulpmes and take the bus to Neustift.

2) Walk to Neustift as follows: As you reach the Kreuzjoch base station, buttonhook sharply to the right on a path eventually signed "Neustift." The trail descends gently as you walk though Grobenhof, its meadows dotted with tiny old barns. Passing the Rastbichl Gasthof on the left, walk ahead to a signed intersection before reaching the main auto road. Turn right, to NeustiftRain. This narrow trail takes you uphill, though a working farm, as it winds up and around to the left in the direction of Rain and Neustift. Reaching an unmarked intersection at Rain, take the ascending road to the right, staying on the heights above Neustift. Turn

left at a fork in the road, descending gradually and switching back and forth until you arrive at the church square.

Walk # 7: Kretrzjoch Top Station to Starkenburger Hutte to Neustift
Walking Easy Time: 5 to 6 hours
Rating: More Challenging

The walk to the Starkenburger Hutte begins with the lift from Fulpmes to the Kreuzjoch Top Station at 6890 ft. (2100 m.) It will take about three hours to hike to the Starkenburger Hutte at 7340 ft. (2237 m.) along a narrow, mountain trail that may be uncomfortable for those of you concerned about balance and footing. This is one of the most popular trails in the area, but there are some rocky sections. Strong walkers should have no problems completing the hike. The descent to Neustift is probably best taken along the jeep trail, down the mountain, to beyond the Kartnellhof Restaurant, walking into the village from there.

    Directions: *Take an early morning bus from Neustift to Fulpmes. See directions in Walk #6.*

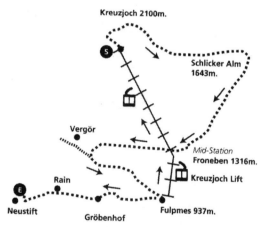

Start: At the Kreuzjoch top station take the trail to Sennjoch and the Starkenburger Hutte—the most traveled trail from the Kreuzjoch. The trail starts with a bit of a scramble—and is marked #4 on your map all the way to Sennjoch. From Senjoch at 7185 ft. (2190 m.) take the easier, most direct trail, also marked #4, (not the dotted red line trail over the mountain), to the Starkenburger Hutte. There are no restaurants or facilities along the way, so make sure you have packed food and plenty of water. After about 90 minutes of walking, the trail proceeds around a rocky prominence and the Starkenburger Hutte is within grasp. Pick up the jeep road descending to Kaserstattalm at 6201 ft. (1890 m.) buttonhooking right on #4, all the way to the Kartnallhof for the descent into Neustift on #3.

ADDITIONAL WALKS IN THE NEUSTIFT AREA:

Walk # 8: The Besinnungsweg (Meditation Trail)
Walking Easy Time: 2 1/2 hours (one way)
Rating: More Challenging

The newest trail in the Neustift area is in the Pinnistal (Pinnis Valley). It begins at the jeep roa above Neder and above the entry to the Obergasse Trail to Neustift— which you take in Walk #1.

This new path ascends about 1000 ft. (300 m.) somewhat quickly. You can access the trail from Neustift by taking the Obergasse Weg, path #2 on your hiking map, to the road. Turn right to the signed entry to this new trail (Besinnungssteig on your map). The entrance is on your left and you climb rapidly with the aid of 300 steps, through the forest and up the mountain, reaching a height of 5250 ft. (1600 m.) passing original sculptures that give you an opportunity to rest and meditate. The trail then descends on a zig-zag path to the sunterrace of the Issenangeralm Restaurant at 4482 ft. (1366 m.). The walk to Neustift is back along the jeep road, through the Pinnistal as in Walk #1, but walk past the Obergasse Weg into Neder, where a left turn brings you past the Elfer Lift station and Neustift.

A WALKING EASY TRAIL

SEEFELD

Seefeld, sitting on a sunny plateau at 3872 ft. (1180 m.), appears to have been created specially for *Easy Walkers*—cooled by mountain breezes and rimmed by rocky crests surrounding meadows dotted with walking trails. This is a cosmopolitan village of 3000 inhabitants, with the Wetterstein and Karwendel mountain ranges forming an imposing backdrop, and the unusual formation of the Hohe Munde towering above the village. A major resort in Austria, Seefeld attracts an international clientele of tourists and hikers—offering a championship golf course, casino, tennis center, concerts in the town park and Parish Church, cable lifts rising to mountain and ridge walks, and a traffic-free village.

Only 15 miles (26 km) northwest of Innsbruck, Seefeld is easily accessible by train, bus and car. Easy-to-reach excursions to Innsbruck in Austria—and Mittenwald, Munich and Garmisch-Partinkirchen in Germany—make Seefeld an enticing stop. Seefeld is a first-class walking and hiking center, with trails attracting all levels of walkers.

TRANSPORTATION TO SEEFELD

By Train—Seefeld is a half hour from Innsbruck and 2 1/2 hours from Munich by train—easily accessible from any area of Austria.

By Car—Driving from the east, take the A12 *autobahn* towards Innsbruck. Turn north before reaching Innsbruck, following signs to Seefeld. From the Salzburg area, take A12 past Innsbruck and drive north into Seefeld.

FAVORITE *WALKING EASY* HOTEL

Hotel Regina
Three-Star, Owner—Monika Egger
A-6100 Seefeld/Tyrol
Inrernet: www.seefeld.at/hotelregina
E-mail: regina.seefeld@nextra.at
    Supervised with the personal touch of Mrs. Egger and her pleasant staff, the Hotel Regina located on a quiet side street, is a five-minute walk from the center of Seefeld. This cozy, comfortable hotel is traditionally furnished and serves a breakfast buffet and traditional family-style dinners. The hotel is very affordable and a under the caring eyes of Monika, provides a family-oriented *Walking Easy* experience.

EXCURSIONS

The Seefeld Tourist Office is located in the main square opposite the church.

Internet: www.seefeld.at

e-mail: info@seefeld.at

Concerts in the church and band shell are held twice a week. A free shuttle bus is available to and from many Seefeld walking areas and lift stations. Pick up a map and schedule at the **i**

1. **Innsbruck**—See "A Trail of Three Cities-Innsbruck."
    Directions: The trip to Innsbruck takes 35 minutes by frequent train from Seefeld.

2. **Mittenwald, Germany**—Only 8 1/2 miles northeast of Seefeld, and just over the German border in Bavaria, Mittenwald is noted for its uniquely painted buildings. (See Walk #4.)
    Directions: *Train service is frequent for this half-hour trip.* **Remember to take your passport!**

3. **Garmisch-Partenkirchen, Germany**—These twin Bavarian towns, lying at the foot of the Wetterstein range, are international winter/summer resorts. At the Garmisch railroad station, the trains of the Zugspitzbahn leave every hour to the Zugspitze, Germany's highest mountain.
    Directions: The train from Seefeld arrives in Garmisch in 45 minutes. **Remember to take your passport!**

4. **Munich, Germany**—Stroll to the center of town and the famous Marienplatz to hear the renowned **glockenspiel**. Walk to the **Isartor** and the **Karlstor**, 14th-century gates of the old city. Take an elevator up the **Town Hall Tower** for a panoramic view of the city. Enjoy the Gothic **Church of Our Lady (Frauenkirche)**, the city's most famous landmark, built in the 1400s. Meander through the shopping streets but don't forget to have a *wurst* in the world-famous Hofbrauhaus, with a Munich beer, of course. Visit the **Old Pinakothek (Alte Pinakothek)**, an immense building housing collections of paintings gathered over hundreds of years, but remember that least four hours are needed for even a cursory inspection of its art treasures.
    Directions: *The trip to Munich takes a little over two hours.* **Remember to take your passport!**

SEEFELD WALKS
Recommended Map: Mayr Wanderkarte #15—Seefeld

Walk #1: Introductory Walk around Seefeld
Walking Easy Time: 1 1/2 hours
Rating: Gentle

This walk can be taken on the day of arrival, to become acquainted with the Seefeld area. You will walk along the main, car-free walking street, filled with cafés, shops and hotels—and around the lake in the direction of Auland, returning to Seefeld along the opposite side of the lake.

Start: Walk south, past the church on the main walking street, until you reach the Wildsee. Walk around the lake on the road for a few minutes and turn right on a signed gravel path towards Auland and Reith. Turn right at the first intersection, through a boggy area around the tip of the lake and back towards Seefeld on the other side of the lake, just past a little restaurant on the shore. Turn left on intersecting road #4a on your hiking map, back through the forest, following signs to the zoo and *kinderspiel*, in the direction of Auland. Turn left towards Seefeld and the lake to meet the original path back into Seefeld.

Walk #2: Gschwandtkopf Top Station to Mösern to Lottenseehutte to Wildmoosalm to Seefeld
Walking Easy Time: 4 hours
Rating: Comfortable

Today's low-level walk begins by taking the Gschwandtkopf Lift and hiking down the back side of the mountain to the village of Mosern. The hike to Mosern— about an hour of pleasant downhill walking—brings you into this village with its magnificent views of the Inn River as it flows through the next village of Telfs and beyond. You will leave for the Lottenseehutte through forest paths, passing the golf course and walking through Wildmoosalm.

Directions: *Take the free Seefeld Dorf Bus to the Gschwandtkopf Lift. Or, at the church square, walk on Klosterstrasse, passing the back of the church. Make the first left turn, following signs to the Gschwandtkopf Lift, past the Sports Center. Purchase a one-way ticket to the top.*

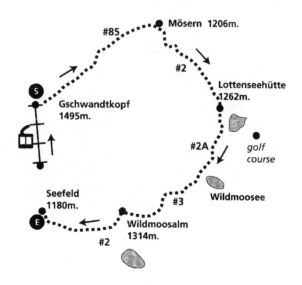

Start: While the top station is only at 4905 ft. (1495 m.), the views are spectacular in all directions. Restaurants and facilities are available. Look for directions on the side of the panoramic map down from the lift station. Follow #85 to Mosern, on your hiking map. The forest trail passes tiny Gschwandtkopf Lake. Soon, the lookout on the right brings initial glimpses of the Inn River and the village of Telfs. Continue on this wide path and turn right at "Mosern #4." At intersecting trails, turn left and take #96 to Mosern, ascending over the Moserer Hohe.

In the village of Mösern, turn left on the main street, crossing the road and passing the Tourist Office. In about 50 yards, turn right and walk up the hill in the direction of Gasthof Menthof. The view from the Menthof's sun-terrace is one of the most spectacular panoramas in the area. Path #2, the Pirchsteig leading to the Lottenseehütte, can be seen from the Menthof sun-terrace—not marked, but easily located—walk up the little trail in back of the restaurant.

After entering onto the Pirchsteig, signs confirm your direction to the Lottensee. Remain on this path through the forest, the trail ascending gently to the Lottensee and the restaurant to the left. Walk back to the main road if you have detoured to the restaurant, following path #2a along the road, with the golf course on the left. There is an option here to take the unsigned, grassy path along the lake (when there is a lake), continuing along the right side of the golf course, and up to the golf club parking area. With either option, continue on the main road, soon becoming a gravel path leading to Wildmoos and its lake, also full only periodically. At the intersection, turn right to Wildmoosalm and Seefeld along path #3. At Wildmoosalm, you have the option of taking the bus to Seefeld or walking back. If you decide to walk, turn right on #2 into the outskirts of Seefeld.

Walk #3: Seefelder Joch Top Station to Seefelder Spitze and Return, Walk Rosshutte Mid-Station to Seefeld
Walking Easy Time: 4 hours
Rating: Comfortable

You will take the Rosshutte funicular from 4049 to 5745 ft. (1234 to 1751 m.), changing for the cable car to the Seefelder Joch at 6805 ft. (2074 m.). The first part of the walk is a hike up to the Seefelder Spitze at 7287 ft. (2221 m.) along the spine of the mountain. You will return to the Seefelder Joch along the same path. After taking the cable car back to the Rosshütte, the walk continues down the mountain to Seefeld.

Directions: *Walk up Andreas Hofer Strasse to the Rosshütte Standseilbahn base station. Purchase a ticket to Seefelder Joch, with a return to Rosshütte, with its large sun-terrace and picnic facilities. At the mid-station, follow signs to the Seefelder Jochbahn for the cable car ride to the top.*

Start: At the Seefelder Joch, walk up the hill towards the large cross, following the ridge trail to 7287 ft. (2221 m.) and the Seefelder Spitze. While this walk is listed as 45 minutes, *Easy Walkers* may take an hour to reach their destination. (It is possible to hike ahead, eventually making a right turn down and around the mountain to the Rosshütte. This trail is rocky and can be steep in places.) If you return to the Seefeld Joch by walking down on the same trail you came up on, take the cable car back to the Rosshütte station. Here, take a new trail called the" Zirbenweg," a 20-minute circle route to the mountain rescue cabin just above the Rosshütte. After returning to the mid-station you have an option for an additional excursion: take the Härmelekopf cable car for a short ride across a deep gorge to the paragliding headquarters of Seefeld—returning to the mid-station in the same manner.

Follow the sign from the mid-station to Seefeld on a wide gravel path, ending at the base station.

Walk #4: Seefeld to Triendlsage to Giessenbach to Scharnitz (Excursion to Mittenwald, Germany)
Walking Easy Time: 3 1/2 hours
Rating: Comfortable

Today's low level walk and excursion takes hikers from Seefeld to Triendlsage at 3691 ft. (1125 m.), into the Lehenwald (forest), past Bodenalm and through the valley to Giessenbach and Scharnitz. This walk takes about 3 1/2 hours, and you should arrive in time to catch a train for the seven minute ride, crossing the German border, to the scenic village of Mittenwald. Do **not** forget your passport.

Mittenwald is a very pretty Bavarian town, where particular care is given to the ornate, hand-painting decorating its church, shops and homes. The village is famous for its violin museum and the crafting of fine, hand-made musical instruments.

Start: Walk on Seefeld's main street, Münchnerstrasse, past the Hotel Eden, turning left on Geigenbühelweg, and following signs to the *panoramaweg*. You'll shortly pass the Panoramagolf Driving Range on the right. At the intersection, continue ahead on #65 to Triendlsage and Bodenalm. At the next intersection, turn left at the sign "Triendlsäge #1." Walk down the hill, following signs to Triendlsäge and Seefeld.

Walking down to the tiny intersection in Triendlsage, make a right turn on the carriage road marked #64 Bodenalm. This level path is an easy walk through the Lehenwald, a tall pine forest in the Drahnbachtal (Drahnbach Valley). Continue, following signs to Bodenalm, walking past this small farm and restaurant on your right.

At the next intersection, continue following #65 on your map, in the direction of Giessenbach and Scharnitz, crossing the Drahnbach River on a little bridge to your left. Continue to the right on #19, passing Giessenbach, all the way into Scharnitz, where you follow signs to the *bahnhof* on the other side of the highway. Trains to Mittenwald leave about 45 minutes past each hour—check the train schedule.

Get off at Mittenwald and be prepared to change your thinking from Austrian schillings to German marks, although many shops are prepared to deal with you in both currencies. Visit the church, built in the early 1700s, with its fine stuccos and murals. The Geigenbau-und-Heimatmuseum (Stringed Instrument Museum), on the street behind the church, displays the different phases of violin-making. The brightly painted houses lining the streets of the Obermarkt are a pleasure to behold, and photographers will appreciate a few hours spent in this "living picturebook," as described by Goethe.

Trains returning to Seefeld depart Mittenwald frequently for the short ride.

Walk #5
Wildmoosalm to Weidachsee to Leutasch/Weidach
Walking Easy Time: 2 1/2 hours
Rating: Comfortable

This pleasurable, mid-to low-level walk provides *Easy Walkers* with a mix of open meadow, mountain paths and forest trails through the beautiful Fludertal (Fluder Valley). A bus runs from Seefeld to Wildmoosalm at 4311 ft. (1314 m.), where the walk begins. The trail altitude does not vary more than 150 ft. (45 m.) over the length of a pretty forest path, the Wurzelsteig, bringing you down to the lake and restaurant at Weidach. After visiting the little village of Weidach you will take the bus back to Seefeld. **NOTE: Afternoon buses run infrequently between Weidach and Seefeld, please check bus schedules before you leave on today's hike.**

    Directions: *Take the bus—usually leaving every hour on the hour—to Wildmoosalm, from the parking area diagonally across from the Hotel Eden, next to the apotheke (drugstore) on Münchnerstrasse. Purchase a one-way ticket to Wildmoosalm.*

    Start: At Wildmoosalm, walk past the restaurant and a little lake on the right, to a signed intersection "Leutasch #3." Turn right and walk uphill on a carriage path for about 25 minutes. Additional signs at the intersection confirm your direction—ahead on #3. Within minutes you'll enter the Fludertal, with stunning views of the Wetterstein mountain range towering behind tall pine forests.

    After about an hour, the path descends to the auto road. Turn left, carefully walking alongside the road, taking the narrow, beaten path along the left side of the auto road, descending down to the road again. Turn left up into the forest on a path marked with a blue and white sign picturing a biker and hiker. You are now on "Wurzelsteig #42," soon to be confirmed by signing. This narrow forest path is blazed in **blue**. This trail lifts gently out of the forest and crosses a meadow, with a small *spielpark* (amusement park) in full view down the hill. Be careful as you walk under a chairlift, and cross over a flume slide and go-cart path, part of the amusement park.

    Entering the forest again, walk to the right immediately on an **unsigned**, blue-blazed path. This path soon crosses a jeep road. Walk ahead following "#42." Reaching an intersection marked "#3 Weidachsee," turn right. The path widens and drops easily towards the lake at Weidach. At the next intersection, turn right on "Seerundgang #3," walking to this lake with its trout farm and fishing piers. The restaurant at the end of the lake is noted for its trout specialties and makes a fine lunch stop if you decide not to picnic.

When ready to leave, walk on the auto road past the restaurant, making a right on the sidewalk at a main road. Continue until you reach the heart of the tiny village—all the way to the main street. Turn right—the bus stop is just below Gasthof Zum See. (The post bus schedule will read "Leutasch/Weidach Gh Zum See")

Walk #6: Seefeld to Moserersee to Auland to Seefeld
Walking Easy Time: 4 1/2 hours
Rating: Comfortable

Today you will leave Seefeld by way of Moserer Mahder #2 in the direction of Mösern, with a walk around the Moserersee at 4213 ft. (1284 m.). The walk continues down to the village of Mosern, around the Gschwandtkopf on Moserer Steig #4, to the village of Auland. This portion of the walk offers fabulous views of the snow-capped peaks of the Austrian National Park. The hike ends with a short ascent to Seefeld, walking around the Wildsee.

ON THE TRAIL AGAIN

Start: Walk past the Seefeld Tourist Office and Post Office on the right, to the main auto road. Pass the Olympic Centre on the left and make a left turn in the direction of the See Kirche. This part of the walk is along the road, but it only lasts for a few minutes. Cross the road a few hundred yards after the See Kirche, making a right turn up the hill, to Mosern #2. At the top of the hill, turn left and continue on Mosern #2. The Tennis School is on the left. Continue on this path in the direction of Mosern. Within a short time, bear right at the fork, again in the direction of Mosern. Passing trail #96, proceed on the path #2 Zum See and Mosern up to the right, shortly reaching the Hotel Olympia. Follow the path ahead, passing the Hubertushof, making a sharp right up the hill to the Moserer See. Always follow the Zum See signs—they lead through the parking lot, over a fence, across a rocky intersection and up to the lake. There you will find a restaurant if you decide not to picnic, and a delightful walking path around the lake.

When ready, retrace your steps through the parking area. Cross the little rocky intersection ahead. Turn right on the road and follow the sign to Mosern, again passing the Hubertushof and the Olympia. Just past the Hotel Olympia, follow the auto road down the hill to Mosern. Cross the highway and turn left on the sidewalk, walking for about 100 yards to enter the path into the forest on the right, marked #4 Auland-1 1/2 hrs. After a few minutes you'll reach a picturesque viewing point with a bench. Turn left up the hill in the direction of Gschwandtkopf, as the path now rises from 3937 to 4295 ft. (1200m. to 1309 m.). Walk past the intersection of #85, the path from the Gschwandtkopf peak. Continue on Moserer Steig #4, always in the direction of Auland.

After about 1 1/4 hours of walking from Mosern, the path descends onto an easy path into Auland. This route offers a spectacular view of the snow-capped peaks of the Austrian National Park to the southeast. Passing the Alpenkonig Hotel on the left, a sign directs you left on the road, to the Englhof Hotel, with a sun-terrace and tantalizing assortment of desserts. Continue walking uphill towards Seefeld for a short ascent on #4. Cross the road at the top, walk straight ahead to the outskirts of Seefeld, and turn left on See Promenade #4 around Seefeld's resort lake, eventually turning right into town.

Walk #7: Salzbachbrucke to Gaistalalm to Tillfussalm to Salzbachbrücke
Walking Easy Time: 3 hours
Rating: Comfortable

This hike in the Gaistal, was discovered by enthusiastic *Easy Walkers* Lyn and Jud Ford. They reported that this comfortable ascent along the river, with magnificent views of the Wettersteins on one side and Hohe Munde on the other, is one of the prettiest walks in the Seefeld area. You will enter the Gaistal (Gais Valley) by walking along the river on the Nordalpenweg, returning to Salzbachbrucke on the higher trail.

Directions: Bus service to Salzbachbrucke in the Leutasch is very limited, so check your bus schedule carefully. If you go by car, we recommend that you park in the furthest of four parking area, as the trail begins near there.

Start: Take path #7 to Gaistalalm, on a comfortable ascent along the Leutascher Ache (river). You'll pass the Hohe Munde and Niedere Munde on your left and the impressive Wetterstein range up on the right. In about 15 minutes, reaching a fork in the trail, stay left, continuing along the river, all the way to Gaistalalm, where you have a few options:

1) Turn right up to the restaurant at Gaistalalm and walk back to the parking area along the Ganghofer Weg.
2) Continue ahead and around through Tillfussalm, passing the restaurant at Gaistalalm, then returning on the Ganghofer Weg.

ZELL AM ZILLER

The narrow-gauge, red-and-yellow regional train *zugs* its way deeply into the Zillertal (Ziller Valley) from the wide valley entrance at Jenbach to Zell am Ziller. This is the preferred Ziller Valley *Walking Easy* base village because of its quiet location on the banks of the Ziller River, proximity to local bus and railroad service, and an outstanding resort hotel.

A mecca for European tourists, and finally being discovered by Americans who are beginning to learn about the charm and easy accessibility of this valley, the Zillertal manages to strike a balance between meeting the needs of vacationers and preserving the dignity and strong sense of tradition inherent throughout this region. A comfortable, pervasive feeling of *gemutlichkeit* seems to emanate from everyone in Zell am Ziller—from the tourist office to the hotel owners.

Mayrhofen, near Zell am Ziller at the end of the Zillertal, is the gateway into picturesque, volcanic valleys called *grunde,* open only in summer and autumn, sealed at their distant ends by peaks usually covered year-round with snow. These U-shaped valleys were formed during the ice ages, gouged out by glaciers. Today these steep inclines are covered by forests, towering above lush green valleys used for farming and grazing—a walker's paradise.

The Zillertal also serves as an entry to the Tuxetal (Tux Valley). Year-round skiers and summer hikers are attracted to Hintertux and its glaciers, which feature a high-level, multi-section lift system. Many Zillertal lifts operate during summer months, transporting walkers to mountain restaurants and miles of marked paths and trails, through tall, pine forests and flower-filled meadows—guaranteed to evoke an annual urge to return to Zell am Ziller.

TRANSPORTATION

By Train—When traveling to Zell am Ziller by train, there is always a change of train in Jenbach to the Zillertalbahn, next to the Jenbach station; follow the Zillertal sign.

By Car—Turn off the A12 *autobahn* at the Zillertal exit and follow signs to Zell am Ziller.

FAVORITE *WALKING EASY* HOTEL

Sporthotel Theresa
Four-Star, Owners—Familie Egger
A-6280 Zell am Ziller Tel: 52 82 22 86 0
Internet: www.theresa.at
E-mail: info@theresa.at

A personal favorite, this wonderful four-star resort hotel (with five-star ambience) features an outstanding kitchen, caring staff, and excellent facilities. From the swimming pools, solarium, fitness room, and extensive spa facilities, to the clay tennis courts with a teaching pro to the superlative cuisine—nothing escapes the eyes of Theresa and Siegfied Egger and their family. They have created a warm, quest-oriented atmosphere in a full service resort catering to leisure seekers and hikers alike.

The Egger family are great hikers and lead walks for their guests. Once you experience the charm of the Theresa you will return for years. Just ask any *Easy Walker*.

EXCURSIONS

The Zell am Ziller Tourist Office is in the center of town on Dorfplatz.

Internet: www.zell.at
e-mail: info@zell.at

Pick up the booklet Zilertaler **Gasterzeitung at** the Tourist Office; all local bus and train timetables are listed in the back. The Wanderticket, or Z-Ticket, is a local 6-day pass for use on Ziller Valley cableways and transportation, valid for 4 of 6 days. Proof of identity with a photo is required.

1. **Zell am Ziller**—The **Pfarrkirche** or parish church, was constructed in the 1700's in an unusual octagonal design, topped by a huge dome.

2. **Mayrhofen**—Only 13 minutes by train from Zell am Ziller, Mayrhofen is at the end of the Ziller Valley.

   Directions: *Trains and buses (conveniently listed on the same schedule) run frequently from the Zell am Ziller train station to Mayrhofen. A steam train operates on this narrow-gauge railway twice a day from May ito October 15. Or, you can walk on the Ziller promenade between Zell am Ziller and Mayrhofen. (See Walk #1.)*

3. **Hintertux Glacier**—This paradise for year-round skiers is at the end of the Tuxertal, reached by bus from Mayrhofen. Gondolas rise to Sommerbergalm at 6890 ft. (2100 m.) and TuxerFerner-Haus at 8728 ft. (2660 m.) the heart of the glacier regions of the Tuxer Alps.

Directions: *Take a bus or train from Zell am Ziller to the Mayrhofen bahnhof Catch the bus to the Hintertux Gletscherbahn.*

4. **Innsbruck**—See "A Trail of Three Austrian Cities—Innsbruck.")
   Directions: *Take a train from Zell am Ziller to Jenbach and change for the train to Innsbruck.*

5. **Krimml Waterfall (Krimml Wasserfillie)**—Located west of Mittersill, these shimmering falls have a drop of 1250 ft., the highest in Europe. (See "Kitzbuehel," Excursion #5.)
   Directions: *Check bus schedules on this route—changes are frequent, **bus service is infrequent.***
   If the Tourist Office in either Zell am Ziller or Mayrhofen runs an excursion to the waterfall, try this option.

6. **Schwaz**—In the 14th and 15th centuries, Schwaz was a copper and silver mining center, well-known as the "silver town of Europe." The silver mine is open, and the mine railway operates through tunnels and underground stalactite formations.
   Directions: *Buses run from Zell am Ziller to Schwaz on the Innsbruck route.*

7. **Rattenberg**—This old fortress town is noted for its historic squares, narrow alleyways, frescoed houses, and the etching and cutting of fine crystal. (See "Alpbach," Excursion #3.)
   Directions: *Take a bus or train to Jenbach and change for the train to Rattenberg/Kramsach.*

ZELL AM ZILLER WALKS

Recommended Map: Mayr Wanderkarte #33—Zillertaler Alpen

Walk #1: Introductory Walk on the Ziller Promenade—Zell am Ziller to Mayrhofen
Walking Easy Time: 2 hours
Rating: Gentle

This introductory walk from Zell am Ziller to Mayrhofen is a pleasant first afternoon's outing. The walk begins in Zell am Ziller, on the Ziller Promenade, ending in Mayrhofen, a busy town at the end of the valley. After exploring Mayrhofen you can walk back to Zell am Ziller or return by bus or train. Mayrhofen is the largest town in the Zillertal and serves as entry point to the *grunde*, or summer valleys, and to Hintertux at the foot of the Tux Glacier.

Start: From the Tourist Office, walk towards the river on Dorfplatz, the main street. Turn left at the river—onto the Ziller Promenade—with the river on your right, following signs to Mayrhofen. After checking out the *konditorei* (pastry shops), the Tourist Office, the local church and shops, you can return to Zell am Ziller by bus or train, or walk back along the Ziller Promenade.

Walk # 2: Rosenalm Top Station to Kreuzjochhutte to Kreuzwiesenhutte to Wiesenalm Mid-station
Walking **Easy Time:** 3 1/2 hours
Rating: Comfortable

Today's high-level walk offers stunning views of the Zillertal, with the peaks of the Zillertaler Alps across the Gerlos Valley, and a visit to two mountain *hutte*. After a 20-minute walk from Zell am Ziller to the Kreuzjoch lift, you will rise to 5722 ft. (1744 m.) in a two-stage gondola.

From Top Station Rosenalm, *Easy Walkers* will take a scenic path ascending to the Kreuzjochhutte at 6267 ft. (1910 m.) walking from there to the Kreuzwiesenhutte at 6300 ft. (1920 m.) with two options to return. You can walk back on the same path to Rosenalm and take the gondola, or continue down the mountain to Weisenalm Mid-Station.

Directions: In Zell, walk towards the i. Turn left on Rohrerstrasse between the i and the Zillertaler Bier Company. Continue on Rohrerstrasse, and after about 15 minutes, walk over the bridge to the lift station. Purchase a one-way ticket to Top Station Rosenalm.

Start: After exiting at the top lift station, turn left and walk down the hill on a jeep path in the direction of the Kreuzjochhutte. Turn right and continue uphill on the dirt road, following signs to Kreuzwiesenalm and Kreuzjochhutte. After walking about 30 minutes (resisting the uphill meadow shortcut to Kreuzjochhutte), you'll come to a signed intersection, with Kreuzjochhutte to the left and Kreuzwiesenhutte straight ahead. Turn left for a 30-minute ascent to the Kreuzjochhutte and its great views of the Zillertal.

When ready, descend on the same path and turn left at the intersection towards Kreuzwiesenhutte on path #11—you should reach the *hutte* in a little over an hour. The views across the valley are worth another refreshment stop on the restaurant's large sun-terrace, usually filled with hikers and sun-worshippers. Here, you have two options:

1) Follow signs to the Wiesenalm Mid-Station on a comfortable forest trail and take the gondola down to Zell.

2) Return on the same path to the lift at Rosenalm, where you take the gondola down to Zell.

Walk # 3: Grune Wand Hutte through the Stillupgrund to Gasthaus Wasserfalle
Walking Easy Time: 2 1/2 hours
Rating: Gentle

Mayrhofen lies on the far end of the Ziller Valley, linked to other smaller valleys, open only in summer, and known as *grunde*. These deep, picturesque valleys lead from Mayrhofen—and one is the site of today's hike—the Stillupgrund. You will visit a beautiful lake/reservoir that reaches across the narrow valley floor, offering hikers a scenic path to the head of this valley.

You'll leave Mayrhofen by private bus for a ride to the Grune Wand Hutte at 4712 ft. (1436 m.). The walk back descends gradually through the valley, with giant waterfalls on either side and friendly cows grazing throughout the *alm*. Reaching the lake and the Alpengasthaus Wasserfalle at 3662 ft. (1116 m.) you will take a private bus return to Mayrhofen and a bus or train back to Zell am Ziller.

Directions: *Leave Zell am Ziller by train or bus to Mayrhofen in sufficient time to catch a mid-morning private bus. After leaving the Mayrhofen train station, turn right along the road. Make your first left turn, and just before the Post Office, note the large sign "Bus Line-Stillupgrnnd" to the right. Follow that street around, into the parking area. The bus stop is next to the i.*

NOTE: Please check times and location carefully. The 45-minute bus ride winds through the narrow entrance of the valley to the Gasthaus Wasserfalle, where you change for another mini-bus, riding deeper into the valley to the Grune Wand Hutte, where the walk begins. (Purchase a round-trip ticket for the first bus and a one-way ticket for the second. There is a separate charge for each bus.)

ZILLERTAL HIKING SIGN

Start: This walk is along a little-used road, starting at 4712 ft. (1436 m.) descending gradually through meadows filled with grazing cows, with the rapidly flowing Stillupbach (Stillup River) on the left. After walking about an hour, the Stilluphaus at 3911 ft. (1192 m.) is available for a rest or refreshment stop. Continuing, walk though and around three small tunnels leading to the lake and the Wasserfalle Restaurant. The return private buses to Mayrhofen usually leave at 30 minutes past the hour. **Check Schedules.** After arriving in Mayrhofen, walk to the train station for the next train or bus to Zell.

Walk # 4: Gschusswand Top Station to Mid-Sation Finkenberg Lift, Lift to Penken, Walk to Gschosswnd Top Station
Walking Easy Time: 4 hours
Rating: More Challenging

After a short ride and visit to Mayrhofen you'll take the Penken lift to the top station at 5906 ft. (1800 m.), and walk along the mountain on a comfortable path to the mid-station of the Finkenberg Lift. From there you'll take the chairlift up to Penken and return to Gschosswand on the higher trail, with fabulous views of the Ziller valley, its surrounding peaks, and summer *grunde*.

Directions: *Take the train or bus from the Zell am Ziller bahnhof to Mayrhofen. Walk up to the main shopping street, and turn right for the ten-minute walk to the Penken Lift Station. Purchase a one-way ticket to the Gschosswand Station.*

Start: On exiting, follow the Penkenhaus #22 sign on to the road under the chairlift all the way to the Almstuberl Restaurant and Finkenberg Chairlift. Take the chairlift one-way, up to the Top Station Penken.

At Penken take the Finkenberger Panoramaweg #23 to the chairlift above Gschosswand. Here you have the option of going to the Penken gondola by riding the chairlift or walking down the path for the return trip to Mayrhofen and the walk to the *bahnhof.*

Walk # 5: Finkenberg to Kreuzlau to Burgstall to Schwendau to Hippach to Zell am Ziller
Walking Easy Time: 4 hours
Rating: Comfortable

Although all walks are nicer when the skies are clear, this mid-level hike can also be taken on a cloudy day. The walk begins in the village of Finkenberg after a short bus ride from Mayrhofen. Walkers will hike along the Leonhard-Stock-Weg above and along the Ziller Valley. The trail then ascends to Burgstall, eventually reaching the picturesque villages of Schwendau and Hippach. From there, the walk is on a level path along the valley floor for an easy stroll into Zell am Ziller.

Directions: *Take a bus or train to Mayrhofen, transferring to the Finenberg bus outside the train station. Buy a one-way ticket to Finkenberg, getting off at the church at Finkenberg-Dorf.*

Start: Walk into the churchyard and follow the #26 Leonhard-Stock-Weg up to the right, on a little road in the direction of the forest. The path soon becomes a grassy carriage road and splits. Follow Leonhard-Stock-Weg #26 as you enter the forest on a pine-covered *bergweg*. Avoid trails 26a and 26b, and continue in the direction of Mariensteig along the Leonhard-Stock-Weg. This trail continues through the forest, where you take path #2 to Mayrhofen, descending to a dead-end main path (overlooking the river and SPAR market). **Turn left** (unmarked #12) and continue to the Zillertal Restaurant.

Walking a little past the restaurant, do not turn left on #2C to Zimmereben, but walk a bit further and ascend left on path #12 to Burgstall, Schwendau and Hippach on the *waldweg*. This trail, blazed white, is easy to follow and eventually arrives at a road. Cross and continue on path #12, to the charming little community of Schwendau. After exploring this village filled with old landmark homes, as well as a herd of goats and sheep in the center of town, walk through the apple and pear trees back to the trail marked #12. The trail leads up and around Schwendau and onto a level, red-blazed forest path for the walk to Hippach. Follow signs to Hippach and turn right at Cafe Waldegg, signed "#7 Hippach," descending though town and making a left turn before the bridge on the path #1 Ziller Promenade to Zell am Ziller. The next hour's walk is along this path, with the river on the right. After passing through Zellberg, turn right at the bridge and walk over the river into Zell am Ziller. In Hippacl/Ramsau, it is possible to take the train or bus back to Zell am Ziller.

Walk # 6: Sonnalmn Top Station to Kotahornalmn to Buhel
Walking Easy Time: 4 hours
Rating: More Challenging

Today's more challenging hike takes you from Sonnalm at 4462 ft. (1360 m.) the top station of the Ramsau chair lift, up to Kotahornalm at 5328 ft. (1624 m.) and its tiny old snack hut, famous for local cheese, sausage, beer and *schnapps*. This isolated farmhouse is an oasis sitting on a high *alm,* welcoming hikers with old-fashioned *gemutlichkeit.* The trail brings you up 866 ft. and finishes with a downhill trek directly to Buhel, a train and bus stop, or to Ramsau where the walk began earlier in the morning. The descending path is not so much steep as it is long, and it will take about 2 1/2 hours to descend 3281 ft. (1000 m.) to Buhel from Kotahornalm. This walk should be taken on a dry day and not after a wet period—the trail can be slippery.

Directions: *Take the bus or train from Zell am Ziller bahnhofto Ramsau, a quick ride in the direction of Mayrhofen. Follow signs to the Ramsberg Lift. Purchase a one-way ticket to Sonnalm, where the walk begins.*

Start: Walk down the path to the front of the lift station, following Kotahorn and Gerlosstein, path #50. This road/trail ascends to Kotahornalm, marked #50. After about a half hour, a sign directs you sharply left, up a steep trail on #50 to Kotahorn—do not take it! Continue ahead up the road, the path becoming a red-blazed trail, still marked #50. Shortly, the path button-hooks steeply up a stepped trail marked "Brandenberg, Steinkogel #50." At the top a sign indicates the path to Brandenberg and Steinkogel to the right. This path also goes to the left, back down the mountain—you must turn right here, following the red-blazed ascending trail. The sign is moveable, so don't be fooled—turn right. Shortly you'll come into a meadow—bear right and walk up the path. Around the turn on the left is an old country farmhouse, providing a warm, cozy place to rest and snack.

When ready, return down to the path and follow signs #51 Mayrhofen, remembering that your final destination is Buhel/Ramsau. Pick up the #51 Ramsau/Buhel path, descending from 5250 to 2133 ft. (1600 to 650 m.) The church steeple in the town of Hippach comes into view as you descend through the forest, arriving at a road. Follow the sign to Buhel, turning left at the dead end and walking to the bus or train station, near one another. Check your bus and train timetable, taking the first to come along for the short ride into Zell am Ziller. The bus station is on the main road, marked by the familiar "H" sign; the tiny train station can be reached by walking through a tunnel and making a left turn. **NOTE: Don't forget to hail the train—it stops by request only.**

Walk # 7: Gerlosstein Top Station to Kotahornalmn to Karlalmn to Kotahornalmn to Sonnalmn, Ramsberg Lift to Ramsau (Optional Walk to Zeil am Ziller along the Ziller Promenade)
Walking Easy Time: 3 to 4 hours
Rating: Comfortable

Our hike today starts at the top station of the Gerlosstein Lift in Hainzenberg, reached by bus from Zell am Ziller. You will walk to Kotahornalm, with its quaint cabin and sun-terrace—a perfect spot for local sausage and cheese—to prepare for a mountain trail rising from 5387 ft. to the Karlalm pasture at 5729 ft. with its fabulous views of the Zillertal and the Tuxer Alps across the way. While it is possible to continue ahead for a descent to Brandberg, Steinerkogel and, eventually, Mayrhofen, we recommend that *Easy Walkers* return from Karlalm to Kotahornalm and take the path to Sonnalm for the chairlift return to Ramsau. From Ramsau you have the option of returning along the Ziller Promenade to Zell am Ziller or, if you prefer, taking the first available train or bus.

Directions: *Bus service to Hainzenberg is limited—check the bus schedule. However, there may bean early morning bus that leaves the Zell am Ziller bahnhof about 9:00 am for the short ride to the lift. Purchase a round-trip ticket to the top station, good for both the Gerlosstein lift and the return Ramsberg chairlift from Sonnalm to Ramsau.*

Start: After leaving the lift station turn right. Walk in back of the restaurant and follow the upper path to Kotahornalm and its rustic restaurant and sun-terrace. A sign directs you to Karlalm on an ascending *bergweg,* eventually entering the forest as the trail climbs up to the Karlalm pasture. While it is possible to continue the descent to Mayrhofen, we suggest returning down the same trail to Kotahornalm, taking path #50 down the mountain to Sonnalm. A little more than half way down, at an intersecting trail from the left, walk ahead over the steps, continuing the descent to the wagon road. Turn right, following the path directly to the Ramsberg chairlift at Sonnalm. Take the chairlift down to Ramsau and walk into the village. Turn left and proceed on the main road for about 300 feet. Cross the road to the train station for a quick ride back to Zell am Ziller. Or, walk over the railroad tracks, turn right and pick up the Ziller Promenade for the 50-minute walk to Zell am Ziller.

ADDITIONAL WALKS IN THE ZELL AREA:

If staying at the Sporthotel Theresa (see "Accommodations" section), Sigal Egger and son Stefan take gnests on great hikes through the countryside.

MIEMING

Tranquil Mieminger Plateau is a sunny, agricultural plain, open to the south and protected in the north by the high, snow-capped peaks of the Mieming mountain range. With over 130 miles (210 km.) of comfortable, mostly level, signed hiking trails winding through lush meadows and picturesque larch forests, around working farms and vast cornfields—this sun-terrace in the heart of the Tyrol is only 22 miles (35 km.) from historic Innsbruck. The dramatic Hohe Munde mountain lies to the north and, if you've hiked around the *Walking Easy* base village of Seefeld, you've trekked on the other side of this uniqely shaped mountain. Another Seefeld hike leads to the village of Mosern—with a view along the Inn River to the village of Telfs, and further, to our new base village on the Mieming Plateau.

Mieming does not offer high, rocky, alpine hiking. Most trails are gentle, rolling paths, with little change in elevation, and will appeal to walkers who prefer easier challenges. The *Walking Easy* Hotel Schwarz however, with its sophisticated array of spa facilities and full board accommodations, is the center of attraction in this area for *Easy Walkers*.

Many paths weave in and around the hamlets of the Mieming Plateau. All trail are signed, and with the aid of the local hiking map, *Easy Walkers* can stroll and bike endlessly in this pastoral setting.

TRANSPORTATION

By Train and Bns—Take an express train to Innsbruck and, outside the train station, at the bus *bahnhf* take a bus to Obermieming (about an hour's ride). Get off at the Hotel Post in Obermieming and follow the sign to the Hotel Schwarz, a few minute's walk. Or, take a local train to Telfs and a taxi to the hotel.

By Car—You can reach the Mieminger Plateau via the Inn Valley highway—4 1/2 miles (7km.) from the Telfs exit and 2 1/2 miles (4km.) from the Motz exit.

FAVORITE *WALKING EASY* HOTEL SCHWARZ

Four-Star; Owners—Franz and Martha Pirktl
A-6414 Mieming; Tel: *52 64 52* **12 0,**
E-Mail: hotel@schwarz.at
Internet: www. schwarz.at

The wellness Hotel Schwarz is a secret waiting to be discovered by Americans and *Easy Walkers* who may prefer a quality, four-star, full resort hotel offering all amenities to pamper their guests. Located on the Mieming Plateau, amid cornfields and potato patches, but close enough to Innsbruck for a one-day sightseeing excursion, the Schwarz experience includes modern spa facilities, outdoor swimming pool and gardens, tennis, children's zoo, and a new golf course at its front door. Your reservation includes a bountiful buffet breakfast and lunch, excellent dinner, and an array of day-long snacks and drinks. The Pirktl family is always attending to the comfort of their guests. It will cost a bit more, but if you want to be spoiled, check into the luxurious, family-oriented Hotel Schwarz.

EXCURSIONS

The Tourist Office (Tourismusverband Sonnenplateau Mieming-Wildermieming) is on the main street of Mieming.
   Internet: www.mieming.at
1. **Innsbruck**—See A Trail of Three Cities—Innsbruck.
   Directions: *Take the bus to the Innsbruck train station, a one hour ride.*
2. **Seefeld**—See Seefeld section.
   Directions: Take the bus to the Innsbruck train station and change/or a train to Seefeld, a *half-hour ride.*
3. **Mittenwald, Germany**—See Seefeld Excursion #2 and Walk #4.
   Directions: *Take the bus to Jnnsbruck and the train to Mittenwald.*

Mieming Walks
Recommended Map:
Mayr Wanderkarte Sonnenplateau #14—Obsteig, Mieming, Wildermieming

---

Walk# 1
Obermieming to Untermieming, throngh the Fiechtertal to Wildermieming to Obermieming
Walking Easy Time: 3 hours
Rating: Comfortable

This comfortable walk begins at the Hotel Schwarz and brings you down through the tiny village of Untermieming and its Gothic church, then into the country-side to Fiecht. These paths offer fabulous views of the Mieming Plateau, and the walk continues though the Fiechtertal (Fiecht valley), returning to Obermieming though the charming village of Wildermieming. The plateau is largely agricultural, filled with working farms and massive cornfields.
   Start: From the Hotel Schwarz, walk to the main road. Cross the street in front of the Gasthof Post and pick up the path to the left of the house, walking

away from the road towards FIECHT. In the rural hamlet of St. Georg, pass the chapel and pick up the wagon path signed UNTERMEIMING. After visiting the church in Untermieming, tturn left at the Gasthof Steigl, following the sign to Fiecht.

As you proceed gently up the hill away from the village and into the country-side, you will see the Hotel Schwarz on the plateau to the left, framed by the Mieminger Berg mountain range. At the top of the rise, turn right following 8A PLATEAUBLICK. After a few minutes on 8A, turn left on *a forest strasse* in the direction of Telfs (the right path leads to Stams). Eventually you'll follow signs FIECHT and GERHARDHOF. At a fork in the path, continue left, descending gently towards Telfs and the Gerhardhof

There will be an opportunity at the fork to go back to Untermieming, but continue, through the Fiechtertal, on #10—to the main auto road. Cross the road, following signs up and around to Wildermieming—not to the Gerhardhof This path continues through the village of Wildermieming, where you can pay a visit to its magnificent church. Pick up the bike path and walk directly back to the Hotel Schwarz. (There are three different roads going though this village, all of which eventually lead to Obermieming and the hotel.)

Walk 2
Obermieming to Wildermieming to the Gerhardhof to Telfs
Walking Easy Time: 2 1/2 hours
Rating: Comfortable

Today you'll walk through Wildermieming into the valley and forest, to the busy town of Telfs, at 2080 ft. (634 m.) with a stop at the Gerhardhof, a delightful oountry inn (closed on Monday and Tuesday). The return to Obermieming is by bus from Telfs.

Start: Turn left as you exit the Hotel Schwarz, walking towards Wildermieming on a country road. Just before Wildermieming the road forks—take the left fork marked WILDERMIEMING #10A. As the road continues you can see the Wildermieming church steeple down on your right. Follow the signs ahead TELFS—1 1/2 HRS. and GERHARDHOF—30 MIN. Continue to follow signs to the Gerhardhof Eventually the road turns around and continues right and then left though the Angertal, in the direction of the Gerhardhof A sign takes you from the wagon path up on a mountain trail to a path contiuing through the forest to the Gerhardhof, a charming mountain restaurant—one and a quarter hours from Obermieming.

When ready, follow the sign in front of the restaurant TELFS—1 1/2 HRS. However, it only takes another hour to reach the suburbs of Telfs. This path from the restaurant is occasionally marked with small signs reading *rund wanderweg.* Follow the road down through the outskirts of Telfs to the main highway. Turn right for the bus stop to Obermieming or spend some time exploring this village before returning by post bus.

Walk # 3
Grunberg Panorama Rundweg, Obsteig Lift to Grunberg, Walk to
Zwischensimmering to Obsteig
Walking Easy Time: 2 1/2 to 3 1/2 hours
Rating: Comfortable

Today's hike begins in Obsteig at the top of the Grunberg chairlift, 4912 ft. (1497 m.) *NOTE:* **This lift does not operate on all days. Please check with the hotel or Tourist Office/or current operating hours.**

   Directions: *Take the local bus from Obermieming to Obsteig. Walk though the village to the chairlift.*

   Start: Exiting the chairlift to your right, the walk proceeds around the Grunberg peak on the Grunberg Panorama Rundweg, #31, around and down to Zwischensimmering at 4321 ft. (1317 m.) where you have the option of continuing down the mountain through Holzerhutte, passing the waterfall, all the way to Obsteig. Or, you can continue around the peak on #31, and take the chairlift down to Obsteig.

   At the base of the chairlift you have two options:
1.   Return to the main road and take the bus to Obermieming.
2.   Take any one of several paths up and around to Obermieming.

Walk #4
Obermieming to Moosalm to Kohlplatz along the Engenbergweg to Arzkasten
to Holzleiten
Walking Easy Time: 3 1/2 hours
Rating: Comfortable

Start: Exiting the Hotel Schwarz, turn right and right again on the first street, walking to the *spielplatz* or playground. Turn left, walking over the river, then right, to the Tennis Hall above Barwies. Turn right as if to Moosalm, 2920 ft. (890 **in.**), but turn right again, ascending to Kohlplatz, 3170 ft (966 m.) Follow the Eggenbergweg on #17 and then #19, rising to Arzkasten, at 3776 ft. (1151 m.). At Arzkasten, follow signs to Aschland and then to Holzleiten. Across the street from the Restaurant Holzleiten, 3567 ft. (1087 **in.**), is the bus stop for your return to Obermieming.

Walk #5
Obermieming to Wildermieming to Strassberghans on15A and Retnrn.
Walking Easy time: 4 hours
Rating: Comfortable

Start: Exiting the Hotel Schwarz, turn left and walk on the country road to Brente. Pass a little chapel on your left, and walk on the path above Wildermieming, where you follow the sign 15A STRASSBERGHAUS. The path is well-defined and ascends gradually on the Strassbergweg from 2855 to 3908 ft. (870 to 1191 m.) It is possible to walk down along the little river to Telfs, but that can be a long, descending hike with a bus return to Obermieming and the hotel. A more pleasant and easier return is along the same path with new views of the plateau.

Walk # 6
A Walking Tonr of Innsbrnck
Walking Easy Time: A Full Day
Rating: Gentle

See A Trail of Three Cities—Innsbuck

Directions: *Take the bus to Innsbruck through the village of Telfs and get off at the main bahnhol/(train station) and bus station. Return to this station later for the bus back to Mieming.* NOTE: Check bus schedules belore today's excursion.

SALZBURGERLAND

BADGASTEIN

The deep, fertile Gasteinertal (Gastein Valley) in Salzburgerland, is nestled between high mountain peaks and borders on Austria's dramatic Hohe Tauern National Park. Badgastein, the valley's social and cultural center, is perched on a steep hillside, and is one of Europe's most famous all-season resorts. Gushing waterfalls and natural springs originate in this beautiful valley and serve as the core of spa activity and as a source of natural energy. The Belle Epoque architecture merges with an updated center where winter and summer sports enthusiasts seek the pleasure of the Gasteinertal's world-famous thermal springs. In summer, ski tracks give way to hiking trails criss-crossing the surrounding mountains.

Bad Hofgastein, Dorfgastein and Bockstein, Badgastein's sister villages, complete the infrastructure of the valley, offering a full range of cultural and sports activities. Concerts are held daily and the turn-of-the-century casino in Badgastein provides evening social activity. Charming country restaurants specializing in local cuisine are located throughout the 55 miles (90 km) of hiking trails. For those *Easy Walkers* who would like to combine a hiking holiday with the advantages of world-class spa facilities, Badgastein is the base village of choice.

Near Badgastein, the valley divides into smaller valleys—the Kotschachtal, home of the tiny village of Grüner Baum; the Anlauftal, where a little rail system enters old, gold-mining tunnels, now the scene of the Healing Gallery; and the Nassfeldtal, entrance to Sportgastein, one of the most scenic alpine areas in Salzburgerland.

TRANSPORTATION TO BADGASTEIN

By Train—Trains depart hourly from Salzburg for the trip to Badgastein.

By Car—Take the A10 *autobahn* south, exiting at Bischofshofen. Drive south and then west on Route 311. At the junction with Route 167, head south, following signs into Badgastein and your hotel. If arriving from the south, exit the

A10 *autobahn* at the Villach/Mallnitz exit (railway car ferry) and follow signs to Badgastein.

FAVORITE *WALKING EASY* HOTEL

Hotel Gruner Baum
Four-Star; Owners-Familie Blumschein
A-5640 Badgastein,
Internet: www.grunerbaum.com
E-mail: info@grunerbaum.com
> This exceptional hotel-spa and mountain retreat is located in the lush Kotschach Valley. The Gruner Baum specializes in a complete range of spa and health-related treatments utilizing Badgastein's hot springs. Mix in a dash of gourmet dining, mountain day walks, and an attentive staff, and you have a perfect vacation setting.

EXCURSIONS IN AND AROUND BADGASTEIN

The Badgastein Tourist Information office is located on Mozartplatz.
Internet: http://www.badgastein.at
e-mail: info@badgastein.at
Upon checking into your hotel you will receive a Guest Card, entitling you to reductions on summer activities. Your hotel and the Tourist Office can provide information about spa treatments.

Public Bundesbus and private Lackner bus (both charging the same amount and sometimes traveling on the same routes), are available throughout the valleys.
1. **Badgastein**—Visit the **Nikolauskirche (Church of St. Nicholas)** and its Gothic frescoes and stone pulpit, along with Baroque tombs and altars. The waterfall of the **Gasteiner Ache** cascades into the center of town with its turn-of-the-century hotels and fashionable shops.
    The 17 thermal springs originating in Badgastein contain radon, reputedly beneficial to certain illnesses. The Healing Gallery is located in Bockstein, in the heart of the Radhaus mountain. A train runs slowly through the old tunnels of gold prospectors. Visitors can "take the cure" at Austria's leading spa with thermal water baths or a ride through the Healing Gallery.
2. **Bad Hofgastein**—At 2850 ft. (869 m.), this well-established spa village lies five miles north of Badgastein. Visit the Gothic Pfarrkirche, built in the 15th century, and note many ancient turreted houses—remnants of wealthy gold-mining days in the Gastein Valley.

Directions: *There are frequent buses available for the short ride between the towns, or you can walk along the river promenades. (See Walk #1.)*

3. **Salzburg**—See "A Trail of Three Cities—Salzburg."
   Directions: *Take a morning train for the hour ride to Salzburg.*

BADGASTEIN WALKS
Recommended Maps:
   1) Gasteiner Wanderkarte—mit Wandernadel-Summer Panorama
   2) Freytag & Berndt—#191—Gasteinertal/Wagrain
   3) Gasteinertal Panorama mit Wanderwegen and Ortsplan

Walk #1: Gruner Baum via the Hohenweg to Bad Hofgastein, Schlossalm Lift to Kitzstein, Walk to Bad Hofgastein
Walking Easy Time: 2 1/2 to 4 1/2 hours
Rating: Gentle

The first part of today's walk is a good introduction to the Gastein Valley, a gentle walk through the forest. This pleasant balcony trail is about 600 ft. (183 m.) above the valley floor. After visiting the charming village of Bad Hofgastein, you will continue by taking the Schlossalm funicular to Kitzstein for a walk down to Bad Hofgastein, a low-to mid-level hike—a good walk for an overcast day.

If you arrive at your hotel mid-day and feel like walking in the afternoon, this walk can be abbreviated by taking the 2 1/2 hour walk to Bad Hofgastein along the Höhenweg and returning to the hotel by bus from Bad Hofgastein.

Start: Start from the tiny village of Gruner Baum; facing the Hotel Gruner Baum, turn left in the direction of Kaiser-Wilhelm Promenade and the Martin Lodinger Weg. Turn right at the fork, following signs to the Martin Lodinger Weg. Follow the road, running adjacent to the Promenade up on the left. At the fork in the road, walk to the right over the bridge, the road occasionally marked

HINT: The meadows may be separated from the path by thin wires. Do not touch them—they are often electrified.

"Martin Lodinger Weg." Continue, but do **not** take the path up to the Gamskarkogel, walk ahead on the small, paved road. This is a good opportunity to view Badgastein perched on the mountain to your left. Cross the bridge by the waterfall and follow the sign left, to the Höhenweg. After about 40 minutes pass Cafe Hubertus and an animal farm.

Continue in a northerly direction, **not** walking down to the Gadaunern. You'll soon reach and pass through the dramatic Gadaunern Schlucht (Gorge). Follow signs down to Café Gamskar, eventually emerging onto a paved road and Bad Hofgastein.

Turn left and then right on the road, and walk towards the church steeple. Walk down and around to the Kirchplatz, passing the Panorama Apartment Hotel. Continue down to Kongresszentrum and the open square with the Tourist Information Office. Walk through the square towards the funicular across the way, crossing over the river and passing the large bus stop.

Purchase a one-way ticket to Kitzstein (in summer, this is the last station—the chairlift to the stop station is closed). Turn left to Angertal and Hofgastein. Do not make a sharp left turn, through the cow fences and past a farm, but continue ahead in the direction of the Angertal, walking over the bridge. You'll shortly come to another sign indicating the Angertal ahead. However, turn sharply left, following a small sign to Bad Hofgastein, on a trail to the road below. The road ends at a house—follow the sign in back to Bad Hofgastein on a descending wagon path through the forest. Turn left at the road and walk down to the main road. Turn left and walk back to the Schlossalmbahn and the bus stop across the road for the return to the Badgastein *bahnhof* and your hotel.

Walk #2: Sportgastein to Nassfeldalm to Veitbauernhütte to Sportgastein to Evianquelle Restaurant (Bockstein) along the Nassfelder Wanderweg
Walking Easy Time: 3/12 to 4 hours
Rating: Comfortable

Reserve the better part of the day for this rewarding hike through the Nassfeld Valley into the largest "prairie" in Austria. The walk starts at Sportgastein, after a bus ride on the Alpenstrasse toll road. The path is through the valley, past small old farmhouses and barns—the alp filled with grazing cows and horses—to the Veitbauernhütte at 5397 ft. (1645 m.). You will return to Sportgastein along the same path and pick up the Nassfelder Wanderweg, winding through the deep valley, all the way to the Evianquelle Restaurant just outside of Böckstein, for the bus ride back to Badgastein and your hotel.

Directions: *Take a morning Lackner or Bundesbus from Badgastein bahnhof to Sportgastein for the 20-minute ride.*

Start: After exiting the bus, walk ahead, through the parking area, to the large Nassfeld Alm sign, passing the Valeriehaus Restaurant up on your right. You'll be walking with the river on your left. This gentle path offers unobstructed views of the Kreuzkogel on the left, and the snow-capped peaks of the Hohe Tauern ahead. In about 45-minutes, passing through Nassfeldalm and by the Moaralm, a small farmhouse offering Austrian specialities, you'll reach Veitbauernhutte, a one-room farmhouse selling fresh milk and other beverages. The trail then ascends the mountain, and we suggest returning on the same path, back to the bus stop at Sportgastein. Continue through the parking area onto the road, until reaching the first tunnel. To the left is the *wanderweg* trail to Bockstein, descending deeply into the valley along the Nassfeld River, all the way to the Evianquelle Restaurant and the bus stop for the return to Badgastein. If you wish to continue walking, pick up the Kaiser-Elizabeth Promenade in Bockstein into Badgastein.

Walk #3: Stubnerkogel Top Station along the Otto Reichert Weg to Bockhartsee to Sportgastein
Walking Easy Time: 6 hours
Rating: More Challenging

Today's full-day hike is demanding and will be challenging for *Easy Walkers*. The difficulty factor is not due to great altitude change, but to the rocky nature of the Otto Reichert Trail around the side of the Tischkogel. The Otto Reichert trail is well-blazed in red and white and easy to follow, however *Easy Walkers* will be scrambling over rocks for a few hours and, if you hike in late June or early July, this trail can be wet, muddy and slippery. The views of the area are quite lovely, but you will be concentrating on your footing on the rocky trail ahead. You'll descend to the Bockhartsee and then walk up to the Bockhartseehütte before descending to the road and the bus stop in Sportgastein.

This hike should be taken **only** by strong walkers who are capable of scrambling over rocks and can handle somewhat steep descents on a trail that can be muddy and is **very** rocky. Allow almost six hours from start to finish, taking in just a little rest time. There are **no** restaurants or facilities along the way, so pack a picnic lunch and lots of water.

HINT: Check bus schedules, both *Bundesbus* and Lackner, to make sure you arrive at Sportgastein before the last bus to Badgastein.

Directions: *Taking a morning bus to the Badgastein bahnhof, walk past the railroad station to the stairs up and over the tracks to the Stubnerkogel gondola. Buy a one-way ticket and get off at the top station at 7317 ft. (2230 m.).*

Start: Walk in the direction of Bockhartsee and the Zitterauer till you come to the sign "Otto Reichert Weg," to the right. The left path goes up and over the Tischkogel. Because of the ascent to 7875 ft. (2400 m.), we chose the Otto Reichert Weg, #132 on the hiking map. This red and white blazed trail stays fairly level, with no major altitude changes, but is very rocky. Continue ahead to Miesbichlscharte, where the trail descends steeply. Follow the red and white blazing to the left at the fork in the path, in the direction of the lake and Sportgastein.

At the lake, take the gravel road up, but before reaching the restaurant, take an unsigned trail on the left that descends down to the road, winding into the bus stop at Sportgastein. Take the first available bus to the Badgastein *bahnhof.*

Walk #4: Gruner Baum through the Kotschachtal to Restaurant Prossau to Gruner Baum
Walking Easy Time: 3 hours
Rating: Gentle

Today's low-level, gentle walk is on a forest path along the Kötschach River to Restaurant Prossau, and the lovely waterfall at the end of the valley. Gently rising from 3494 to 4167 ft. (1065 to 1270 m.) at the restaurant, the trail begins to steepen as you ascend towards the waterfall and the end of the valley. Many stop at the sun-terrace of the restaurant, enjoy refreshments and the view and return on the same path.

Start: From Grüner Baum, walk on the main, paved path into the Kotschach Valley and the Hohe Tauern, the Austrian National Park. This forest trail ascends easily, and after about 1 3/4 hours, you'll reach the restaurant at Prossau, with a sun-terrace and wonderful view of the waterfall. If you wish, continue on a trail into the forest for another half hour to the end of the valley—staying under the huge stone walls of the mountain. Return to Grüner Baum on the same shaded, forest path.

Walk #5: Graukogel Top Station to Palfner See to Palfner Hochalm to Badgastein
Walking Easy Time: 4 hours
Rating: More Challenging

NOTE: The Graukogel chairlift does not open until the second week in July. You will take two chairlifts to the Graukogel top station at 6411 ft. (1954 m.). You will return to the Graukogel top station for the trek to the Palfner See and the descent to Badgastein or Gruner Baum.

Directions: *Take the bus to the Graukogel lift station in Badgastein. Buy a one-way ticket to the top and board the single chairlift, changing to a double chairlift rising to the top statio*n.

Start: At the top station it is possible to ascend steeply to the Hüttenkogel at 7320 ft. (2231 m.) for a quick view. Return to the top lift station and walk past the Graukogel Restaurant on #527, to the Palfner See at 6805 ft. (2074 m.). On the way to the Palfner See you have the option of shortening the hike by turning right on #527 and continuing down to Palfner Hoch Alm, instead of walking up to the Palfner See and then down to Hochalm on #526. In either case, the walk continues down the mountain to Badgastein. It is possible to pick up the Hardt Weg just before Badgastein, turning right all the way to Gruner Baum.

Walk #6: Stubnerkogel Mid-Station along the Bocksteiner Hohenweg to Bockfeld Alm to Bockstein to Badgastein on the Kaiser-Elisabeth Promenade
Walking Easy Time: 3 1/2 to 4 hours
Rating: Comfortable

Today's mid-level walk begins with the Stubnerkogel lift, rising to the mid-station. You will walk along the Bocksteiner Höhenweg, passing through Hirschkarkogel, with great views of the Gastein Valley. This path eventually descends into the village of Bockstein, home of the Thermal Galleries. From Bockstein, you will return to Badgastein on the Kaiser-Elisabeth Promenade.

Directions: *Take the bus to the Stubnerkogel lift. Purchase a one-way ticket and get off at the mid-station.*

Start: Follow path #129 on your map on the Bocksteiner Hohenweg, ascending from 5857 to 6569 ft. (1785 to 2002 m.) through Zitterauer Alm, descending to the Bockfeld Alm at 5046 ft. (1538 m.), eventually down to Bockstein at 3711 ft. (1131 m.). In Bockstein, follow signs to the Kaiser-Elisabeth Promenade for the gentle walk back to Badgastein.

KAPRUN/ZELL AM ZEE

The lakeside village of Zell am See, founded by monks in the eighth century, sits at the doorway of Austria's National Park Hohe Tauern and the dramatic, twisting Grossglockner mountain road. Kaprun, Zell am See's more charming and intimate sister village, is nestled nearby, close to the 10,509 ft. (3203 m.) Kitzsteinhorn. Here the brilliantly-engineered Gletscherbahn (Glacier Railway) and a series of cableways rise to the Alpincenter at 8045 ft. (2452 m.), reputably the largest winter and summer glacier skiing area in Austria. The world's highest cable car support takes you to Bergstation Kitzsteinhorn at 9938 ft. (3029 m.), where a tunnel walk leads to the Glocknerkanzel and an observation terrace facing the Grossglockner, Austria's highest mountain. The valley beyond Kaprun and the Kitzsteinhorn ends abruptly at the mammoth walls of the Mooserboden and Wasserfallboden Reservoirs, part of Europe's largest hydro-electric network utilizing the world's largest platform funicular—the site of a *Walking Easy* hike and excursion.

Trails encircle and connect Kaprun and Zell am See, serviced by local bus transportation and lifts to scenic lookouts and trailheads. The Kaprun/Zell am See area is a complete destination vacation, offering all the water sport activities associated with Lake Zell, as well as those walking adventures preferred by mountain ramblers. What a find for the outdoorsperson who likes to do both!

TRANSPORTATION TO KAPRUN

By Train and Bus—At Zell am See, transfer to the hourly Kaprun Bundesbus, leaving across from the Zell *bahnhof*—(a 15-minute drive)**By Car**—Drive to Zell am See and follow signs to Kaprun.

FAVORITE *WALKING EASY* HOTEL

Hotel Tauernhof
Four-Star, Owner—Familie Gschwantner
A-5710 Kaprun
Internet: www.tauernhof.at
E-mail: info@tauernhof.at

> The Hotel Tauernhof is conveniently located in a quiet location, just a five-minute walk to Kaprun Center, where bus transportation to Zell am See and area lifts are available. Breakfast is a plentiful buffet. Dinner is well prepared and includes contemporary and traditional Austrian cuisine. The hotel

includes an indoor pool and is a favorite of hikers in the area. The Gschwantner family is always present. You'll enjoy!

EXCURSIONS IN AND AROUND KAPRUN

The Kaprun Tourist Information Office is located in the center of the village.
Internet: www.kaprun.at
e-mail: info@kaprun.at
You can buy a reduced-rate National Park Ticket as an incentive to use the area's environmentally friendly, public transportation system.

1. **Zell am See**—Situated on the shores of a deep glacial lake, Zell am See is an important summer and winter resort, with a small but interesting Old Town to explore. The 12th-century **Constable's Tower (Kastnerturm)** was once used as a grain silo. The Romanesque **Parish Church (Pfarrkirche)** was built in the 11th-century. The 16th-century **Castle Rosenberg** was once an elegant residence and is now home to the Town Hall and an art gallery. Check out the **Folklore Museum** in an ancient tower near the town square. Lake Zell, 2 1/2 miles long and one mile wide, offers all types of swimming and boating facilities.
    Directions: *Buses run hourly between Kaprun and Zell am See.*

2. **The Grossglockner Road**—The Grossglocknerstrasse, the longest and most scenic Alpine highway in Europe and the gateway to Austria's Hohe Tauern National Park, is a fantastic drive of about 30 miles—rising from 2483 ft. (757 m.) to its highest point at 8220 ft (2505 m.). Because of the altitude rise and the multitude of hairpin turns, take the bus from Zell am See instead of driving. (See Walk #7.)

3. **Salzburg**—See A Trail of Three Cities—Salzburg.
    Directions: *Take a bus from Kaprun, arriving in Zell am See in time to catch the train to Salzburg.*

4. **Kitzbuehel**—Once an old mining town, Kitzbuehel is now a fashionable winter and summer resort. (See Kitzbuehel chapter.)
    Directions: *Take a bus from Kaprun to Zell am See, and the **local** train to the **Kitzbuehel-Hahnenkamm** station—about a 90-minute trip—a few minutes walk into the heart of town.*

5. **Sigmund-Thun Klamm**—In the Ice Age, the Kaprun Valley was covered by a glacier. As it melted it left behind a deep notch—105 ft. (32 m.) deep, and 1050 ft. (320 m.) long—through the Sigmund-Thun Klamm (Gorge), where the Kaprun River flows into the valley. (See Walk #3.)
    Directions: *Take the bus from Kaprun to Sigmund-Thun Klamm.*

KAPRUN/ZELL AM SEE WALKS
Recommended Maps:
1) Freytag & Berndt—Wanderkarte—Kaprun/Zell am See
2) Wanderkarte Zell am See/Kaprun—Fremdenverkehrsverband
3) Kapruner Wander-un Tourenführer (Alles Da)

Walk #1: Introductory Walk—Kaprun to Guggenbichl on the Guggenhohenweg, to Kaprun Castle to Kaprun (Optional Walk, Kaprun Castle to Mayereinoden to Kaprun)
Walking Easy Time: 2 1/2 to 4 hours
Rating: Comfortable

This mid-level walk, which can be taken on the afternoon of arrival, rises comfortably from 2494 to 2953 ft. (760 to 900 m.). You will reach Guggenbichl about 30 minutes after ascending from Kaprun, with fabulous views past Zell am See and the snow-capped peaks of the Hohe Tauern. After walking through the cool forest, you will descend on a trail to Kaprun Castle, with a return on the road to Kaprun. If time permits, the walk can be extended from the castle towards Mayereinoden and back to Kaprun.

Start: Walk to the *gemeindeamt* (village hall) in Kaprun. Cross the street and follow "Guggenhöhenweg #10." Walk up the street and turn left at the *wanderweg* sign. Walk over a small bridge and continue up the street to the right, to Guggenhohenweg #10. This little-used road takes you up through the meadows in about 30 minutes to the *jausenstation* (snack bar) at Guggenbichl, perched on the side of the hill. Continue the ascent on a *forest strasse,* a wagon road through the woods. Soon, path #10, The Mountain Way, ascends to the right on a red and white blazed path. Or, you can continue ahead on the wide wagon path, meeting the #10 mountain path in about a half hour. At this point, turn left on a narrow, descending, zigzagging, red and white blazed forest trail to the castle. A left turn on Schlosstrasse takes you back to central Kaprun.

If you wish to extend today's walk, locate path #12 to Mayereinoden near the castle, returning to Kaprun via the path along the Salzach River, found by walking towards Zell am See, along the road. Turn left before the river on the Romantik Way, back to Kaprun.

Walk #2: Maiskogel Top Station to Glocknerblick to Unterberg Alm to Maiskogel to Kaprun on the Güterweg
Walking Easy Time: 2 to 4 hours
Rating: Comfortable

Today's walk is a mid-level hike from the top of the Maiskogel Lift to the Glocknerblick (an outstanding panoramic viewpoint) and back. You will then proceed to Unterberg Alm, with a return to Maiskogel for a gentle descent on the Güterweg, through the Schaufelberg meadows, to Kaprun.

Directions: *Take the Kaprun bus to the Maiskogel lift station and buy a one-way ticket to the top.*

Start: For hardier *Easy Walkers*, try the short but somewhat steep ascent to the Glocknerblick, just to the left as you exit the lift station. You'll find fabulous views of the Kaprun Valley. Descend in the direction of Unterberg Alm, from 5479 to 5128 ft. (1670 to 1563 m.), and walk back to Maiskogel Alm on path #25 on your map. For those who prefer not to ascend the Glocknerblick, follow the sign to Unterberg Alm on a gently ascending path, returning along the same path for fresh views of the Zell am See area.

With either option, at the top Maiskogel lift station, take path #3, the Guterweg, by walking under the ski lift tunnel. Do **not** go down path #1 (the steeper way to Kaprun), but continue on the gently descending wagon road on #3, with the sign marked *"nach* Kaprun, 2 hours." At an intersection with path #1, stay on #3 all the way and continue on the road as it zig-zags down past the Kaprun church. Turn left at the high school, into Kaprun.

Walk #3: Excursion to Alpine Reservoirs of Kaprun and Walks at Mosserboden Dam (Optional Valley Walk)
Walking Easy Time: 1 1/2 to 4 hours
Rating: Comfortable

Reserve a clear day for this full day's exciting excursion, to view the dramatic, snow-covered Glockner mountain range of the Hohe Tauern—many peaks over 10,000 ft. (3000 m.).

Directions: *Take a morning Kaprun Bundesbus to Kesselfall/Alpenhaus, the last stop, and purchase a combination ticket for the buses and funicular to the top station at Mooserboden Reservoir. These buses take you through a tunnel to Lärchwand, where you board one of the world's largest inclined lifts, large enough to take a bus up the mountain, rising 1414 ft. (431 m.). Another bus takes you past the Limberg Dam and the Wasserfallboden Reservoir, up to Mooserboden at 6693 ft. (2040 m.); the* *entire trip takes less than an hour! This incredible system of reservoirs and dams provides hundreds of millions of kilowatt hours of electricity for this section of Europe. Completed in the early 1950's, it changed the face and ecology of the Kaprun Valley, and now attracts millions of tourists from around the world.*

Start: After arriving at Mooserboden, walk past the monument, over the first and second sections of the dam. The views are astounding—icy glaciers and high mountain peaks. Visit central Europe's only glacier museum. Upon returning to the main restaurant and trail signs, follow the half-hour Alpenblumenweg Path for a short walk among the alpine flowers.

Return to the bus stop for the trip back to Kesselfall/Alpenhaus and the Bundesbus to Kaprun. If it is early, you can take a gentle meadow and river walk, never far from the main road, back to Kaprun. This path, #13 on the hiking map, can be entered from the parking area on the left side of the road, at the Kesselfall bus stop. The path for this two-hour return walk descends gently and can be interrupted easily at bus stops along the way, indicated by an H on your map.

Walk #4: Kitzsteinhorn Alpincenter (Glacier Excursion) to Kreefelder Hutte to Maiskogel on the Alexander Enzinger Weg
Walking Easy Time: 4 hours
Rating: More Challenging

The following excursion and walk at the Kitzsteinhorn at 9938 ft. (3029 m.), its glacier and the Alpincenter at 8045 ft. (2452 m.) was a prime target for us. Unfortunately, a July mountain blizzard wiped out our plans, and while a few hardy summer skiers seemed to enjoy this phenomenon, all hiking trails were closed due to snow conditions. Instead, we enjoyed hot chocolate, threw snowballs and returned to the more friendly environs of the bottom station, walking back to Kaprun on a very pretty forest and meadow path along the Kapruner Ache (River), visiting the Sigmund-Thun Klamm (Gorge) on the way. This is an all-day excursion and hike, and an early start is advised.

Directions: *Take a morning bus to the Gletscherbahn and purchase a round-trip ticket to the Kitzsteinhorn (the return ticket to be used at the Maiskogel Lift). Take the underground funicular railway to the Alpincenter and transfer to the cable car to the Kitzsteinhorn Top Station. A ten-minute walk brings you to the glocknerkanzel, an observation terrace where you will meet the Grossglockner, Austria's highest mountain, and other major alpine peaks in Austria's National Park. This particular spot is called "the window to Hohe Tauern." You can take a summit lift to the glacier plateau to experience a glacier walk to the Hocheiserwand observation point. When ready, return to the Kitzsteinhorn top station and take the cable car to the Alpincenter to begin today's hike.*

Start: Follow signs to the Kreefelder Hütte and the long mountain hike along the Alexander Enzinger Weg, via Stangenhohe and the Glocknerblick, to the Maiskogel Lift. This is basically a downhill trek from 7530 ft. (2295 m.) to 5053 ft. (1540 m.) at the Maiskogel Top Station, where you take the lift down to the base station and a bus back to Kaprun.

For those *Easy Walkers* who prefer not to take the long hike to Maiskogel after the activities at the Kitzsteinhorn top station, the glacier and the Alpincenter, return to the base station on the Gletscherbahn, and if you have not taken the Kaprun valley walk and visited Sigmund-Thun Klamm, this might be a good opportunity to do so. The path can be found in back of the lowest Gletscherbahn parking area.

Walk #5: Schmittenhohe Top Station to Breiteckalm to Zeller Bergbahn Middle Station to Zell am See
Walking Easy Time: 4 hours
Rating: Comfortable

A cable car rises to the 6562 ft. (2000 m.) Schmittenhohe, with spectacular views of the mountain ranges of the Hohe Tauern and the Kitzbuehel Alps.You will walk to Breiteckalm, then to the *mittelstation* of the Zeller Bergbahn at 4469 ft. (1362 m.), continuing to walk down to Zell am See. However, at the mid-station you have the option of riding down on the gondola.

Directions: *Take a bus to the last stop in Zell am See at the "PA." Transfer to the Schmittenhohe bus and at the lift station, buy a one-way ticket to the top.*

Start: Walk to the back of the restaurant and up to the chapel. Follow trail #6 to Breiteckalm at 5807 ft. (1770 m.), on a little-used jeep road. Just before arriving at the Glocknerhaus Restaurant at 5194 ft. (1583 m.), turn left onto a meadow trail, following a sign to Zell am See. This short, grassy trail through the pastures leads to the road. Turn left and walk down to the Zeller Bergbahn Mittelstation at 4469 ft. (1362 m.). Continue walking down to Zell am See at 2484 ft. (757 m.), on the zigzagging road, still path #6 on your map. You also have the option of taking the gondola down to Zell am See. With either option, at the bottom, turn right and walk to the *bahnhof* for a visit to Zell am See and the bus back to Kaprun.

Walk #6: Schmittenhohe Top Station, on the Hohenpromenade to Sonnkogel to Sonnalm to Zell am See (Optional Excursion to Zell am See)
Walking Easy Time: 3 hours
Rating: Comfortable

The Erlebnisweg Hohenpromenade from the Schmittenhohe Top Station to the Sonnkogel Top Station, is a comfortable path with numerous display boards providing historical and environmental information about the Schmittehohe area—in the midst of spectacular scenery.

Directions: *See Walk #5*

Start: At the Schmittenhohe Top Station at 6562 ft. (2000 m.), walk around to the back of the restaurant to the tiny chapel with its group of hiking signs. Take path #10 to the right, over the Höhenpromenade to Bergstation Sonnkogel—the chairlift top station at 6017 ft. (1834 m.)—a 50-minute, gentle walk. Depending on the month, this botanic *weg* is bordered by a multitude of mountain flowers and berries, with views of the Kitzbueheler Alps, Zell am See and its lake. When the path forks, you have the option of taking a meadow trail which descends to the mid-station at Sonnalm. However, we suggest walking straight ahead and following the sign to the Sonnkogel Bergstation and restaurant—another five minutes. At Sonnkogel you have a few options:

1)   Take the triple chairlift down to the mid-station.
2)   Walk around the back of the restaurant, past the lift station. Pick up the wagon road going to Schmiedhofalm and then down to the Sonnalm mid-station at 4518 ft. (1377 m).

At Sonnalm mid-station you have a few more options:
1)   Take the gondola to Zell am See and the bus stop.
2)   Or, descend on the road to Zell am See and the bus stop.

If time permits, walk through the pedestrian shopping streets of Zell am See and turn down to the lake front. Walk for as long as you wish in either direction, on the See Promenade along the lake's shores. To return to Kaprun, take the bus across the street from the Zell am See *bahnhof.*

Walk #7: Glacier Walk (Excursion to Hohe Tauern in the Austrian National Park via the Grossglockener Road)
Walking Easy Time: 1 to 3 hours
Rating: Comfortable

This is an excursion to Austria's largest glacier, at the foot of the Grossglockner, Austria's highest mountain, in the magnificent Austrian National Park—a full day's outing with an **early** start necessary. You will take the bus from Kaprun to the Zell am See train station where you board a special bus, riding to the last stop at Kaiser-Franz-Josefs-Höhe, visiting the glacier for a short walk. If time permits, you can walk on the upper ridges adjacent to the glacier before returning by bus to Zell am See and Kaprun.

The Hohe Tauern looks as it did 1000 years ago—plants and animals in a protected alpine wilderness. In the heart of the park lies Austria's tallest mountain, the Grossglockner, at 12,457 ft. (3797 m.), and her largest glacier, the Pasterze, six miles (10 km.) long. With 120 peaks rising over 10,000 ft. (3000 m.) and 169 glaciers, the park is one of Europe's most beautiful and enthralling high alpine regions.

Directions: NOTE: The following are approximate times, subject to change. *Take the 8:25 am bus from Kaprun, arriving at the Zell am See bahnhof at 8:40. Outside the train station, transfer to the 8:53 Bundesbus, arriving at Kaiser-Franz-Josefs-Hohe at 11:04 am. The Grossglockner Road is one of the most famous excursions in Austria and the best* viewing opportunities are from seats on the **right** side of the bus.

Start: After getting off the bus at the last stop, Kaiser-Franz-Josefs-Hohe, walk towards the glacier. A short funicular ride will take you to the bottom station for your glacier walk. At the bottom station there is a steep, 15-minute scramble down to the glacier itself—remember that you also have to climb back up from the glacier to the funicular base station to return to the top. **CAUTION: After reaching the glacier, follow the steps cut into the ice, holding on to the guide ropes, advancing up to the forward alert ropes.** Leave ample time to climb back up to the funicular, where there may be a wait for the ride to the top.

If time permits, note the following options:

1) The park service provides an interesting and informative 20-minute film on the wonders of the Austrian National Park.

2) Walk along the side of the glacier. Walking distance depends on how much time is left before the bus leaves. Walk through a short tunnel leading to a wide, level path, with the glacier on your left. The Hofmanshutte is about a two-hour round-trip walk.

Please remember that you **must** be at the bus stop by 2:35 pm if you want to take the 2:45 bus, returning to Zell am See at 4:32 pm to catch the 5:25 bus to Kaprun. The next (and last bus) leaves Kaiser-Franz-Josefs-Höhe at 3:45 pm, arriving in Zell am See at 5:32, where you change for the 6:25 pm bus to Kaprun—the end of a long, exciting and memorable day in the Austrian National Park. **Check current bus schedules**.

A TRAIL OF THREE CITIES

WALKING EASY IN SALZBURG, INNSBRUCK AND VIENNA

The historic cities of **Innsbruck** and **Salzburg** are close enough to most Austrian *Walking Easy* base villages so that you can take a comfortable, one-day excursion, and return to your hotel for dinner. **Vienna**, too far away from our base villages for a one-day excursion, is included for those *Easy Walkers* who wish to spend additional time exploring this landmark city.

INNSBRUCK

The imperial city of Innsbruck, the crossroads of Europe, is a stone's throw from the famous Brenner Pass and the dramatic Dolomites of Italy. Surrounded by snow-capped mountains, it is close enough to the *Walking Easy* base villages of Seefeld, Neustift, Alpbach, Zell am Ziller and Kitzbuehel for a comfortable, one-day city tour of its charming Old Town. An historic and cultural center, Innsbruck was the home of the Hapsburgs, Austria's royal family, who were responsible for developing this capital of the Tyrol into an important architectural and arts center.

The Innsbruck Tourist Office is located at Burggraben 3, at the corner of Herzog-Friedrich-Strasse—the colorful, cobblestone, main street of Old Town. This pedestrian-free zone houses shops and street cafes and is the heart of today's city-walk.

Innsbruck—One-Day *Walking Easy* Itinerary
Directions: Take the train or bus from any nearby *Walking Easy* base village to Innsbruck. While it is possible to take a local bus or taxi to **Altstadt,** the historic city center, Innsbruck's main train and bus station are only a few minute's walk.

Start: Exit the train station, cross the main street, Sudtiroler Platz, and turn right. Continue on Sudtiroler to Museumstrasse and turn left. Walk about four blocks to Burggraben, bearing left to the famous pedestrian streets of Old Town. Turn into Herzog-Friedrich-Strasse and walk towards the **Stadtturm (City Tower)**, dating from 1440, located on the right, just before the Golden Roof. Note the tower's imposing 16th-century cupola. Climb to the top for a great view of Innsbruck. Continue to the **Goldenes Dachl (Golden Roof)**, a loggia covered with over 2500 fire-gilt copper tiles on a 15th-century residence. As you face the **Golden Roof**, turn left towards **Helblinghaus**, situated on the left side of the street. This 15th-century Gothic townhouse is decorated with Baroque pastel stuccoes. The street continues with a variety of shops.

Retrace your steps back to the Golden Roof and turn left to the Baroque **Dom zu St. Jakob (St. Jacob's Cathedral)**, featuring Lucas Cranach's famous painting of the Madonna over the main altar. Turn right after leaving the cathedral and cross the street to the 16th-century **Hofgarten**. It is possible to hire a horse-drawn carriage at the entrance to the park for a more leisurely view of old Innsbruck. After leaving the park, walk past the columned **Landestheatre**, originally the court's 17th-century Opera House. Just past the theater is **Leopold's Fountain** with its equestrian statue.

Across from the Landestheatre and fountain is the **Hofburg**, the imperial palace. Visit the state rooms—guided tours in English are given throughout the day. Exiting the palace, cross the street to the 16th-century **Hofkirche (Court Church)** with 28 bronze figures inside—the famous "Black Knights." As you exit Court Church turn left, continuing on Burggraben, walking around to the entrance of the pedestrian street. Walk past the Tourist Office and turn left on Maria-Theresien-Strasse, the main shopping street. Continue past the 18th-century **Anna Column**, commemorating the successful Tyrolean resistance against a Bavarian invasion. Proceed to the 18th-century **Triumphal Arch,** erected in honor of the marriage of Leopold II. Just before the arch, turn left on Saturner Strasse and walk directly to the bus and train station—ending your tour of the highlights of Innsbruck's Old Town.

SALZBURG

Easy Walkers staying in the base villages of Badgastein can take an easy, one-day visit to Salzburg, the city of Mozart. Like Vienna and Innsbruck, Salzburg is a comfortable city to walk in, and boasts an impressive list of must see landmarks in its Old Town. Architecturally, Salzburg is a gem, with its 17th-and 18th-century houses, hotels and shops.

Salzburg—One-Day *Walking Easy* Itinerary

Directions from Badgastein: Take a morning bus to the Badgastein *bahnhof* and a direct train to Salzburg—a one-hour train trip.

Start: In the Salzburg train station, follow signs to the **i** the Salzburg Tourist Office. Purchase a **24-Hour Salzburg Card** with a city map, for free use of all public transportation and free entry into Mozart's Birthplace, the Hohensalzburg Fortress, the state rooms at the Residenz and numerous museums, galleries and memorials.

Walk outside the train station towards the main traffic street, turn right and board bus #5, 6, 51 or 55, getting off at the fifth stop for entrance to the **Alter Markt**, just after crossing the Salzach River. Follow crowds through to the **Alter Markt**, a square filled with street vendors and tourists. As you walk forward, note the famous Café Tomaselli, for a mid-morning snack. Bear around to **Residenz Platz**, an open square with an impressive Baroque fountain, location of the **Residenz Palace** and **Residenzgalerie,** containing European paintings and 15 historic rooms; bordered by **Salzburg Cathedral** with its magnificent marble facade. Entrance to the Cathedral, which you will visit later, is off **Dom Platz.** Walk towards the large statue of **Mozart** in Mozartplatz, just past the eighth-century **St. Michael's Church** on your left. Sounds of music will probably welcome you to the square, as choral and instrumental musicians from around the world perform, adding to the pleasure of listening to the 18th-century, world-famous **Salzburg Glockenspiel.** On the day we visited Mozartplatz, we heard a young violinist, a Scotch bagpiper, a trio from Moscow and an accordionist from Hungary.

Walk back towards and around the Cathedral and into **Cathedral Square** in order to gain entry to this famous Baroque church. The **Hohensalzburg Fortress** towers over Cathedral Square. Cross the large square and walk towards the railway and the castle, entering Festungsgasse and the entry to the funicular. If you have purchased the Salzburg Card, the funicular ride is free. Towering 400 feet above the Salzach River, this ancient fortress is the largest completely preserved citadel in central Europe. While on the fortress grounds, visit the **Burgmuseum** with its collection of medieval art and the **Rainermuseum**'s displays of arms and armor. Conducted tours of the fortress are given daily, check for hours of English-speaking departures.

Return from the fortress by way of the funicular, turning left immediately upon reaching the bottom station. Walk through an ornate gate into **St. Peter's Cemetery,** where Mozart and Haydn are buried. Enclosed by arcades and housing numerous artistic wrought-iron gates, it is located at the foot of the stone wall of the Monchsberg, across from early Christian **catacombs** (tours are available). However, pay **St. Margaret's Chapel** a visit before walking through the cemetery and exiting onto a long street and the eighth-century **Franziskaner Kirche**, one of Salzburg's oldest churches.

Continue past the Concert Hall, crossing Herbert-van-Karajan Platz, and turn right on **Getreidegasse**, the famous walking and shopping street—#9 is **Mozart's Birthplace** and the **Mozart Museum**. Getreidegasse leads to the **Alter Markt** where you first started. Turn left onto the main street, and left again, crossing the bridge. Turn left on the main shopping street, a few yards to the bus stop. If you have time, detour into the **Mirabell Gardens**, designed in 1690, with its groups of sculptures, the humorous Dwarves Garden, the Maze, the Hedge Theater.

Take bus #1,2,5,6 or 55 back to the railroad station for your return—ending an exciting one-day excursion to Salzburg.

VIENNA

Vienna is an encyclopedia of architectural styles—a mix of majestic palaces, churches, culturally diverse museums and colorfully landscaped parks. And, all are within comfortable walking boundaries, criss-crossed by pedestrian streets and serviced by safe, clean, convenient public transportation. Vienna is like a tray of delectable pastries—sample a few, then return when time permits a more extensive visit.

If you decide on a short visit to Vienna, please refer to "Must See Vienna," and choose those places of interest that appeal to you, depending on the amount of time you have.

Vienna Transportation

Vienna's excellent public transportation network includes buses, trams or trolley cars, and a subway (U-Bahn). Choose any discount ticket, which can be purchased in most tobacco stores and major underground stations. **All** tickets can be used for **all** transportation lines at any time.

1. **The Vienna Card**—Take any transportation for a period of 72 hours—with the additional benefits of reduced rates in museums and theaters. This card can be bought at your hotel and the Tourist Office.
2. **The 72-Hour Pass**—It provides unlimited transportation **only**, for 72 hours, and can be bought at *tabac* shops.
3. **Single Tickets**—Can be purchased from a coin-operated ticket machine on the tram or bus.
4. **24-Hour, One-Day Pass**—This pass can be bought at *tabac* shops.

Must See Vienna

The main Vienna Tourist Information Office is located behind the Opera House at Karntnerstrasse 38.

1. **Ringstrasse (Ring Boulevard)**—This great boulevard circles Vienna's old city for almost three miles. For a city orientation, board Tram #1 by the Opera House and enjoy the sights as the tram circles the Ring. Get off at the stop of your choice to begin sightseeing. We recommend beginning at the Hofburg Palace.

2. **The Hofburg Palace Complex**—The imperial palace of the Habsburgs is a vast complex. It contains about 2600 rooms, but only 20 are open to visitors.

   A) **Schatzkammer (Imperial Treasury)**—Reached from a stairway in the Swiss Court, you will be dazzled by the display of imperial treasures. An English brochure and audio tour are available.

   B) **Kaiserappartements (Imperial Apartments)**—Enter by the rotunda of Michaelerplatz under the dome of St. Michael's Gate. The emperors and their families lived on the first floor of the Chancellery wing amid ornately carved furniture. English brochures are available.

   C) **Spanische Hofreitschule (Spanish Riding School)**—Written requests for the 80-minute performances on Tuesday through Saturday at should be mailed at least two months in advance to: Spanische Reitschule, Hofburg, A-1010, Vienna, Austria. Do **not** include the price of the tickets. Tickets for training sessions (no reserved seats), are sold at the entrance on Josefsplatz, Gate 2.

   D) **Vienna Boy's Choir**—Mass is sung in Die Burgkappelle (Imperial Chapel of the Hofburg), through the Schweizerhof entrance, every Sunday from January through June and from mid-September through December at 9:15 am. Line up early for standing room. Write for tickets at least 60 days ahead of time to: Hofmusikkapapelle, Hofburg, A-1010, Vienna, Austria. Do **not** include the admission cost. Tickets may then be picked up at the Burgkapelle. During May, June, September and October, the Vienna Boys' Choir performs at the Konzerthaus every Friday at 3:30 pm. Tickets can usually be obtained at your hotel.

   Directions to the Hofburg Palace Complex: *Take Tram #1, 2, D or J to Burgring. From there, locate the Hofburg on your city map.*

3. **Opera House**—The State Opera House was opened in 1869 as the first of the grand buildings to be built on the Ringstrasse, and it was rebuilt after WW II. English-language guided tours are offered in July and August, daily at 2:00 and 3:00 pm (**check current schedules**).

   Directions: *Take Tram #1 and exit at the Opera House. Or, take the U1, U2 or U4 subways to Karlsplatz.*

4. **Kunsthistorisches Museum (Museum of Fine Arts)**—Across from the Hofburg Palace, this art collection of the Habsburgs, is one of the most important in the world. Plan at least three hours to view just a few of this museum's treasures.
   Directions: *Take tram #1, 52, 58, D, J, or the U-Bahn to Volkstheatre stop.*
5. **St. Stephen's Cathedral**—The 12th century saw the beginning of this cathedral, the geographic, historic and spiritual center of Vienna. Damaged over the centuries by fire, conquest and WW II bombings, it has been rebuilt and restored. The cathedral is filled with paintings, sculpture and intricate altars—combining to make St. Stephen's one of the great Gothic cathedrals of the world. Climbing the 344 steps of the South Tower offers a panoramic view of Vienna, the Vienna Woods and the Danube. The North Tower ascent is by elevator for a viewing of the cathedral's great church bell. Brochures in English are available.
   Directions: *Take U-Bahn line 1 or 3 to Stephansplatz. Walking from the Hofburg, locate Kärntnerstrasse on your city map and walk towards the cathedral's spires.*
6. **Die Deutschordenkirche (Church of the Teutonic Order)**—On Singerstrasse, near St. Stephen's Cathedral, this Gothic church was built by the Order of the Teutonic Knights in 1395. Note its beautiful 16th-century Flemish altarpiece. Visit the Treasury on the second floor.
   Directions: *Take U-Bahn line 1 or 3 to Stephansplatz and locate Singerstrasse on your map.*
7. **Peterskirche (St. Peter's Church)**—Situated on Peterplatz, St. Peter's is the oldest and most lavishly decorated Baroque church in Vienna.
   Directions: *Take U-Bahn line 1 or 3 to Stephansplatz and locate Peterplatz on your map.*
8. **Schonbrunn Palace**—This is the second-largest palace in Europe, with magnificent grounds, a zoo and a coach museum. Located out of the city proper, it was built between 1696 and 1712. Its 1441 rooms constitute Vienna's most impressive palace, second in Europe only to Versailles. There are over 40 rooms open to the public. The beautiful Schonbrunn Gardens are also a treat. Located next to the Palace, these immense gardens house the Gloriette, the Palm House, the Butterfly House, the Carriage Museum and the Zoo. A guided tour is necessary to see the apartments, available in English at 9:30, 10:30 and 11:30 am. (Try to make the less crowded 9:30 am tour.)
   Directions to Palace: *Take U-Bahn green #4 line towards Hütteldorf and exit at Schonbrunn station. Follow the signs outside to Schloss Schonbrunn.*
9. **Belvedere Palace**—On Prinz-Eugen Strasse 27, located on a hill above Vienna, is another of Vienna's magnificent palaces. Walk through the lovely gardens to arrive at the palace, with its two great staircases in two buildings—

Unteres and Oberes Belvedere. Lower Belvedere (Unteres) includes the Museum of Baroque Art and the Museum of Medieval Austrian Art, while the Upper (Oberes) Belvedere houses the Austrian Gallery of 19th-and 20th-Century Art and provides an excellent view of the city from its top floors. Directions: *Take Tram D to Schloss Belvedere.*

10. **Stadttempel (Synagogue/City Temple)**—At Seitenstettengasse 4, this "Biedermeier jewel" was built in 1824 and renovated in 1988, 50 years after its near-destruction by the Nazis. It was the only synagogue to even partially survive WWII.

    Directions: *Take U-Bahn line 1 or 3 to Stephansplatz. Walk straight ahead on Rotenturmstrasse, turning left on Fleischmarkt. Walk up the stairs at the end of the street and turn right on Judengasse, then right on Seitenstettengasse to the synagogue.*

11. **Stadtpark (City Park)**—This lovely park is situated off the Parkring. On summer evenings, the orchestra at the *Kursalon,* an elegant café-restaurant on the south side of the park, plays Strauss waltzes.

    Directions: *Take Tram #1, #2, J or T to Stadtpark.*

12. **Prater Amusement Park**—Situated between the Donau (Danube) River and its Canal, the Prater is a fun place to spend a few evening hours. The Riesenrad, a giant Ferris wheel built in 1897, is near the park entrance.

    Directions: *Take the U-Bahn red line 1 towards Kagran and exit at Pratersten.*

13. **Wienerwald (Vienna Woods)**—Bordering Vienna on the north and west, the famous Vienna Woods are 500 square miles of green rolling hills, intersected by a network of color-coded walking paths, usually at the end of public tram and bus lines. Grinzing, at the edge of the Vienna Woods, is the home of many *heurige,* or wine taverns—a village of old, winding streets, and houses built around courtyards where visitors eat, drink wine and listen to music—designated by a green branch hanging over the front door.

    Directions: *Take Tram #1 towards Schottentor and change to Tram #38 to Grinzing. In Grinzing you can take Bus #38A through the Vienna Woods and up the hill to Kahlenberg. This trip takes about an hour each way.*

14. **Uhrenmuseum der Stadt Wien (Municipal Clock Musuem)**—Located at Schulhof 2, and founded in 1690, an old mansion houses a collection of over 3,000 watches and clocks, from primitive to the more modern—a must-see for clock collectors.

    Directions: *Take U-Bahn line 1 or 3 to Stephansplatz and check your city map for directions.*

15. **Dorotheum Auction House**—At this 300-year-old auction house, antique *objets d'art,* paintings, furniture and jewelery may be viewed before the auction. It's like being in a museum, only better, because everything is close at hand for inspection. Worth a visit if you are a lover of art and antiques.

Directions: *From the Opera House on Philharmonicstrasse, walk through Albertinaplatz on to Augustinerstrasse, making a right turn on Dorotheergasse to number 17.*

16. **Vienna Jewish Museum**—This expanded and newly re-opened museum is housed in the 18th-century Eskeles Palace at Dorotheergasse 11, located near the Dorotheum Auction House. The museum contains the Max Berger Collection of Judaica, with ancient texts, scrolls, and ritual objects, and works and photos by Jewish authors.
Directions: *See #15 above to Dorotheum.*

Vienna Restaurant Favorites—Comfortable, Casual and Moderately Priced

Figlmuller—Wollzeil 5, Tel: 512-61-77, no reservations. Restaurants serving local cuisine can be found on almost every street in Vienna, but a favorite of the authors for *schnitzel* is Figlmuller (closed in August). This is a *beisel* or wine tavern, and serves one of the largest *schnitzels* in Austria. A mixed salad, a *schnitzel* and a glass of local wine make a great Viennese dinner.
Directions: *Walk on Karntnerstrasse, past St. Stephen's in the opposite direction of the Opera House, and turn right on Wollzeille. Follow the signs through a 500-year-old arcade to the restaurant, only a few blocks from the cathedral.*

Gigerl—Blumenstockgasse 2, Tel: 513 44 31, no reservations. This is a small, very casual restaurant in the center of the city near Stephansplatz, serving buffet-style food, typical Viennese dishes and local wines. In warm weather the outdoor area is enjoyable.
Directions: *Walk past St. Stephen's on Karntnerstrasse in the direction of the Opera House and make a left on Heihburggasse. Take a first right turn to Rauhenststrasse and a quick right on Blumenstockgasse.*

Ma Pitom—Seitenstettengasse 5, Tel. 535 43 13, reservations not required. This bright, modern, airy restaurant serves excellent "designer" pizzas, many variations on the theme of pasta, and a diet-breaking *tiramasu* for dessert. It is away from the hectic tourist area restaurants and is a favorite with locals.
Directions: Walk past St. Stephen's on Kärntnerstrasse away from the Opera House. Turn left on Fleischmarkt and walk to the end of the street, up the stone steps, turning right on Judengasse and right on Seitenstettengasse.

Cavaliere—Köllnerhofgasse 4, Tel: 513 83 20, reservations not required. Near the Cathedral, this informal Italian restaurant specializes in pasta, and is a favorite with residents of the area. A green salad and linguine with bolognese sauce is a delicious and satisfying meal.
Directions: On Karntnerstrasse, walking away from the Opera House, turn right on Fleischmarkt and right on Kollnerhofgasse. The restaurant is on the left side of the street.

Coffeehouse and Café Favorites

Central—At Herrengasse 14, Central is decorated in late-Empire style. This café is across from the Spanish Riding School. In the 19th century it was a meeting place for Austria's best-known writers.

Directions: *Take Tram #1, 2, D or J to Burgring: from there, locate the Hofburg on your city map. Café Central will be across the street.*

Demel—At Kohlmarkt 14, its Baroque, black marble tables have seated almost every visitor who comes to Vienna. Afternoon tea or coffee with unique pastries has become a tradition with Vienna tourists. An expensive snack, but a "must do" at least once in Vienna.

Directions: *From Stephansplatz, walk on Graben and make a left on Kohlmarkt. Demel is on the right side. From Herrengasse and the Hofburg complex, turn right on Kohlmarkt and Demel will be on the left side.*

Landtmann—Located at Dr.-Karl-Lueger-Ring 4, and over 115 years old, the beautiful Landtmann still attracts a mixture of politicians, actors and writers. The café offers coffee and pastries plus full meals.

Directions: *From the Opera House, take Tram #1, getting off at the Burgtheater. The café is across from the Rathausplatz, just past the Parliament building.*

INDEX

978-0-595-41330-0
0-595-41330-7

Made in the USA
Lexington, KY
25 July 2011